The Unmaking of the Arab Intellectual

The Unmaking of the Arab Intellectual

Prophecy, Exile and the Nation

Zeina G. Halabi

EDINBURGH
University Press

To Khaled Saghieh

Edinburgh University Press is one of the leading university presses in the UK. We publish academic books and journals in our selected subject areas across the humanities and social sciences, combining cutting-edge scholarship with high editorial and production values to produce academic works of lasting importance. For more information visit our website: edinburghuniversitypress.com

Edinburgh University Press Ltd
The Tun – Holyrood Road
12 (2f) Jackson's Entry
Edinburgh EH8 8PJ

First published in hardback by Edinburgh University Press 2017

Typeset in 11/15 Adobe Garamond by
Servis Filmsetting Ltd, Stockport, Cheshire

A CIP record for this book is available from the British Library

ISBN 978 1 4744 2139 3 (hardback)
ISBN 978 1 4744 2900 9 (paperback)
ISBN 978 1 4744 2140 9 (webready PDF)
ISBN 978 1 4744 2141 6 (epub)

Contents

Figures

Series Editor's Foreword

The Edinburgh Studies in Modern Arabic Literature is a new and unique series which will, it is hoped, fill in a glaring gap in scholarship in the field of modern Arabic literature. Its dedication to Arabic literature in the modern period, that is, from the nineteenth century onwards, is what makes it unique among series undertaken by academic publishers in the English-speaking world. Individual books on modern Arabic literature in general or aspects of it have been and continue to be published sporadically. Series on Islamic studies and Arab/Islamic thought and civilisation are not in short supply either in the academic world, but these are far removed from the study of Arabic literature qua literature, that is, imaginative, creative literature as we understand the term when, for instance, we speak of English literature or French literature, etc. Even series labelled 'Arabic/Middle Eastern Literature' make no period distinction, extending their purview from the sixth century to the present, and often including non-Arabic literatures of the region. This series aims to redress the situation by focusing on the Arabic literature and criticism of today, stretching its interest to the earliest beginnings of Arab modernity in the nineteenth century.

The need for such a dedicated series, and generally for the redoubling of scholarly endeavour in researching and introducing modern Arabic literature to the Western reader has never been stronger. The significant growth in the last decades of the translation of contemporary Arab authors from all genres, especially fiction, into English; the higher profile of Arabic literature internationally since the award of the Nobel Prize for Literature to Naguib Mahfouz in 1988; the growing number of Arab authors living in the Western diaspora and writing both in English and Arabic; the adoption of such authors and others by mainstream, high-circulation publishers, as opposed to the academic publishers of the past; the establishment of prestigious prizes, such as the International Prize for Arabic Fiction (the Arabic Booker), run by the Man Booker Foundation, which brings huge publicity to the shortlist and winner every year, as well as translation contracts into English and other languages – all this and very recently the events of the Arab Spring have heightened public, let alone academic, interest in all things Arab, and not least Arabic literature. It is therefore part of the ambition of this series that it will increasingly address a wider reading public beyond its natural territory of students and researchers in Arabic and world literature. Nor indeed is the academic readership of the series expected to be confined to specialists in literature in the light of the growing trend for interdisciplinarity, which increasingly sees scholars crossing field boundaries in their research tools and coming up with findings that equally cross discipline borders in their appeal.

With both the Arab national and cultural projects unrecognisably different today from what they were at the late decades of the nineteenth century and early ones of the twentieth (the *nahda* or awakening period) and with all the metamorphoses that these interdependent projects have undergone from that time to the present day, a reassessment of the role of the Arab intellectual – the writer, the novelist, the poet, the filmmaker is overdue. From the very beginning of the *nahda*, the Arab intellectual has borne the burden of the educator, the moderniser, the connector between East and West, the importer and adaptor of foreign thought and values, the very prophet of a brave new world.

This essentially romantic perception of the role of the intellectual, whether as self-perceived by the intellectuals themselves, or as projected on them by society, was bound to be subverted by the multi-faceted disasters that befell the Arab world since at least the second half of the twentieth century, i.e. more or less since the end of colonialism. The failure of democracy, the dictatorships that replaced the rule of imperial powers in the post-independence era, the defeats in wars with Israel, the economic failure, the civil wars, and more recently the fiasco of the Arab Spring – all this was inevitably to cause the perception of the intellectual as prophet to implode, to become redundant, ironic, a false prophecy.

This is what Zeina G. Halabi is attempting to explore in this study.

Chapter by chapter she juxtaposes authors and texts (and indeed films and directors) from the past with others from the present to demonstrate the conceptual change in the mission of the writer as prophet, bringing the discussion right up to the Arab Spring with its further implications for the role of the intellectual.

Professor Rasheed El-Enany, Series Editor,
Emeritus Professor, University of Exeter;
Professor of Modern Arabic & Comparative Literature,
Doha Institute for Graduate Studies

Note on Translation and Transliteration

I have followed the style and transliteration guidelines of the *Chicago Manual of Style* (15th edn) and the *International Journal of Middle Eastern Studies*. For Arab authors' names, I have chosen the most commonly used transliteration in English. I have transliterated the glottal stop ء as ʾ and the consonant ع as ʿ. Whereas my translation of poetry and the Quran includes all accents on word endings (e.g. rabbikā alladhī khalaqā), my transliteration of prose text includes only internal vowels (e.g. rabbik alladhī khalaq). I have indicated either in the body of the text or in the notes when the translation is my own.

Acknowledgements

When I first came across Tarek Butayhi's painting *Waiting for Youssef* (2013), which now adorns the cover of this book, I was struck by the man sitting on the low chair. His gaze and posture exude a troubled aura. Staring straight at us, the character appears resilient yet disenchanted; disenchanted yet resilient. His presence evokes urgency, an injunction to reflect on the crisis that he endures in silence. His face was all-too familiar: he is the Syrian painter Youssef Abdelke. It is curious how Abdelke, whose *oeuvre* I do not engage in this book, features so prominently on its cover. But the ambivalence that this painting captures, at the intersection of generational deference and dissent, speaks to this book on numerous levels.

To my mind, Abdelke's generation of Syrian, Palestinian and Lebanese intellectuals were all the protagonists of the story I saw unfolding in 1990s Beirut. It was a time of disenchantment, as intellectuals reckoned with a set of political *posts*-: the post-war Lebanese era of redefining militancy following the devastation of the civil war and the post-Oslo moment of thinking of the slippery notion of peace in Palestine and the remaining prospects for national liberation. It was also the post-Gulf War juncture in which Arab intellectuals observed in shock the disintegration of a unified Arab position on Iraq. Intellectuals were introspective and retrospective as they wrestled with the very questions that would ultimately animate this book: What remains of the legacy of the intellectual, when the theorised and anticipated future did not, in fact, materialise? From that moment began a long chain of questions that I was fortunate enough to explore in conversation with a host of thought-provoking interlocutors.

This journey was enriched by the support and generosity of my friends and family in Beirut. I thank Azza el-Zein, Michelle Obeid, Nisrine Mansour and Alya Karame for pointing to the end of the tunnel each time I was in doubt; Samer Frangie for his overwhelmingly generous and rigorous feedback on drafts and proposals; and Fadi A. Bardawil for his feedback, particularly as I wrote the introduction. Khaled Saghieh's own trajectory has inspired my work in ways that I cannot describe here; I am indebted to his wisdom and patience. I thank my family, Laila, Rania, Lana and Omar Halabi, for their constant flow of love and support.

My mentors and colleagues at the University of Texas at Austin continued to support my project even after I graduated. This book would not have been possible without Mahmoud al-Batal and Kristen Brustad and the Arabic programme they founded more than a decade ago. I hope to convey a semblance of their passion in these pages. Tarek el-Ariss has been there since the first moment I was intrigued by Arab intellectuals and their experience of loss in literature. His advice, brilliance and own work on Arab literary modernity accompanied me as I wrote this book. Yoav Di-Capua, the inimitable storyteller, grounded my work in intellectual history and showed me how this book is a story waiting to be told. His humour and rigour are what I hope to channel here. Since her first smile across the classroom, Angela Giordani has read my work, pitched in her vast knowledge of modern Arab thought, and has not ceased to embrace me with love. I thank Benjamin Koerber, the humorous *sajjāᶜ*, for helping me render in English the rhymed prose that I analyse in Chapter 1, and Blake Atwood for reading drafts upon proposals, making suggestions with eloquence and care, always reminding me to keep track of the comparative thread.

At the University of North Carolina, I would like to thank the College of Arts and Sciences for granting me a course release and the Research and Study Assignment that allowed me to complete the book, as well as the UNC Junior Faculty Development Award that funded the initial research. The University Research Council's Publication Grant was essential to the production of the book. I am grateful to Nadia Yaqub for her feedback on my work and for creating the most favourable working environment for a junior faculty. I thank Robin Visser for reminding me of all the ways in which my project is part of a global narrative on the shifting sand on which intellectuals stand and for her conviction that this book will see the light of day. I thank my colleagues Dominique Fisher, Mark Driscoll, Sahar Amer and Gang Yue for their generous advice as I began preparing the manuscript for publication.

At Duke, miriam cooke understood the stakes of this project from the outset. Her support, comments and advice were invaluable. I thank Bruce Lawrence, Erdağ Göknar, Helen Solterer, Ellen McLarney and Didem Havlioglu for reading the manuscript and pointing to all the ways in which the argument could shine.

My affiliation with the Freie Universität Berlin, the Center for Arab and Middle Eastern Studies at the American University of Beirut, and the Orient Institute in Beirut allowed me to reach out to a wide community of scholars and have access to some of the most distinguished libraries and archives. In 2012–13, the postdoctoral fellowship 'Europe in the Middle East – the Middle East in Europe' at the Forum Transregional Studien in Berlin gave me the opportunity to complete the book and engage an exceptional community of Arab scholars who may not have been able to collaborate otherwise. I have deep gratitude to Georges Khalil, who knows not only how to gather a unique group of artists, humanists and social scientists and make an intellectually stimulating programme happen, but also how to continue conversations, even after the programme ends. I thank Hanan Toukan for her generous feedback on proposals and drafts and Friederike Pannewick for inviting me to present on the various stages of my work and for editing with Georges Khalil a section of Chapter 3 that appeared as 'The Day the Wandering Dreamer Became a Fida'i: Jabra Ibrahim Jabra and the Fashioning of Political Commitment', in Georges Khalil and Friederike Pannewick (eds), *Commitment and Beyond: Reflections on/of the Political in Arabic Literature since the 1940s* (Wiesbaden: Reichert, 2015), pp. 156–70, reprinted with the permission of Reichert Verlag.

I thank Elias Khoury, first, for making available *al-Mulhaq*, the cultural magazine that gave me a sense of political direction in 1990s Beirut; and second, for reading my interpretation of his legacy, two decades later, and remaining an extraordinary interlocutor. My deep gratitude goes to Michael Allan, Samira Aghacy and Ken Seigneurie for their invaluable and thought-provoking comments on the manuscript. I thank Muhsin al-Musawi for his support of this project and for editing an earlier version of Chapter 2 that appeared in 'The Unbearable Heaviness of Being: The Suicide of the Intellectual in Rabiᶜ Jābir's *Rālf Rizqallāh through the Looking Glass*', *Journal of Arabic Literature* 44, no. 1 (2013), pp. 53–82. Reprinted by permission of Koninklijke Brill.

I would like to extend my gratitude to the editor of the series, Rasheed el-Enany, for his enthusiasm and support for this project and Nicola Ramsey and the editorial team for the remarkable work they have done. I am grateful to Simone Bitton and Elia Suleiman for providing me with the stills from their films and the permission to use them. Tarek Butayhi's kind permission to use his painting has bestowed the book with the mystique of the man sitting on the low chair.

Preface

At that moment, the future became your approaching past!

Mahmoud Darwish, *In the Presence of Absence*

In 'We, the Intellectuals' (2013), the Palestinian artist Oraib Toukan reflects on the intricate relationship between intellectuals and the politics of cultural institutions in a post-2011 Arab world. She recounts an incident in 1997 when Mahmoud Darwish (1941–2008) read 'In Ritsos's Home' to a packed auditorium at the Royal Cultural Centre in Amman, Jordan.[1] Upon speaking the verses 'O Palestine / name of the earth / and name of the heavens / you shall prevail', he was interrupted by a few zealous listeners, who chanted thrice – perhaps not so spontaneously – 'Long Live His Majesty King Hussein the Great!' Predicated on power and authoritarianism, the injunction to Jordanian nationalism reveals an orchestrated sabotage of Darwish's verse, one that sets the power of the king against the poet's prophecy of Palestinian emancipation. Toukan recalls:

> Darwish simply cleared his throat with a firm 'ahem' and moved on to his next verse. 'In Pablo Neruda's home, on the Pacific coast, I remembered Yannis Ritsos', he read. 'I said: What is poetry? He said: It's that mysterious event, it's that inexplicable longing that makes a thing into a specter, and makes a specter into a thing'. Flash-forward to now and a 'Long Live the King' interruption today would certainly cause a writer to pack up, leave, reject, refuse, and decline invitations from the institution thereafter. There are simply more cultural institutions to choose from – more thinkers, more artists, more spaces, more patrons, more of everything, really ... Moral authority has been democratized. Anyone can speak truth to power; besides, power knows the truth.[2]

Toukan's account of Darwish's poetry reading enfolds three temporalities, of which the past is the first. Before he began reciting 'In Ritsos's Home', Darwish briefly described the circumstances behind the poem. He had been in Chile on a visit to Pablo Neruda's (1904–73) 'lavish' home, when he remembered the Greek dissident poet Yannis Ritsos's (1909–90) 'modest' dwelling in Athens.[3] Struck by the contrast between the living conditions of the two poets, particularly the former's proximity to power and the latter's alienation from it, Darwish poetically reconstitutes the trials of his friend Ritsos, enfeebled by fascism and military rule and exiled at home. Darwish relates past conversations with Ritsos about prisons, poetry and Palestine; more precisely, about the *future* of prisons, poetry and Palestine. Back then, the two poets, alienated and disenfranchised, anticipated a future in which prisons have disappeared, oppression has ended and Palestine has prevailed. The poet's prophecy draws on the power of the word to achieve collective salvation. He not only speaks truth to power but also speaks of emancipation in the name of the displaced and the disenfranchised.

The second temporal layer is the future. The event that Toukan narrates takes place in 1997, or in the wake of Darwish's past conversation with Ritsos. Toukan's temporality – or the future of justice and emancipation that both Darwish and Ritsos had impatiently anticipated – evokes cognitive dissonance, for it mismatches the reality of Darwish as he stands interrupted by the invocation of authoritarian forces. While Darwish reminisced about his exchange with Ritsos, it was clear that Palestine – at least the Palestine in Ritsos's and Darwish's past hopes – did not, in fact, prevail. By the time Darwish stood reading his poem in the post-Oslo Accords era of the 1990s, emancipation and justice had been reconsidered. The Palestinian political and economic elite had returned to the West Bank and Gaza and fostered a discourse of realpolitik, which ultimately pacified and bureaucratised the Palestinian liberation struggle. In other words, Darwish's poetry reading indicated that the future that he and Ritsos had predicted never materialised. In their hoped-for future, power co-opts dissidence twice over: feigning political tolerance by inviting the Palestinian national poet while assigning chanters to sing the praises of the monarch once the poet pronounces Palestine free ('O Palestine/ … / You shall prevail'). Here, the sabotaging of Darwish's verse at the Royal Cultural Centre reveals his prophecy's predicament.

Toukan speaks from the *future* of Darwish's past exchange with Ritsos. We are in 2013, years after Darwish was hosted at the Royal Cultural Center. Toukan's contemporary world abounds with bloody uprisings, military coups, and intellectuals not uncomfortable around centres of power. As they are connected in cultural institutions that contribute to the construction and dissemination of truth, intellectuals materialise in their capacity of 'agents of regimes of truth', of mediators of ideology and their enactment.[4] It is a contemporary juncture in which 'moral authority has been democratized', as Toukan observes, where legitimacy is no longer the prerogative of the prophet-poet as the sole representative of the national cause.[5] Visual artists, activists, filmmakers, curators, graffiti artists and other cultural actors assume that role and speak for a cause, unbound by national, linguistic or generic boundaries. More significantly, Toukan's contemporary moment, which is also the future of Ritsos's and Darwish's prophecy, has proven that speaking truth to power is no longer prized as an act of courage, simply because 'power knows the truth', having heard it all before.[6] If scandals of leaked diplomatic documents, torture, abuse and state-orchestrated war crimes have shown us anything, it is that even when power has been exposed, scandalised and shamed, it is still unyielding.

The incident of Darwish's poetry reading is nestled between a past of prophecies, a present in which they have not materialised, and a future that has not come. As Toukan recalls Darwish recalling, in turn, his prophecy of national and poetic emancipation, she brings multiple realities to the fore. She invokes Darwish's past embodiment of political commitment in poetry and juxtaposes it with a post-Oslo conjuncture that domesticated and neutralised radical politics, which has engendered a temporality of stalled uprisings and aborted revolutions. Toukan thus confronts Darwish's past – significantly, his prophetic past – with her present as she witnesses the receding of ideologies of emancipation, particularly as they manifest in cultural politics. Toukan's sensibility stems from the cognitive dissonance of observing the power of the intellectual's prophecy and tracing its demise. It begins by discerning, as David Scott words it, 'the temporal disjunctures involved in living *on* in the wake of past political time, amid the ruins, specifically, of postsocialist and postcolonial futures past'.[7]

Toukan movingly captures in this short passage a contemporary disenchantment with the afterlife of the Arab intellectual's prophecy. In Toukan's contemporary juncture – the future of the intellectual's prophetic past – the intellectual-prophet can barely say anything new about prisons, poetry and Palestine, for it all has already been said. More significantly, hers is a present temporality that reveals how the intellectual's prophecy has become futile, replaceable and redundant for 'there are simply more cultural institutions to choose from – more thinkers, more artists, more spaces, more patrons, more of everything, really'.[8] As she demystifies the intellectual's authority to speak truth to power in the name of a stateless people, Toukan gestures to Foucault's refiguring of the intellectual's contemporary role. 'The intellectual discovered,' Foucault writes, 'that the masses no longer need him to gain knowledge: they *know* perfectly well, without illusion; they know far better than he and they are certainly capable of expressing themselves'.[9] No longer the lone voice speaking truth to power, the prophetic intellectual that Toukan portrays carries tragically the burden of his aborted prophecy, stranded in a dystopic present, unable to move to the future. Intertwined and enmeshed, the prophetic past, the dystopic present and the stalled future are temporalities that operate as a reminder of the intellectual's interrupted journey toward emancipation.

Darwish's own words on the power of poetry are pertinent in this context. He identifies poetry as 'that inexplicable longing that makes a thing into a specter, and makes a specter into a thing'.[10] Akin to his poetry, Darwish is the inexplicable spectral prophecy that hovers over Toukan's contemporary text, just as Ritsos hovered over Darwish's poem in 1997. In Toukan's description of the scene, the intellectual is elevated to the realm of the abstract, and then turned into a thing, an objectified figure that inhabits poetry, prose, Palestine and everything in between. And yet, he appears at the poetry reading as a remainder of his past self, emblematising the aspirations, contradictions and predicament of the Arab intellectual-prophet. In this context of consecutive disenchantments and the cycle of objectification and demystification, what remains, then, of the Arab intellectual's prophecy that Darwish channelled so well? Oraib Toukan's layered depiction of Darwish, first as Ritsos's prophetic interlocutor and later as an interrupted speaker, evokes a discursive dissent that I map in post-1990s literature depicting intellectuals.

Notes

1. Entitled 'Ka-Haditha Ghamida', the poem appeared in Mahmoud Darwish, *La Ta^c^tadhir ^c^Amma Fa^c^alt*. My translation from the original Arabic.
2. Toukan, ' "We, the Intellectuals" '.
3. Darwish, 'Fi Bayt Ristus'.
4. Foucault, 'The Political Function of the Intellectual', p. 207.
5. Toukan, ' "We, the Intellectuals" '.
6. Ibid.
7. Original emphasis. Scott, *Omens of Adversity*, p. 2.
8. Toukan, ' "We, the Intellectuals" '.
9. Foucault and Deleuze, 'Intellectuals and Power', p. 207.
10. Darwish, 'In Pablo Neruda's Home', p. 308.

Introduction:
In the Beginning was the Word

So ascend with your people, higher and farther than what the myths have prepared for you and me. Write, yourself, the history of your heart, from the moment Adam was struck with love, until the resurrection of your people.

Mahmoud Darwish, In the Presence of Absence

In *The Unmaking of the Arab Intellectual*, I identify the 1990s as a critical historical juncture following which writers began displacing the figure of the intellectual-prophet that had governed Arabic literature in the modern era. If the end of the Cold War engendered collective scepticism over the viability of Marxism, the end of the Gulf War and the dismemberment of the Palestinian resistance indicated the demise of a unified pan-Arab position toward Iraq and the question of Palestine. Writers experienced these profound transformations, in the context of the collapse of the secular nation-state – exemplified by the violent sectarianism of the Lebanese civil war (1975–90) – as the last instalment in a series of consecutive political defeats that had begun in the early 1960s and culminated in the 1967 war. More significantly, the dislocation of the nationalist, socialist and pan-Arab ideological paradigms, which had framed literary and intellectual discourse in the twentieth century, transformed the ways in which writers conceived of the intellectual as both the carrier and embodiment of a prophecy of teleological change and progress. As those paradigms that provided ideological underpinning for emancipation receded, the time came to rethink what constitutes the political in the contemporary era.

The dissent I identify in contemporary literature begins by constructing an effigy of the prophetic intellectual that Mahmoud Darwish personified so well, an effigy that carefully elevates him as the embodiment of emancipation ideologies and subsequently points to the limits of his discourse. Almost identical to that which it aims to parody, the effigy is then voided of its signifiers. But burning, in this sense, is not an act of rupture, erasure and silencing, but rather an act of exorcism, of unmaking. It probes the loss of the prophecy and declares the end of an era. It is a séance in which intellectual ghosts are summoned and later asked to leave. I show how, as contemporary Arab writers reflect on the ideological transformations of the intellectual, they are critical yet reverent. They evoke the power of his iconography, yet point to its limits; they channel its romantic undertones, yet delight in cynicism. In sum, they remind us of the future of his prophecy and reconstruct its demise. The literary deconstruction of the Arab intellectual's prophecy has implications on what the intellectuals say, on how they say it and in whose name.

Crossing generational, linguistic and generic thresholds, the works of the Lebanese novelists Rabee Jaber (Rabī' Jābir; b. 1972), Rashid al-Daif (Rashīd al-Ḍa'īf; b. 1945) and Rawi Hage (b. 1964); the Saudi novelist Seba al-Herz (Ṣibā al-Ḥirz; b. 1983); and the Palestinian cineaste Elia Suleiman (b. 1960) exemplify this aesthetic and political turn. Although identifying with different historical generations and espousing distinct aesthetic sensibilities, these authors participated in a dialectical appropriation of the archetype of the Arab prophetic intellectual by engaging the legacy of forebears like Jurji Zaidan (1861–1914), Jabra Ibrahim Jabra (1919–94), Edward Said (1935–2003) and Mahmoud Darwish and simultaneously pointing to their faltering power. As they embrace a self-reflexive, nonsecular and affective mode of criticism, these writers reject the objectification and the ideological codification of the intellectual and ultimately question the viability of the modernist principles associated with the archetype's construction. In fictionalising and subsequently burning an effigy of the modern, secular, nationalist and exilic intellectual, they elicit a counter-discourse of criticism that questions intellectuals as knowledge producers and disseminators. This book will reveal how notions pertaining to the intellectual-prophet as a modernising subject, political commitment as a literary ethos, exile as a catalyst for change, and nationalism and secularism as ideologies of emancipation have lost their critical vigour and become symptomatic of a defunct political discourse and, in turn, the locus of dissent. Espousing a distinct conception of what constitutes the political, contemporary authors relocated their critique from an explicit logocentric, teleological, secular-nationalist discourse to one that is anachronistic, transnational, nonsecular and latently affective that predicates the political on the personal. It is significant inasmuch as it invites us to conceptualise that which we call 'the contemporary'.

In *The Unmaking of the Arab Intellectual*, I thus make the hitherto opaque conjuncture of the 1990s legible by highlighting the political critique inherent in a presumed post-political aesthetic moment. Specifically, I counter the available critical corpus that reads late-twentieth-century Arabic literature as an apolitical and fragmented discourse insofar as it transgresses the ethos of political commitment, *iltizām*, and the archetype of the modernist intellectual that channels it. I show how, as contemporary writers lost their precursors' faith in the secular modern nation-state, rational political action and the Arab subject that emerged out of these structures, they articulated a new vision of a political collectivity and subjectivity – one on which I draw to theorise the uncharted field of contemporary Arabic literature.

I see this book as an examination of the remainder of the postcolonial moment and a return to the legacy of the Arab intellectual-prophet as the embodiment of emancipation ethos. I do not aim to generate a historiography or a literary inventory of the different and consecutive representations of the intellectual since the 1990s. Neither do I aim to restate the now-tired condemnation of the apolitical nature of contemporary Arabic literature, and much less to declare the political over and expired. Rather, I suggest that the contemporary invites us to engage in a practice of criticism that is inherently retrospective and evaluative, putting into question the very foundation of what constitutes the modern Arab intellectual legacy. I suggest a methodology that ultimately generates a politics of reading that locates the political in contemporary Arabic literature.

The Making of the Intellectual-prophet

Simone Bitton (b. 1955) opens her documentary *Mahmoud Darwich: As the Land is the Language* (1997) with a long drive down a desert road. A man is captured in high angle as he contemplates the overwhelmingly barren landscape. The narrator wonders:

How to film exile? A Palestinian poet looks out over his homeland from the slopes of Mount Nebo, on the eastern bank of the Dead Sea and the River Jordan. It was from here that Moses is supposed to have contemplated the Promised Land, which he was never to enter. Palestine is just across the river; so near, yet so far.[1]

From the outset, Bitton is consumed by the same fascination with exile that accompanied the greatest Palestinian exilic poet and intellectual, Mahmoud Darwish, in his arduous trajectory. She shares his anxiety about signifying and representing exile. Throughout the documentary, Bitton approaches Darwish's exile from its different signifiers: exile as mass exodus; exile as estrangement from one's native tongue; exile as alienation at home; and ultimately, exile as the intertwinement of them all, particularly in her portrayal of Darwish's exile in Paris. Although Bitton broaches the different

Figure I.1 Mahmoud Darwish standing on Mount Nebo in Jordan overlooking the West Bank in Simone Bitton's *Mahmoud Darwich: As the Land is the Language* (1997).

Figure I.2 Mahmoud Darwish standing on Mount Nebo in Jordan overlooking the West Bank in Simone Bitton's *Mahmoud Darwich: As the Land is the Language* (1997).

significations of exile in the documentary, she particularly attends to exile as a state of transcendental and allegorical displacement.

Bitton opens her first scene at the original moment of exile at Mount Nebo, where Moses stood looking over the Promised Land for the first time. The biblical motifs of the desert, Mount Nebo and River Jordan are cinematographically rendered in a wide-angle shot that recalls the divine gaze looking down, not without sympathy, at the tragedy of the exilic people. As in the scriptures, the Prophet speaks Truth in the name of his wandering people and shall lead them to the Promised Land. The power of this kind of 'mythic utopism', Ken Seigneurie writes, is in 'its capacity to kindle nostalgic and utopian sentiments all at once by recoding an image of the past as simultaneously a utopic image of the desired future.'² In other words, the scene validates the transcendence of the Palestinian question, entrusts it to the poet-prophet, who shall carry it to the Promised Land of the future. Bitton, however, sabotages the narrative of Zionism, for the land in question is not Israel, but Palestine; the chosen people are not the Jews, but the Palestinians; the messenger of truth is not a prophet, but a poet; indeed, the prophet is not Moses, but Mahmoud Darwish. As the poet-prophet of today's wandering people, Darwish comments on the significance of standing on the prophetic site:

> The dialogue I have with myself here is a dialogue with the absent part of me. I see Absence so closely that I can touch it. I can embrace it or reject it, as if I were there. As if my spectre [*shabaḥī*] here addresses my essence [*jawharī*] there.[3]

Standing on Mount Nebo overlooking Ramallah, Jerusalem and Jericho, which are in his field of vision yet outside his reach, the poet-prophet describes the poetics of fracture that exile engenders. Exile, as Muhsin J. al-Musawi describes it, 'turns the speaker into a damaged creature and transforms home-land into a site of silence and death.'[4] As the proverbial exilic space brings him close to that which is near yet unreachable, Mount Nebo invites Darwish on a self-reflexive commentary on the state of existing in absence, on his uproot-edness from home. Exilic absence, for Darwish, splits the self into binaries along here/there and embrace/rejection. Most importantly, absence leads to the dichotomous representation of the exilic spectre in contrast to a rooted essence (*shabaḥ* v. *jawhar*).

This scene is perhaps one of the most revealing portraits of Mahmoud Darwish. Invoking the prophetic iconography that colours Darwish's poetry, it evokes notions of displacement, absence, and the privilege of representa-tion, about who speaks for the wandering people and in what ways. As it dialectically reconstructs exile, this opening scene portrays the mythical yet tragic journey of the poet-prophet, the question of temporality, and the dif-ferent conceptions of time that frame the experience of exile. Palestine is thus revealed across three successive temporalities: it is historical inasmuch as it is embedded in biblical tradition and historical memory; it is a present signi-fier of displacement and loss; it is ultimately projected into the future by the spectrality of the exilic poet-prophet. The scene is thus about the intertwine-ment of the lyrical and the political, the personal and the collective, and the spectral and the messianic, all of which set the parameters of the prophetic intellectual.

But here is where the enmeshment of the poet-prophet, Palestine and the manifold sense of temporalities take on a metanarrative dimension. We watch Bitton representing Darwish as he represents the Palestinians in 1997 from the vantage point of a contemporary moment of coups, revolutions and civil wars that have taken their toll on the intellectual that Darwish evoked so well. As such, in the wake of all the horrors they have witnessed, viewers face the incongruity of two fields of meaning: the mythical-utopism of the exilic intellectual-prophet that Bitton channels on the one hand, and the materiality of the intellectual's positioning in relation to power, which Oraib Toukan reveals in her depiction of Darwish, on the other. The visual and allegorical incongruity of these distinct representations of the intellectual-prophet ushers in the questions that animate this book: how has the motif of the intellectual – coded theologically and teleologically – been reconfigured in contemporary literature? What can it tell us about the afterlife of the intellectual? I ask, specifically, what does the contemporary representation of the Arab intellectual reveal about the ways in which writers understand both their past and present temporality? Answering these questions begins by laying out the aesthetic and epistemic contours of the Arab intellectual, specifically those revealed by Bitton's scene.

The question of what exactly constitutes the intellectual has long animated the field of political sociology. Points of contention between the different typologies of the intellectual revolve around the material conditions that mould intellectuals and their consciousness. The first of these questions is whether intellectuals form a distinct social class; and the second is whether intellectuals can, in fact, transcend their class of origins. Between Julian Benda and Antonio Gramsci lies an entire critical corpus that puts forward distinct typologies that are particularly pertinent to the contemporary era. They take into account post-Marxist readings of notions of class and class formation; post-capitalist visions of global actors; and a post-statist reading of history.[5] Other approaches examine the ways in which intellectuals battle with ontological questions about what it means to exist in a postcolonial Arab world[6] and how to create a field of meaning for others by processes of translation,[7] adaptation and speaking back to loci of power. Such approaches build on previous calls by Michel Foucault and Pierre Bourdieu to examine the intellectuals' self-fashioning and the ways in which they are interpellated by structures of power, including those of the cultural field itself.[8] Foregrounding the self-fashioning of the intellectual, Edward Said deplores the lack of attention to 'the image, the signature, the actual intervention, and performance, all of which taken together constitute the very lifeblood of every real intellectual.'[9]

In dialogue with these aforementioned approaches, I examine the literary afterlives of the Arab intellectual by engaging modes of self-fashioning, (self-) representation, and performativity at specific historical junctures. The questions that I ask here and in the following chapters are concerned with the ways in which contemporary Arab writers, emblematic of different literary and historical generations, have conceived and represented the archetype of the intellectual since the 1990s. It is important to begin by showing precisely the dominant tropes that had framed the literary depiction of intellectuals and that contemporary writers have subsequently undone, deconstructed and transcended. I begin by exploring a series of interrelated questions: what is at the core of the intellectuals' prophecy? How do they articulate it? And in whose name? Here, I turn again to Darwish as the quintessential poet-prophet who reflected on and simultaneously embodied these questions.

Mahmoud Darwish's prolific poetic project was one of national emancipation, indeed, but also one that carried a humanist and universal outlook on the questions of alienation, displacement and exile. He spoke of his challenge to transcend the local and specific and engage a poetics of the absolute. It was his way to 'inscribe the national on the universal,' as he writes, 'so that Palestine does not limit itself to Palestine, but that it may found its aesthetic legitimacy in a vaster human space.'[10] His was a project of universalising the particular by making legible the Palestinian question as a human narrative of displacement, and particularising the universal by tracing the yield of a universal humanist discourse of emancipation on the Palestinian tragedy. As such, Darwish carried in his project the ethos that the Arab Enlightenment legacy bequeathed to his generation.

The nineteenth-century Arab Enlightenment era, known as the *nahda*, invited Arab intellectuals to reflect on methodological and conceptual approaches by which they could reconcile acquired Western epistemologies with those drawn from Arab and Islamic heritage. The age of the *nahda* prescribed a model of emancipation predicated on modern epistemologies that range between a selective reconciliation with tradition, and a forward-looking embrace of Western sciences and modes of governance. Such teleological narratives are permeated by humanism that conceives of the subject as the master of a word that ushers in freedom and emancipation. Endowed with a universal ethos and self-identified as modern subjects, *nahḍa* intellectuals laid the contours of the emerging Arab subject.[11] When Jurji Zaidan began construing and nurturing a modernising Arab Ottoman readership,[12] Farah Antun (1874–1922) was thinking of the universal and universalising ethos of socialism,[13] whereas Nazira Zeineddine (1908–76) was conceiving of a modern Islamic female subjectivity that is simultaneously pious and responsive to the modernising injunctions of her times.[14] These *nahḍa* intellectuals took on the challenge, as Darwish would do years later, of particularising what was believed to be universal (justice; freedom; progress), by inscribing it within cultural and political specificities. They simultaneously carried a responsibility that stems from the 'shared idea of a universal subject', of universalising the particular by evading the conceptual boundaries of Arab and Islamic exceptionalism. It was, thus, a collective task of describing their respective historical juncture and prescribing a model of salvation, liberation and redemption. Hence, the Arab age of *nahḍa* put forward an understanding of man as a rational being and a master of the word, one who will usher in a future of emancipation.

The modern Arabic literary canon has thus channelled the aspirations and anxieties of writers and their protagonists as they navigated their troubled path toward modernisation. Arab writers have narrated the push and pull between tradition and modernity and the power struggle embedded in the East/West nexus as they wrestled with foreign and native coercive powers, all within secular-nationalist frameworks that articulate different conceptions of the political. In the wake of profound educational reforms and the emergence of modern educational institutions and cultural platforms, the *nahḍa* historian and man of letters Jurji Zaidan, who coined the term *nahḍa*, conceived of the writer as a generalist (*kātib ʿāmm*) who drew on Western epistemologies to construe a modern Arab identity and literary narrative. Later, men of letters (*udabāʾ*) including Taha Husayn (1889–1973) questioned further the role of the *nahḍa* intellectual and articulated an unwavering modernist vision of culture, one that is not necessarily at odds with the question of colonial influence. The *udabāʾ*'s attention to aesthetics rather than confronting the notion of colonial liberation, which began unfolding, became the object of criticism by an emerging generation of politically conscious intellectuals. Marxist intellectuals like Hussayn Muruwwa (1907–87), Mahmoud Amin al-Alem (1922–2009) and Raif Khoury (1913–67) drew on Jean Paul Sartre's notion of engagement in literature and identified themselves as proponents of literature of commitment (*iltizām*) at the intersection of Marxism and third-worldist emancipation. They, and other intellectuals of different Marxist confessions, articulated what Yoav Di-Capua calls 'an attack, personal as well as generational, on Taha Husayn and his class of intellectual mandarins'.[15] With the emergence of anticolonial movements, the proponents of a liberal reconciliation with colonial cultural influence were at fault. Indeed, those were the 'years when revolutionary futures were not merely possible but *imminent*; not only imminent, but *possible*', to borrow David Scott's words.[16] The anticolonial, pro-Palestinian, and pan-Arab revolutionary discourse that laid out a future of possibilities persisted throughout the 1960s.

Although the 1967 Arab defeat by Israel bolstered a palimpsest of literary voices – from Ghassan Kanafani's (1936–72) conception of 'resistance literature'[17] to Elias Khoury's (b. 1948) codification of the writer as an allegory of the nation in crisis – the depiction of the Arab intellectual as a modern and modernising force persisted.[18] Perhaps it became even more urgent in the wake of setbacks, beginning with the collapse of the United Arab Republic (1958–61) and not ending with the Lebanese civil war. Such historical junctures turned the critical focus from imperialism and class struggle as units of analysis to the question of culture exemplified by the resilience of sectarianism. The intellectual shifted, as Fadi A. Bardawil observes, from the vanguard of Marxist and nationalist militants, to 'an individual critic, who has lost his revolutionary organizational moorings, becoming the lone guardian of the Enlightenment temple'.[19] As such, the question of professing a teleological reading of progress became all the more crucial. Abdel Rahman Munif (1933–2004) lays out the predicament of the Arab intellectual as the embodiment of an Enlightenment ethos that is both salvation and resistance:

An Arab writer is a fida'i, a resistance fighter. In countries where freedom of opinion does not exist, parties are not allowed, where a constitution probably does not exist, all those who are able to express themselves are obliged to put up resistance. Their function is to enlighten the people, to make them aware of the justice and injustice, as long as legal and commonly accepted political institutions are lacking.[20]

Navigating the rough path of decolonisation, on the one hand, and the power of endogenous structures of oppression, on the other, politically committed writers turned to language and thought and confronted the impending danger of erasure of selfhood by 'forging a historic possibility', as Said writes.[21] In a context of crises and systematic processes of erasure, that of peoples and memories, the role of Arab writers, he adds, was 'to be one of *making* the present in such a way as, once again, to *make* it in touch with past authenticity and future possibility.'[22] Put differently, the word and text were indiscernible from the prophecy. Thus, in his mission to create an Arab present that ultimately ushers in a future of possibilities, the Arab intellectual continued to speak, as Foucault writes, 'the truth to those who had yet to see it, in the name of those who were forbidden to speak the truth: he was conscience, consciousness, and eloquence.'[23]

The Arab intellectual's continuous engagement of the universal/particular dialectic invites a discussion about what Foucault calls 'conscience', especially in his positioning in relation to power. Power is understood here within the Foucauldian tradition as that which 'tends to render immobile and untouchable those things that are offered to us as real, as true, as good', whether that of the state, political groups or cultural institutions.[24] Resistant to the seduction of power, the intellectual embodies a spirit that is, Edward Said reminds us, 'in opposition rather than in accommodation'.[25] He speaks in the name of the marginalised and the disenfranchised, disturbing the status quo, challenging institutional power in all ways possible by making connections that are otherwise silenced and denied.[26] Intellectuals in Said's mind are those who ask questions that are embarrassing, heterodox. They challenge dogma without, however, reproducing it.[27] In sum, they identify power and position themselves facing it, fashion themselves in opposition to it, in order to be able to speak truth to it. Said's tackling of the question of power is central to his conception of the intellectual as one who, because of his alienation from centres of power, is permanently located in exile, literal but more significantly, metaphorical. Exile is a metaphoric state of displacement that removes intellectuals from the enclave of power to its margins, which ultimately allows them to foster a critical approach to power with the word as their tool.[28] Darwish, again, illustrates the intellectual's resilience to the seduction of political power.

In the wake of the establishment of the Palestinian Authority and the initiation of the process of state building in the West Bank and Gaza, Yasser Arafat (1929–2004) reinvented himself from the leader of guerrilla warfare to the president of a semi-autonomous fragmented political entity that is the West Bank and Gaza. It was imperative, as it is legitimising, that the most prominent Palestinian intellectual participated in that transition. Darwish confirms to Simone Bitton rumours about how he rejected Arafat's offer to join in his cabinet:[29]

> He asked me 'What harm did it do when Malraux became a Minister in De Gaulle's cabinet?' I said there are at least three differences: First, France is not the West Bank and Gaza. Second, the circumstances of Charles De Gaulle are not those of Yasser Arafat. And third, André Malraux is not Mahmoud Darwish … negligible differences. But if Palestine were to become a great state like France, and Yasser Arafat were to have Charles De Gaulle's power, and I were to reach Malraux's stature, then I would rather be Jean-Paul Sartre.[30]

Here, the intellectual subverts his comparison to Malraux's endorsement of political power and conveys his ambivalence about Arafat's authority and autonomy. Only when Palestine is autonomous and Arafat is as uncompromising as De Gaulle was, will the intellectual consider reconciling with power. But even then, the model of the intellectual that Darwish admires is not Malraux's (1901–76), but rather that of Jean-Paul Sartre. Here, Darwish reminds Arafat and subsequently his audience, that as a minister of cultural affairs during the uprising of May 1968, Malraux had been on the other side of political power; not alongside but facing Sartre, the visionary of political commitment and the anticolonial intellectual leading the protests. Unlike Malraux, whose remains lie in the French Pantheon, Sartre refuses to be co-opted by power; his rejection of the 1964 Nobel Prize for Literature scandalised the European cultural establishment. The intellectual that Mahmoud Darwish has in mind is more akin to his friend and interlocutor Edward Said, one who relishes critical distance from power despite, or perhaps because of, his unrivalled cultural and symbolic capital.[31]

The Enlightenment mission that Arab intellectuals took upon themselves could hardly have been possible without the assumption of representation. Speaking in the name of a silent and silenced other is intimately linked to the notion of authority, of who is entrusted with the prophecy and who is entitled to create a field of meaning for others and speak in their name. In that sense, the intellectual is an individual, as Said imagined him, 'endowed with a faculty for representing, embodying, articulating a message, a view, an attitude, philosophy or opinion to, as well as for, a public.'[32] Intellectuals construct a language – literary, poetic and philosophical – that speaks truth to power,[33] for 'knowing how to use language well and knowing when to intervene in language are two essential features of intellectual action,' he reminds us.[34] The faculty of representation, of speaking in the name of absolute values and for the sake of the disenfranchised promised victory, is a critical constituent of Darwish's intellectual prophecy.

The legitimacy of Darwish, the intellectual-prophet, stems precisely from his power to represent, enlighten and lead the voiceless. Like intellectuals who 'represent themselves to themselves', by depicting the personal plight of estrangement and exile, Darwish demonstrates precisely how representation may be poetically articulated and performed.[35] By 1970, Darwish had become 'the poet of the [Palestinian] Resistance' (shāʿir al-muqāwama). Following the publication of four influential poetry collections, his name became the signifier of both Palestinian nationalism and poetry.[36] Darwish admits his ambivalence about the weight that the term 'national poet' implies:

> It depends on what is meant by 'national.' If a national poet is a representative, I don't represent anyone … But if what is meant is that the national poet is the one who expresses the spirit of the people, I accept that, that is beautiful. Every poet in the world dreams that his voice will also be the voice of others.[37]

Darwish pushes back against the entrapment of political representation and ushers in his own concept of representation embedded in a romantic nationalist rhetoric. He refers to representation as the task of conveying 'the spirit of the people', of carrying the voice of the oppressed and the disarmed, those exilic wanderers to whom Simone Bitton referred in the opening scene. As such, the intellectual's word is endowed with the power of achieving collective salvation as it represents the plight of the silenced and the marginal, particularly during moments of national crisis. Darwish demonstrates the representative powers of the prophecy, yet again.

In 1983, Darwish stood on a podium in a crowded hall in Algiers before the Chairman of the Palestinian Liberation Organization, Yasser Arafat, and hundreds of Palestinian leaders representing different political factions. A few months earlier, in the summer of 1982, Lebanon had witnessed one of its worst episodes of the civil war. The Israeli siege of Beirut ultimately led to the fall of the city and the withdrawal of thousands of Palestinian militants, fida'is, to the sea, eventually to Tunisia where the PLO relocated. Left on their own and without protection from local and regional allied forces, thousands of the remaining Palestinian refugees of Sabra and Chatila camps were massacred by Lebanese Christian militias. The tragedy of 1982 engendered multiple experiences of loss: it was the loss of Beirut, the city that had sheltered the Palestinian resistance; the loss of vulnerable refugees and heroic fida'is; and the loss of Arab solidarity with the Palestinians. Displaced again, Palestinian refugees were left powerless but for the word of their poet-prophet. In a dramatic moment exuding resentment, pride and grief and verging on sacrilege, Darwish reads – rather, recites – an epic poem about the 1982 siege of Beirut. 'In Praise of the Tall Shadow' (*Madih al-Zill al-ᶜAli*, 1983) captures the tragedy of the capitulation of the fida'is and the horror of the camp massacres. Drawing on perennial poetic genres – from boast, panegyric, invective, to elegy – Darwish poetically reconstructs the dramatic fall of the Palestinian freedom fighter, the fida'i. In an auditorium in Algiers, packed with fida'is, leaders of the PLO and allies of the Palestinian liberation struggle, Darwish stands on the podium and gestures to the Quranic Surah, 'The Blood Clot':[38]

Recite:

In the name of thy fida'i who created, [applause]

created horizon of a boot. [applause]

In the name of thy fida'i who renounces

Their world

To His first calling,

The very first.

…

In the name of thy fida'i who begins

Recite![39]

The reading ends in standing ovation. Arafat walks toward Darwish and embraces him as numerous cameras capture the moment when leaders of the PLO bury their differences and unite around the indisputable representative of the Palestinian people in exile. As he speaks in the name of the fida'i-God ('In the name of thy fida'i'), as one would invoke God in prayer ('In the name of God') and prostrates before his might, Darwish reiterates his own power as the poet-prophet yet again. As he deifies the fida'i, he consecrates himself as the prophet entrusted to carry the fida'i's word and lead his people through exile. By enacting the poet-prophet, Darwish uses the word, precisely the verse, as the medium of the ethos of emancipation. Darwish, here, gestures to Sartre's conception of the politically committed writer and yet transcends him by pointing to the emancipatory potential of poetry. He uses verse to speak in the name of the fida'i, for the exilic Palestinian people, and to Israel and Arab regimes of oppression. He speaks not only truth but also *liberation* to power. Darwish's enactment of representation in this recitation draws on the age-old dialectics of tradition and modernity by revisiting, so as to point to its contemporaneity and timeliness, the premodern Arab poetic tradition. As he enacts the poet of the tribe who communicates, in verse, the aspirations, pride and anxieties of his people, Darwish channels the greatest tenth-century Arab poet, al-Mutanabbi (915–65). But unlike al-Mutanabbi, Darwish does not speak in the name of power but in the name of the disenfranchised. When he is offered power, Darwish rejects it, unlike his Abbasid predecessor, who, Elias Khoury writes, 'exhausted his entire life searching for its mirage.'[40] Rather than channelling Malraux and al-Mutanabbi, Darwish embraces Sartre and ʿUrwa Ibn al-Ward (d. 607), the ṣaʿālīk, brigands of poetry and philosophy. Such are the ways in which the intellectual's prophecy is embedded in a theological iconography. It draws on the topos of the exilic prophecy, of theologically coded spaces (e.g. Mount Nebo), a timeless spectrality fostered by displacement (e.g. jawhar/shabaḥ), the centrality of the prophetic word in a teleological discourse of salvation.

The self-fashioning and depiction of the intellectual evoke all these biblical signifiers, and yet do not relinquish the worldly. The literary infatuation with the messianic tradition, with its iconography and rootedness in local mythologies, its elevation of the word arises from the post-Enlightenment worldview of the intellectual. Nahḍa intellectuals, whether Zaidan, Ahmad Faris al-Shidyaq (1805–87) or Butrus al-Bustani (1819–83), sifted the mythological from the metaphysical in order to construe a vision of a post-Enlightenment man reconciled with his religious heritage but fundamentally materialist in his sensibilities. This conception of the role of the Enlightenment subject has bequeathed a literary tradition that is mostly sceptical of religious authorities and institutions, as al-Musawi observes, due to their perceived normalisation of state practices of coercion.[41] The intellectual's articulation of spirituality, agnostic and anxiety-ridden, has thus remained distant from metaphysics and secular in its dispositions.

This multi-layered portraiture of Darwish yields an understanding of the intellectual-prophet as the embodiment of Enlightenment values. This intellectual uses the power of the word not only to speak truth but also to advocate emancipation to local and colonial coercive powers. To borrow Said's words again, the prophecy is 'an individual vocation, an energy, a stubborn force engaging as a committed and recognizable voice in language and in society with a whole slew of issues, all of them having to do in the end with a combination of Enlightenment and emancipation or freedom.'[42] The intellectual's legitimacy stems precisely from his distance from structural power. He represents the disenfranchised, which lay at the fringe of power by means of the word. The intellectual thus carries a communal history, is beset by a tragic present, which he sees unfolding into a promising future. Darwish, Rashid Khalidi writes, 'always carried himself with a reserve that seemed to bespeak an inner sorrow, as if he perceived wrenching tragedies deeper than the rest of us could fathom.'[43] This conception of the transcendence of the poet is rendered not only in Darwish's poetry but also in the visual representation of his works. For instance, the cover art of Darwish's penultimate book, *In the Presence of Absence* (2006; English trans. 2011), mimics a tombstone, 'but it is a tombstone promising an eternal presence in words,' writes Sinan Antoon.[44]

As such, Mahmoud Darwish emblematises, not without ambivalence, the figure of the modern Arab intellectual that I address in this book. As the poet-prophet standing on the allegorical Mount Nebo, this figure is prophetic, representative and righteous. The poet-prophet is a modern force and a force of modernity, an intellectual who secularises the divine by means of his omnipotence, his unmatched ability to lead change; he is omniscient in knowing how to do it; and most importantly omnipresent. The intellectual is omnipresent because he is spectral, endowed with an insurmountable power, not only to clearly identify and embody that which constitutes the Arab experience of modernity, but also to continue to hover over an uncertain future that is the contemporary. But what exactly constitutes this moment that I call contemporary? And how does, then, the distorted, interrupted and disfigured legacy of the Arab intellectual inhabit it?

Aftermaths

Darwish describes his positioning as a Palestinian intellectual in this multi-layered, multi-temporal vision of history: 'I have found a *terra firma* saturated with history. I draw my strength from it because I look through the prisms of past and future. Thus, the present appears less fragile, more like a passage toward a more certain history.'[45] Darwish draws his power and resilience in the face of tragedy from a stable consonance of three interlaced temporalities: the present tapping a saturated history of tragic losses, which necessarily engenders a future of emancipation. The agreement between the different temporalities to which Darwish refers is striking in its fluidity, tranquillity and consistency. But what happens when this sense of consonance is disturbed, when this temporal order no longer flows?

An illustration of disturbed temporalities is Paul Klee's *Angelus Novus*, a painting that captivated Walter Benjamin due to its forceful disturbance of temporal quietude:

A Klee painting named Angelus Novus shows an angel looking as though he is about to move away from something he is fixedly contemplating. His eyes are staring, his mouth is open, his wings are spread. This is how one pictures the angel of history. His face is turned toward the past. Where we perceive a chain of events, he sees one single catastrophe which keeps piling wreckage upon wreckage and hurls it in front of his feet. The angel would like to stay, awaken the dead, and make whole what has been smashed. But a storm is blowing from Paradise; it has got caught in his wings with such violence that the angel can no longer close them. The storm irresistibly propels him into the future to which his back is turned, while the pile of debris before him grows skyward. This storm is what we call progress.[46]

Benjamin writes here about the disquiet of temporalities. The past is uncertain, the present is unstable, and the future may not come. If read in the context of the intellectual's prophecy, Benjamin's interpretation of *Angelus Novus* destabilises the temporal logic that frames the mission of the intellectual-prophet endowed with the word in order to usher us to a the Promised Land that is the future. The faith in historical change that drew specifically on the coherent and stable division of time into past/present/future has become unbearable in its teleological reasoning, or as David Scott writes, 'that old consoling sense of temporal *concordance* is gone.'[47]

The end of the Cold War engendered collective scepticism over the viability of both Marxism as an episteme and socialism as a mode of governance. The receding of the institutional left ushered in a collective sentiment of disillusionment in the role of the state in leading progress. Twentieth-century Europe witnessed therefore the demise of a political ethos of redemption, of a conception of the Sartrian politically committed intellectual, as one endowed with the power to prophesy redemption and usher the collectivity into a world emancipated from 'historical necessity'.[48] The intellectual was granted the right to speak 'in the capacity of master of truth and justice' and was self-fashioned as 'the spokesman of the universal'.[49] In other words, as Lyotard maintains, twentieth-century Europe witnessed the end of the 'Enlightenment model of politics as the site of a secular redemption.'[50] A corollary of the demise of the Enlightenment ethos is the diminishing relevance of the question of representation that stipulates a mode of creating and interpreting a field of meaning and speaking in the name of a disenfranchised other. Foucault's injunction against intellectual prophecy stems precisely from the ethical implications of representation as an act that prevents represented subjects from speaking for themselves. In this sense, the role of the intellectual as a universal intellectual – intervening within ethical parameters and creating a field of meaning for others, most importantly embodying conscience and consciousness – was, for Foucault, a vestige from the past.[51] Gilles Deleuze concurs on the receding role of the Enlightenment intellectual. Blurring the distinction between a speaking and an acting subject, theory and praxis, Deleuze returns to the 'theorising intellectual', who is 'no longer a subject, a representing or representative consciousness'.[52] Representation for Deleuze 'no longer exists; there's only action – theoretical action and practical action which serve as relays and form networks.'[53] The disturbance of this teleological understanding of history and praxis engendered, thus, a collective disillusionment not only with Enlightenment principles and representation ethos, but also with the intellectuals who had articulated them.

If the past had been merely a set of unfulfilled promises and the future a temporality that will never materialise, in what ways have writers experienced the present? David Scott probes the predicament of previous epistemological models when they are made obsolete and voided of their emancipatory power. In *Omens of Adversity* (2014), he examines the failure of the revolution and emancipation hopes in Grenada by looking at the notion of temporality, specifically at the intricate rapport of the troubled past, its interplay in the present, and its legacy in the future. He delves into the notion of the 'aftermath', a temporal experience of ideological ruins and disenchantment. The aftermath is an experience of the present, not as a transitional temporality, or what Said described as interstitial temporality between a past and a future and fertile with possibilities, but one in which time has become paralysed, 'stranded in a postrevolutionary present that has nowhere to go'.[54] The tragedy of being abandoned in the contemporary, that of reckoning with a present temporality that abounds with the aftermath of unfulfilled prophecies, a present that is going nowhere, is hardly a phenomenon restricted to Arab intellectuals; it is the constitutive element of the collective memory of modernist intellectuals who carried specifically the mission of emancipation and representation. Although being 'stranded in the present' is not exclusively an Arab predicament, the Arab experience of the post-1990s colours the tragedy of the collective sentiment of loss in particular ways. I approach the contemporary Arab moment as a collective experience of history and time defined along the parameter of consecutive 'posts-', such as post-war Lebanon (1990), post-Gulf War (1991) and post-Oslo Accords (1993).

The era of aftermaths and 'post-' that is pertinent to this book begins with the end of the Lebanese civil war. The war erupted in 1975 following years of mobilisation, ideological then military, around questions that had preoccupied post-independence intellectuals: how do we conceive of a Lebanese modernity, one that is reconciled with its Arab past and at the same time cautious of premodern sectarian and tribal structures of identification? Along this line of questioning, consecutive generations of intellectuals, all born between 1930 and 1950, found in Arab nationalism, Marxism, the Palestinian liberation struggle, or their intersection, the hope for a future liberated from structural modes of economic and political oppression. They steered their vision away from the question of culture by embracing materialist readings of sectarianism and modern feudalism and looked at nationalism, Arab and Palestinian, as a unifying ethos. Engulfing all and sparing none, the civil war mutated from a conflict that may have been ideologically rationalised into one driven by brute sectarianism that ultimately rearranged and neutralised pre-war ideological fault lines. Consequently, Lebanese militant intellectuals-turned-novelists, who had once espoused a nationalist and/or Marxist discourse of emancipation, found themselves at a double loss: first was the loss of the nationalist and Marxist ideological prospect, the realisation of its futility and permeability to the sectarian order; then came the loss of their own voice as catalysts for change and emancipation.

With the suspension of conflict in 1990, Lebanese intellectuals turned their gaze inwards, to their wounded self-image. It was a moment of introspection, of looking at what caused this abysmal loss of the self, and collective doubt, or at least, one of 'a-certainty' (al-lā-yaqīn) as Elias Khoury coined it.[55] It was a reflexive move, similar to that which Yasin al-Hafiz (1930–78) had articulated earlier, 'a reflexivity of defeat, a tragic reflexivity, rather than an epistemological reflexivity or a reflexivity of struggle,' Samer Frangie observes.[56] 'It was a reflexivity aiming at understanding why ideologies and theories failed or cannot be applied, while being on the side of these theories and ideologies. It was a reflexivity torn between the knowledge that it produced and the inability to act that it led to,' Frangie adds.[57] While *culture*, as an epistemological notion, had been sidelined in the 1960s in favour of a materialist positivist reading of history, it returned in full force as the war unravelled and became a dominant paradigm in the 1990s.[58] The question became, then, about what is it in culture that allows such violence and resistance to change. As such, novelists like Rashid al-Daif re-examined their respective sectarian, tribal and regional ties, not as critics and rebels, but this time as disenchanted subjects reckoning with the angst of breaking with traditional structures of identification. But there were other intellectuals, such as Khoury, who were less interested in culture as a unit of analysis, but rather in the collectivity as it materialises in the wounded national community prevented from mourning its losses. So began a process of examining collective memory, reconciliation and trauma and conceiving of the literary text as a site for the construction of a new ethos of writing.[59] It was a moment of loss, indeed, but also one of reconfiguring what it means to be an intellectual in a watershed era. As the post-war cultural scene emerged from the ruins of modernisation ideologies and the ashes of prophetic modernism, the intellectual was either mourned or construed as a messianic figure, a crucible of the pains of his national community. Chapter 1 on Jurji Zaidan and Rashid al-Daif and Chapter 2 on Elias Khoury and Rabee Jaber reveal the ways in which the Lebanese intellectual and his prophecy are transgressed and reconfigured in the post-war era.

As the Lebanese civil war ended, the Gulf War began. The sectarian violence of the civil war was not alone in fostering deep anxieties about the yield of modernist teleologies. Iraq's invasion of Kuwait and the subsequent retaliation of the Allied Forces against Iraq were the final blow in a series of consecutive political defeats of Arab nationalism as an ideology of unification and emancipation, an experience of defeat that was first felt with the ebbing of Nasserism. The splintering of a unified anticolonial and anti-imperialist Arab position began in the wake of the 1978 Camp David Accords. With the signing of that historic yet controversial treaty, Egypt became the first Arab state to recognise Israel – to the shock of many militant Arab intellectuals. A few days following the treaty and before he attempted suicide, the Syrian playwright Saadallah Wannous (1941–97) writes: 'We are both the mourned and the mourners.'[60] He adds: 'Our homeland and Cause are in the coffin, so are the hopes of our lives.'[61] As he expresses a collective disenchantment with the fragmentation of a unified Arab position toward Israel that had begun following the 1967 war, Wannous laments both the loss of Arab unity and the incapacity of intellectuals as they stand counting their losses.[62] The paradoxical position of being both the mourner and the mourned has since engendered a poetics of collective defeat sustained throughout the consecutive losses that intellectuals have witnessed: from the capitulation of the Palestinian resistance in Beirut in 1983, the sectarianisation of the Lebanese civil war, all the way to the demise of inter-Arab solidarity during the Gulf War. Wannous, among other intellectuals, experienced the Gulf War as a reminder of previous ones. He describes it as a political but also somatic experience of defeat that forever scarred his body. It was so devastating, he believes, that it caused the terminal illness that later took his life.[63] The ideological void ushered in by the ebbing of pan-Arab worldviews reintroduced Islam as the old, yet new, paradigm that is both imminent and possible. As such, the post-nationalist moment brought in defeat, indeed, but it also reconciled with a religious epistemological tradition that has been left out of the field of vision. The rise of a religious sectarian worldview and the idealisation of the religious militant intellectual are the focus of my analysis in Chapter 4 on the individual mourning of collective loss in *The Others* (2006; English trans. 2009) by the Saudi novelist Seba al-Herz.

In the wake of the collapse of the USSR, the end of the Lebanese civil war and the Gulf War, the Palestinian question had returned, particularly after the events of the First Intifada (1987–91). The Oslo Accords between the Palestinian Liberation Organization and the State of Israel in 1993 stipulated a new political and legalistic understanding of the Palestinians' displacement and their right of return. The establishment of the PLO in 1965 and the defeat of Egypt, Syria and Jordan following the 1967 war initiated a liberation rhetoric that infused a new life to the legacy of the exilic intellectual. The intellectual of the time was a proponent of resistance literature that Ghassan Kanafani theorised, a politically committed intellectual who brings forward the question of 'cultural resistance', marrying theory and praxis. For the militant intellectual who thinks emancipation and enacts it, the emphasis 'is on the political as the power to change the world. The theory of resistance literature is in its politics,' Barbara Harlow writes.[64] However, following the successive military setbacks – from the tragic events of the 1970 Black September war in Jordan to the renewed exile of Palestinian intellectuals from Beirut in 1983 – all paths led to political settlement. Moving from the national liberation trope of the 1960s and 1970s and the nation-building trope of the 1980s, the 1993 Oslo Accords ushered in an era of settlement and negotiation, exemplified in the building of a state bureaucracy within the boundaries of a non-sovereign political entity. The paradox of emancipation under occupation becomes flagrant in Ramallah, 'where people live under Israeli colonialism, on the one hand, and with hallucinations of a postcolonial condition, on the other,' as Hanan Toukan aptly describes it.[65] This will be the post-Oslo era, in which political pragmatism, neoliberalism and growth under occupation overrule national liberation.

At stake in this political and discursive mutation is the legitimacy of the exilic intellectual, who returned, not to the Palestine of Darwish's poetry and Kanafani's short stories, but to the 'Palestinian Territories', a neologism evoking neither emancipation nor autonomy. As such, the exilic Palestinian intellectual experienced the Palestinian idiosyncratic notion of return ('awda), not as a collective restoration of the injustice of population transfer, but as a legalistic, sanitised, selective return of capital to a Palestinian proto-state. In this context of the aborted emancipation and false return of the wandering people, the portrait of the exilic and militant intellectual has been reconfigured by a new generation of writers who seek to give voice, as Kamran Rastegar argues, 'to those aspects of Palestinian experience which are irreconcilable to such a project of codifying a national narrative.'[66] Turning their gaze to the evasive notion of the Palestinian ordinary, writers and filmmakers have taken us to Israeli checkpoints, roadblocks, walls and sieges, while others re-examined the notion of exile by decentring the figure of the exilic intellectual and voiding it of its signifiers. The Palestinians' experience of daily life under occupation and the urgency of the question of the ordinary have deeply transformed the ways in which Palestinian writers imagine militance, heroism and resistance. The novelist Alaa Hlehel ('Alā' Ḥulayḥil; b. 1974) observes how the demise of an overarching and uniting Palestinian liberation project has led to the emergence of anti-heroic dystopic motifs in literature and cinema that point to the inadequacies of exisiting paradigms for reading contemporary Palestinian literature.[67] Chapter 3, on Rawi Hage and Elia Suleiman and their portrayal of the exilic intellectual, retraces that discursive shift arising from the generational disenchantment with the post-Oslo era.

The aftermath of such decisive historical junctures has engendered an unnamed, unqualified and inconspicuous contemporary era that is defined not by what it is, but relationally, by what it lacks and what it transgresses and classifies as past. Thus, the remainder of Arab ideologies of emancipation and modernisation has generated a present that is paralysed and beset by a generationally transmitted incapacity and a collective sense of paralysis.[68] It is an experience of the aftermath in which the anticipated future 'could no longer be imagined as a horizon guaranteed by the memory of the past, and the present could no longer be experienced as a mere interval in the passage from remembered past to immanent future,' Scott writes.[69] Lacking resolution, the present or contemporary literary moment stagnates at the intersection of cynicism, irony and melancholic affect, mistakenly read as a testament to the end of the political. Against the backdrop of this conception of the contemporary, one that lies at the intersection of a legacy of unfulfilled prophecy and a necessity to redefine and appropriate the political, the portrait of the Arab intellectual-prophet will be disturbed and redefined.

Scope

The questions that inform this book stem from new prospects that Arabic literary criticism has ushered in. Recently, Roger Allen announced that there would be no third edition of *The Arabic Novel*, the widely read and taught critical introduction to Arabic literature from the nineteenth century to the early 1990s.[70] This is partly because, he maintains, Arabic literary criticism has taken for granted assumptions of linguistic, generic and regional unities that can no longer justify a new edition. He suggests, therefore, a re-evaluation of the nomenclature that has governed Arabic literary criticism by embracing critical methodologies that question the foundation of what constitutes the 'modern', 'Arabic' and 'literary' in the construct of 'modern Arabic literature' and its epicentre, the novel.[71] Such destabilisation of the tenets of the field of Arabic literary criticism simultaneously both responds to and influences emerging studies that have problematised Arab literary modernities, questioned the centrality of nationalist paradigms, and dislocated the strict boundaries between genres and disciplinary denominations. I draw on this critical opening in *The Unmaking of the Arab Intellectual* by introducing a dialogic, multidisciplinary and cross-generational approach that examines the prism of the past, present and future in the contemporary depiction of intellectuals. In line with influential studies in the field of Arabic literary criticism, I suggest an alternative vision of criticism, one that revisits the canonical paradigm of the intellectual-prophet, and in so doing salvages precisely the perspectives, texts, authors and genres, which have been either critically dismissed or discounted from literary historiographies and taxonomies of the contemporary era.

As it examines the afterlife of the modern Arab intellectual, *The Unmaking of the Arab Intellectual* traces the ways in which contemporary Arab novelists have deconstructed and resignified the intellectual's legacy. In so doing, it gestures to the critical corpus pertaining to the self-fashioning of the modern intellectual from the nineteenth-century Arab Enlightenment era to the modern times. The scholarship on the emergence of the *nahda* intellectual has proliferated in the last decade. One could read this growing critical attention as a reinscription of sidelined, discounted and erased articulations of the modern onto the telos of Arab Enlightenment. The renewed interest in *nahda* canonical intellectuals such as Jurji Zaidan, Rifaa al-Tahtawi (1801–73) and Ahmad Fares al-Shidyaq are instances of such significant contributions. The re-examination of subaltern subjectivities has preoccupied other *nahda* scholars such as Leyla Dakhli in her work on the emergence of early Syrian and Lebanese women intellectuals in the context of the 1908 Ottoman reforms and Lital Levy in her work on Esther Azhari Moyal (1873–1948), the little-known Lebanese-Jewish intellectual.[72] Other scholars, like Dyala Hamzah, approached a historiography of *nahda* intellectuals by probing the emergence of a public sphere, in which *nahda* intellectuals were constructed and which they constructed in turn.[73] Others articulated a new critical theory by embracing the challenge of dialectically engaging historical materialism and poststructural discourse analysis, as the work of Stephen Sheehi demonstrates.[74] In addition, a revisionist concern has preoccupied scholars including Shaden Tageldin and Tarek el-Ariss, who examined the construction of Enlightenment subjectivities by looking at the interplay of affect, bodily inscription and externalisation of *nahda* values, all the while destabilising visions organising the world around East/West, tradition/modernity and conquest/subservience, among other binaries.[75] In Chapter 1, on Rashid al-Daif's historical metafiction, I re-examine the canonicity of the *nahḍa* intellectual by reading al-Daif's contemporary return to Jurji Zaidan, particularly to the moment Zaidan began construing a modern and modernising intellectual sensibility.

Not only is *The Unmaking of the Arab Intellectual* concerned with *nahḍa* as a move to make sense of the contemporary return to the *nahḍa* intellectual, but it also engages the literary corpus pertaining to the self-fashioning and representation of the postcolonial Arab intellectual. The postcolonial Arab intellectual's multiple setbacks, disenchantments and arduous journey toward emancipation have been largely collapsed into the 1967 *naksa* telos. Conceived as a moment of deep rupture, the *naksa* has been the dominant paradigm that informed Arab thought and Arab literary criticism in prior decades. In the wake of the 1967 war, Arab intellectuals engaged in a collective introspection, in which they reflected on all reasons – cultural and political – that facilitated the defeat that ultimately reorganised their understanding of themselves and their temporalities. Around 1967, intellectuals such as Abadallah Laroui (b. 1933), Georges Tarabishi (1939–2016), Mohamed Abed al-Jabiri (1935–2010) and Sadek Jalal al-Azm (1934–2016), to name a few, turned their gaze to the problematic notion of culture.[76] The question was about what it is in Arab cultures that prevented Arabs' progress into modernity. At fault were Arab traditionalism, resistance to change and attachment to metaphysical epistemologies. Despite the panoply of perspectives that range between a renewed attachment to the rational model and a disenchanted return to religious politics, the emphasis on the 1967 war has been constant. One can read this emphasis in intellectual historiographies that have promoted such periodisation as a cardinal point to map the reverberations of the *naksa* on Arab thought and philosophy.[77] In literary criticism, too, 1967 has been read as the beginning of an era that ushered in new critical paradigms, as Edwar al-Kharrat (1926–2015) maintains in *The New Sensibility* (*al-hasāsiyya al-jadīda*).[78] More recently, a similar framework has appeared in Fabio Caiani's approach to postmodern literary techniques;[79] in Samira Aghacy's conception of a shattered masculinity; and Muhsin J. al-Musawi's tracing of an Islamic literary sensibility.[80] What these perspectives have in common is a conception of the *naksa* as a moment of rupture that generates new critical paradigms and aesthetic sensibilities.

The *Unmaking of the Arab Intellectual* builds on – as a means of probing – the available readings of the 1967 war and suggests an alternative reading of the *naksa* that is simultaneously, if not paradoxically, tragic and generative. Looking beyond Egypt, one may read the reverberations of the 1967 war as, rather than a juncture of defeat and rupture, a moment that grew on the 'fecundity of crisis' as Samer Frangie argues as he maps the intellectual transformations of the socialist nationalist intellectual Yasin al-Hafiz.[81] For the Palestinians, the empowering of the Palestinian guerrilla warfare led, as Anouar Abdel-Malek writes, to replacing 'the armoury of criticism with the criticism of arms', as I show in the chapter on Jabra Ibrahim Jabra.[82] In the Lebanese context, the 1967 defeat, in fact, radicalised all political discourse until the 1980s when secular and left-wing militant intellectuals realised that the war had indeed turned sectarian, as Chapter 1 on al-Daif demonstrates. *The Unmaking of the Arab Intellectual* thus conceives of the post-1990s as a new era of emerging political and literary sensibilities, an era that I call the contemporary.

Furthermore, *The Unmaking of the Arab Intellectual* recognises the importance of bringing multiple sets of critical literatures together. It draws not only on debates within North American and European scholarly circles, but also on the vast critical corpus in French, English and Arabic that is embedded in the intellectual milieus of the texts and their authors. The emphasis on a transnational approach is inherent to the ways in which I examine the depiction of the Arab intellectual. My inclusion of the Anglophone writer Rawi Hage takes advantage of critical perspectives that traverse disciplinary boundaries by making the 'Arabic' component of Arabic literature more inclusive of transnational, diasporic, Francophone and Anglophone literary experiences as the works of Syrine Hout and Michelle Hartman suggest.[83] Furthermore, as I explore works from Lebanon, Palestine and Saudi Arabia, I present a transnational reading of contemporary Arabic literature, in which I challenge the strict adherence to a nation-state approach at probing the transformation of canonical tropes. This becomes particularly salient in Chapter 4 on literature by Saudi women, in which I suggest a new mapping of the Arab world, one in which the Gulf becomes the locus of not just economic but also intellectual power that dislocates the secular-nationalist paradigms that have informed the literary canon as well as its reception and circulation.

But one may wonder why Egypt and the Maghreb, the latter so under-represented in Anglophone Arabic literary criticism, are not part of my focus. It is true that there is a distinctive Levantine character in the choice of these texts by mostly Palestinian and Lebanese authors, local and diasporic. However, I concur with Roger Allen who argues for a need among critics, especially in Western academe, to 'focus our attention on more variegated studies that examine particular genres and sub-genres, regions and their cultural particularities, and critical approaches.'[84] Considering Allen's call, I found it necessary to question the unit of 'Arabic' in Arabic literature and probe local and regional literary economies that inform different critical and literary sensibilities. *The Unmaking of the Arab Intellectual* points to the ways in which the question of Palestine and its corollary notion of political commitment – which are particularly urgent in the context of the Arab Levant – have transformed the ways in which intellectuals have conceived of themselves and their peers after the watersheds. As such, this approach calls for the need to engage in local debates and intellectual genealogies that inform the texts. Chapter 2 on Rabee Jaber and Elias Khoury recognises the importance of drawing on endogenous intellectual debates of the early 1990s in order to identify the scope and implications of Jaber's intervention.

Although it concerns itself with contemporary fiction, the book branches out to several other genres and media. The majority of the texts that I analyse in *The Unmaking of the Arab Intellectual* are novels, yet they are always read against the backdrop of a wider ecology of genres that includes poetry, essays, op-eds, obituaries, eulogies, literary magazines, memoirs and visual media such as films, recorded interviews, poetry readings and documentaries, among others. I join other scholars in avoiding a genre-centred criticism restricting itself to one genre read within a given nationalist framework. From this standpoint, the question of genre becomes central. As *The Unmaking of the Arab Intellectual* branches out to film, it demonstrates that the contemporary reconfiguration of the intellectual-prophet is not exclusive to literature. But one should acknowledge the concern about comparing two different media, the danger of collapsing the visual, the cinematic and the artistic to the textual. What prompts, one may wonder, a comparative reading between a visual medium such as a feature film and prose? How can we, at the end of the day, read Elia Suleiman's visual language against the prose of Jabra Ibrahim Jabra or Edward Said, or place Simone Bitton's documentary in dialogue with the vast critical corpus pertaining to Mahmoud Darwish? Elia Suleiman's first feature film, *Chronicle of a Disappearance* (1996), has received considerable attention – none of which, to my knowledge, pertains to the depiction of the intellectual. The choice to include Suleiman and Bitton stems from my belief in the importance of branching out to cross-disciplinary readings without, however, collapsing the visual to the literary. Akin to other cineastes, Suleiman and Bitton are part of a rich and complex local cultural field and global art network. Visual artists, indeed, they are also interlocutors within global and local dialogues pertaining to literature, history and philosophy. Hanan Toukan rightly observes how 'Arabic literary texts have historically been used as both the subject or the object of the artwork itself in various ways: as narrative or statement, as recorded speech and even as sculpture or performance', and how more recently they have been recuperated by young contemporary artists 'as a central vehicle for articulating counter-hegemony.'[85] Pointing to the literary in the visual text will, thus, reveal the critical possibilities inherent in various works of visual art. Such interdisciplinary transgeneric reading would unveil the critical potential of films, such as Kamal Aljafari's (b. 1972) *Port of Memory* (2010) and *Recollection* (2015), which may be read as a visual archive stemming from and informing Palestinian literature concerned with safeguarding collective memory.[86] In Lebanon, how can we make sense of the evolution of cinema and photography in the early 1990s, without, again, reading it against the backdrop of Lebanese fiction utterly consumed by the question of collective memory and post-war trauma?[87] In such instances, documentaries, feature films and videos are not only visual but also literary, and *The Unmaking of the Arab Intellectual* examines their literariness.

My approach is also intergenerational without espousing a strict understanding of the notion of generation, as I share Elizabeth Kendall's caution against the gratuitous use of the concept of 'generation'.[88] The term has been widely used in Arabic literary criticism to classify and describe historical and literary groups from the 'Sixties Generation' (*jīl al-sittīnāt*) to the most recent denomination, the 'Nineties Generation' (*jīl al-tisʿīnāt*). It is crucial to remember, as Kendall argues, that authors such as Jabra Ibrahim Jabra and Rashid al-Daif may identify with two or more generations. Thus, we cannot refer to the constructs 'contemporary writers' or '1990s generation of writers' with ease. The concept of generation, as I refer to it, is rather particular to the cultural and political specificity of the intellectual milieus – not necessarily national – that each chapter discusses. Generational nominations are, thus, not only temporal, pertaining to specific historiographic delineations, but also idiosyncratic, evoking a collective reckoning with a decisive historical juncture characteristic of the political milieu from which they hail. Examples of such classifications are the '*nakba* Generation' (*jīl al-nakba*) in the Egyptian context, the 'Disenchanted Generation' (*jīl al-khayba*) with which a generation of previously militant Lebanese intellectuals have identified, and the 'Dreamers' (*al-ḥālimūn*), the Iraqi generation of modernist artists and *udabāʾ* as they were depicted later.

The Unmaking of the Arab Intellectual is by no means a literary history of the contemporary representations of the intellectual (committed; exilic; dissident; Islamic; nationalist; communist) or an examination of the construction of symbolic capital and its circulation in various national cultural fields. This is not to say that studies that have engaged in such typologies are not valuable. On the contrary, they have contributed immensely to tracing the historical depth of the literary representation of the intellectual-prophet. Instead, my approach is selective, as it looks closely at the inner workings of specific texts, the limited number of which may raise doubts about how such a small selection is capable of making truth claims about Arabic literature in the last two decades. In addition, the texts chosen in this book are not meant to be exhaustive in illustrating all the ways in which Arab intellectuals have been represented in contemporary fiction since the 1990s. Indeed, one could name several other contemporary works of Arab fiction and film in which the intellectual is not only a dominant trope but also a site of ambivalence and criticism. I chose these texts among many others because each is emblematic of its specific cultural field (e.g. Rabee Jaber and Elias Khoury of the post-war Lebanese literary field); of a specific mode of subversion (e.g. irony in Rawi Hage and Elia Suleiman); or of a retrospective and anachronistic reconfiguration of the *nahḍa* intellectual (e.g. Rashid al-Daif on Jurji Zaidan). I show how each in turn and all together refigure the prophecy of the intellectual.

The selectivity of texts has allowed me to conduct close reading in order to build a deeper and more complex argument and refine my interpretations and, in so doing, has shown precisely the depth of the political critique inherent in these works. In *The Unmaking of the Arab Intellectual*, I steer away from a cursory, survey-based analysis and view the novels and film that I study as texts that constitute, in and of themselves, a fertile ground for theory. My approach thus relies on close readings that reveal the nuanced political critique inherent in exemplary works that have either received limited critical attention (e.g. Al-Daif and Jaber) or have been repeatedly read within a critical lens that fails to attend to their discursive transgression and political intervention (e.g. Al-Herz, Suleiman and Hage). By conducting close readings, I point to the interplay of aesthetics and politics to show what exactly has been omitted, silenced and displaced in these texts. Such an approach unearths the critical voice of Arabic literary texts, often sidelined by historicist, sociological and anthropological readings that are not always attentive to the texts' aesthetic value. My selection of texts and approach are different facets of this project that ultimately aims to redefine what constitutes the counter-canonical move in contemporary Arabic literature.

Chapters

In the chapters that comprise this book, I approach the depiction of the Arab intellectual from different methodological and conceptual angles. The following chapters do not constitute a teleological narrative, for each can be read on its own and in no particular order. Together, though, they ultimately build a thematic unity and contribute to what I hope is a coherent reconstruction of literary dissent from the archetype of the Arab intellectual-prophet. In Chapter 1, I examine the contemporary reconfiguring of the East/West and modernity/tradition binaries that framed critical discourse pertaining to the *nahda* intellectual. True to his self-reflexive narratives, the disenchanted novelist Rashid al-Daif fictionalises in *Tablit al-Bahr* (Paving the sea, 2012) the consecrated *nahda* intellectual Jurji Zaidan in a historical metafiction about a nineteenth-century Syrian intellectual and his troubled encounter with Western modernity. Countering the tepid reception of the novel, which missed the nature of al-Daif's critique, I reveal the ways in which the novel articulates contemporary ambivalence toward hegemonic historical narratives by displacing Zaidan's secular, nationalist and modernist legacy.

I return in Chapter 2 to a critical moment in post-war Lebanon in which the novelist Elias Khoury wrote tirelessly against the systematic erasure of collective memory and conceived the intellectual's word as the remaining hope for salvaging lost memory. While it mobilised the post-war intellectual scene, Khoury's dominant ideological and literary discourse on collective memory was the object of the emerging novelist Rabee Jaber's critique as he reinterpreted the suicide of a prominent Lebanese intellectual by rejecting the politicisation of his death.

I map in Chapter 3 the revisiting of the archetype of the exilic intellectual. Jabra Ibrahim Jabra had conceived of exile, particularly that of the Palestinian intellectual, as a tragic state of individual displacement that simultaneously works as a catalyst for modernisation and change. Jabra's romanticisation of the exilic intellectual, which Said later channelled in his conception of exile and secular criticism, was transgressed by Rawi Hage and Elia Suleiman. As I stage this unlikely transnational, cross-generational and multidisciplinary exchange between Jabra and Said on the one hand and Suleiman and Hage on the other, I reveal the ways the contemporary novelist and cineaste turn to metafiction, irony and play as strategies that ultimately demystify the Arab intellectual in exile.

Chapter 4 addresses the legacy of the Arab modern intellectual by examining his striking absence. Specifically, I take issue with the dismissive, essentialist and Orientalist critical interpretations of Seba al-Herz's *The Others* and read it as a novel that stages a unique exploration of the psychological and physical traces of three decades of political violence within the Shi°i community of Saudi Arabia. As I discuss the emergence of a Shi°i sectarian transnational rhetoric that challenges the secular-nationalist attributes of the modern intellectual, I point to the pervasiveness of the political critique inherent in what has been indiscriminately branded 'Saudi women's literature'. The only chapter that does not stage an intergenerational literary parallel, Chapter 4 points to the rupture that women writers, particularly in the Arabian context, have exhibited. The intellectual depicted here is more opaque, less articulate, lying at the intersection of the somatic traces of memory.

I emphasise in the conclusion in Chapter 5, as I contend throughout the book, how the literary unmaking of the intellectual is not an eschewal of the political, but rather a move to redefine and recode the political in ways that are congruent with the contemporary political moment. Specifically, I show how the displacement of canonical tropes associated with the archetype of the prophetic Arab intellectual is not a necessary process of destruction and elimination, but rather a means to make visible the complexities and fault lines of the modernist discourse of Arabic literature since the *nahda*. Finally, I briefly probe the ongoing Arab uprisings and ask whether the radical critical and political discourse they have engendered rejected further the archetype of the modern Arab intellectual or, on the contrary, rearticulated it as an indispensable catalyst for change.

Notes

1. My translation from the original Arabic. Bitton, *Mahmoud Darwich*.
2. Seigneurie, *Standing by the Ruins*, p. 9.
3. My translation from the original Arabic. Bitton, *Mahmoud Darwich*.
4. Al-Musawi, *Trajectories of Modernity*, p. 167. For an extensive analysis of the poetics of exile in the poetry of Darwish, Abdel Wahhab al-Bayati and Adunis, among others, see al-Musawi chapter 6, 'Envisioning Exile: Past Anchors and Problematic Encounters', pp. 162–217.
5. For a discussion of these different notions, see Kurzman and Owens, 'The Sociology of Intellectuals'.
6. Yoav Di-Capua's work on the Arab reception of existentialism exemplifies this scholarship. See Di-Capua, 'Arab Existentialism'.
7. For travelling theories, texts and the question of translation, see, for instance, Bardawil, 'When all this Revolution Melts into Air'; Litvin, *Hamlet's Arab Journey*; Elshakry, *Reading Darwin in Arabic, 1860–1950*.
8. See Foucault and Deleuze, 'Intellectuals and Power'.
9. Said, *Representations of the Intellectual*, p. 13.
10. Darwish, 'Mahmoud Darwish', p. 81.
11. Lyotard, 'The Wall, the Gulf, and the Sun: A Fable', p. 3.
12. See Chapter 1 for a detailed examination of Jurji Zaidan's legacy.
13. See Khuri-Makdisi, 'Inscribing Socialism into the Nahda' and *The Eastern Mediterranean and the Making of Global Radicalism, 1860–1914*.
14. See cooke, *Nazira Zeineddine*.

15. On the generational dissent from the *udabā*ʾ, see Di-Capua, 'The Intellectual Revolt of the 1950s and the "Fall of the Udabaʾ"'. For an intellectual genealogy of the concept of political commitment, see Klemm, 'Different Notions of Commitment (*Iltizam*) and Committed Literature'.
16. Original emphasis. Scott, *Omens of Adversity*, p. 4.
17. Barbara Harlow reads Ghassan Kanafani's conception of 'resistance literature' against the backdrop of a wider anti-imperialist literature of cultural resistance hailing from the post-Bandung Third World. Harlow, *Resistance Literature*, p. 30.
18. See Chapter 2 for an extensive analysis of Khoury's conception of the writer.
19. Bardawil, 'The Inward Turn and its Vicissitudes', p. 102.
20. Quoted from Khalil, Pannewick and Albers, 'Introduction: Tracks and Traces', p. 14.
21. Said, 'Arabic Prose and Prose Fiction after 1948', p. 64.
22. Original emphasis. Ibid. p. 49.
23. Foucault and Deleuze, 'Intellectuals and Power', p. 207.
24. Foucault, 'Power, Moral Values, and the Intellectual', p. 1.
25. Said, *Representations of the Intellectual*, p. xvii.
26. Ibid. p. x.
27. Ibid. p. 11.
28. Ibid. p. 63.
29. Darwish resigned from the PLO executive committee following the 1993 Oslo Accords between Israel and the PLO, which he criticised for being risky. See Sinan Antoon's analysis of Darwish's poetic critique of the Accords in Antoon, 'Mahmud Darwish's Allegorical Critique of Oslo'.
30. My translation from the original Arabic. Bitton, *Mahmoud Darwich*.
31. Although Darwish's friends insisted that he should be buried in his hometown, al-Birweh, the Palestinian Authority demanded that he be buried in Ramallah. Today, the mausoleum of Mahmoud Darwish is located in the Muqataa district, not far from Arafat's mausoleum.
32. Said, *Representations of the Intellectual*, p. 11.
33. Ibid. p. xvi.
34. Ibid. p. 20.
35. Ibid. p. xv.
36. Darraj, 'Transfigurations in the Image of Palestine in the Poetry of Mahmoud Darwish', p. 58.

37. Yeshurun, '"Exile Is So Strong Within Me"', p. 55.
38. 'Recite: In the Name of thy Lord who created, created Man of a blood clot' (Quran 96:1–2).
39. My translation from the original Arabic. Simone Bitton featured an excerpt of the poetry reading in *As the Land is the Language*, the longer version of which is widely available online. There are a few yet significant changes between the first and later editions of the poem. In the recent edition, the poem reads: 'Recite: / In the name of thy fida'i who created / created horizon of his wound / In the name of thy fida'i who renounces / Your world'. Compare between Mahmoud Darwish, *Madih al-Zill al-ᶜAli* and Mahmoud Darwish, *Al-Aᶜamal al-Ula*. Darwish often spoke of his dissatisfaction with his earlier poetry, *Madih* being the most memorable of the time. One could read his ambivalence about his earlier poetry in his poetic testament: 'How you trained yourself to reside in adventure, how you were burned by the embers of dualities, and how you struggled to endure opposites. You avoided defining a thing by its opposite, because the opposite of wrong is not always right. Homeland is not always daylight and exile is not night ...' Darwish, *In the Presence of Absence*, p. 42.
40. Khoury, 'The Poet is Dead', p. 101.
41. Al-Musawi, *Islam on the Street*, p. xviii.
42. Said, *Representations of the Intellectual*, p. 73.
43. Khalidi, 'Remembering Mahmud Darwish', p. 74.
44. Darwish, *In the Presence of Absence*, p. 6.
45. Darwish, 'Mahmoud Darwish', p. 83.
46. Benjamin, *Illuminations*, pp. 257–8.
47. Original emphasis. Scott, *Omens of Adversity*, p. 6.
48. Readings, 'Foreword', p. xviii.
49. Foucault, 'Truth and Power', p. 126.
50. Ibid. p. xix.
51. See Foucault, 'The Political Function of the Intellectual'.
52. Foucault and Deleuze, 'Intellectuals and Power', p. 206.
53. Ibid. pp. 206–7.
54. Scott, *Omens of Adversity*, p. 24.
55. Khoury, 'Thaqafat Maᶜbaᶜd al-Iltizam'.
56. Frangie, 'Historicism, Socialism and Liberalism after the Defeat', p. 351.
57. Ibid. pp. 351–2.
58. Fadi A. Bardawil examines this collective introspection, particularly in the works

of Yassin al-Hafiz and Sadek Jalal al-Azm, beginning from 1967. See Bardawil, 'The Inward Turn and its Vicissitudes'.

59. See, for instance, Khoury's op-eds during Israel's invasion of Beirut in 1982 in Elias Khoury, *Zaman al-Ihtilal*.

60. My translation from the original Arabic. Wannous, *Al-Aʿmal al-Kamila*, p. 493.

61. نحن الجنازة والمشيعون معاً. بعضٌ مني في التابوت، وبعضي الآخر يجرجر وراءه الأذيال...يا أيتها الإذاعات، ويا أيها الحكام، قليلاً من الصمت، فالتابوت وطن وقضية، وأماني عمر.
Ibid. p. 493.

62. Friederike Pannewick points to the First Gulf War as the turning point in Wannous's stance on political commitment, which will be gradually replaced by critical introspection and an inversion of ethical and political perspectives manifest in his play *Al-Ightisab* (Rape, 1989). Pannewick, 'From the Politicization of Theater to Individual Humanism'.

63. In an interview with the Syrian director Omar Amiralay (1944–2011), Wannous observes: 'I have the impression that our life is an endless series of setbacks. The last setback was especially painful. I believe that it caused the cancer I'm suffering from. With the setback, I mean the Gulf War. It killed our last hope. It is no coincidence that my first tumour appeared at that time. To be more precise: as the US was bombing Iraq.' Quoted in ibid. p. 228.

64. Harlow, *Resistance Literature*, p. 30.

65. Toukan, 'On Delusion, Art, and Urban Desires in Palestine Today', p. 209.

66. Rastegar, *Surviving Images*, p. 100.

67. Hlehel, 'Al-Riwaʾi al-Filastini'.

68. Scott, *Omens of Adversity*, p. 6.

69. Ibid. p. 109.

70. Allen, 'Rewriting Literary History', p. 250.

71. Ibid. p. 249.

72. Dakhli, *Une Génération d'intellectuels Arabes*. Also Levy, 'Partitioned Pasts'.

73. Hamzah, 'Introduction', p. 1.

74. Sheehi, 'Towards a Critical Theory of Al-Nahdah', p. 277.

75. El-Ariss, *Trials of Arab Modernity*, p. 172.

76. For a primer on these debates see the introduction of Massad, *Desiring Arabs*; and Kassab, *Contemporary Arab Thought*. Samer Frangie discusses the disenchantment of the Syrian Marxist intellectual Yasin al-Hafiz and specifically this question. See Frangie, 'Historicism, Socialism and Liberalism'.

77. See Kassab, *Contemporary Arab Thought*, and Abu-Rabiʿ, *Contemporary Arab Thought*.

78. Kharrat, *Al-Hasasiyya Al-Jadida*. Also see Deheuvels *et al.*, *Intertextuality in Modern Arabic Literature since 1967*.

79. Caiani, *Contemporary Arabic Fiction*.

80. Al-Musawi, *Islam on the Street*.

81. Frangie, 'Historicism, Socialism and Liberalism', p. 237.

82. Abdel-Malek, *Contemporary Arab Political Thought*, p. 19. On the emergence of the PLO and the rise of Palestinian armed struggle, see Sayigh, *Armed Struggle and the Search for State*. On the radical and radicalising effect of the Palestinian guerrilla in south Lebanon, see Meier, 'The Palestinian Fidā'i as an Icon of Transnational Struggle'.

83. See Hout, *Post-War Anglophone Lebanese Fiction*; and Hartman, *Native Tongue, Stranger Talk*.

84. Allen, 'Rewriting Literary History', p. 250.

85. Toukan, 'Whatever Happened to *Iltizām*?', pp. 335–6.

86. See Limbrick, 'Contested Spaces'; and Yaqub, 'Refracted Filmmaking'.

87. For an analysis of nostalgia, trauma and memory in wartime and post-war Lebanese feature films, see Seigneurie, *Standing by the Ruins*, particularly chapter 2: 'Speak Ruins!' In photography, the post-war work of Fouad Elkoury comes to mind, particularly his photographic collections *Beirut City Center* (1991) and *Traces of War* (1994–1997) and film *Civil War, the Film* (2012).

88. Kendall, *Literature, Journalism and the Avant-Garde*, pp. 2–3.

I

Requiem for the Enlightenment

My son, you have a dream
Follow it with the night given to you!
And be one of the dream's attributes
Dream and you will find paradise in place!

Mahmoud Darwish, *In the Presence of Absence*

Since its inception, the Lebanese novel has drawn on the seminal trope that has preoccupied Arab intellectuals since the *nahḍa*: the intricate question of the contact with the West and the tradition/modernity nexus. Arab intellectuals' encounters with the West and their ensuing questions pertaining to modernisation, autonomy and emancipation are intrinsic to the ways in which the novel has evolved. Ken Seigneurie observes that 'insofar as it was a prestigious element of modernity that lay in Arab hands, the novel was a privileged mediator between the Arab world and modernity.'[1] The 1967 *naksa* resulted in a political and military defeat that Arab intellectuals, particularly in Egypt, interpreted as a symptom of a defective appropriation of *nahḍa* principles. The epistemological, ideological and aesthetic implications of the ensuing collective process of introspection have left novelists struggling with a paradox: the impossibility of fully appropriating the edicts of the *nahḍa* and the impossibility of eschewing them entirely.

Ambivalence toward the troubled Lebanese modernity has haunted post-war novels. The Lebanese civil war (1975–90) was a pivotal era in which novelists questioned their prevailing modernist convictions and reconfigured the protagonists that channelled them. Such questioning of political commitment as a literary ethos continues to frame the Lebanese novel in the post-war era, as does the archetype of the intellectual as a modern and modernising subject. The Lebanese intellectual community includes writers who began their literary career as militants alongside different socialist and nationalist pro-Palestinian military factions but reassessed their convictions a few years into the war as their ideological vectors were overshadowed by sectarianism. The question of how to respond to the demise of revolutionary ideologies animated the writings of novelists like Elias Khoury, Jabbour Douaihy (b. 1949), Hassan Daoud (b. 1950) and Rashid al-Daif. They wrote extensively about the archetype of the intellectual facing the interplay of violence, collective amnesia and the ascendance of sectarian identities over what remains of secular idealism. The novelists who had espoused a firm belief in binaries such as tradition/modernity, theory/praxis, or progressive/retrograde were the most transformed by the collapse of ideological referents and the growing anomie of the civil war. Sobhi Boustani observes how 'men who have been proven incapable of absorbing modernism and to harmoniously wed the innate to the acquired, reality and theory, have lost the war on all levels.'[2] As such, in the last few years of the war, but particularly in the Lebanese post-war era, the novel became the platform upon which previously militant and politically disenchanted writers expressed their disillusionment with the pre-war ideological identifications that the civil war had violently exposed. Thus, as Seigneurie rightly argues, the Lebanese war novel emerged as a response to the collapse of realist literature of commitment.[3]

Disenchanted with modernist tropes and aesthetics, novelists lamented their own fractured psychological and ideological portrait by fictionalising the Lebanese intellectual. The themes that frame post-war literature revolve around two fundamental questions: how can the vanguard of modernism possibly survive a civil war organised along premodern structures of identification? What remains of literary humanism following the banality of evil that imbued the civil war? In order to answer these questions, novelists reverted to history, and particularly to the fault lines of the *nahḍa*, as a way to deconstruct its modern legacy. The recent novels of Rashid al-Daif, Rabee Jaber and Hoda Barakat (b. 1952), among others, reveal a collective interest in the genealogy of discursive violence as they examine vernacular narratives that antedate the civil war trauma. Their works evoke history, not nostalgically, but rather critically through their recourse to postmodern narrative tools such as parody, irony and play.

Al-Daif's intellectual trajectory testifies to the transformative impact of the Lebanese civil war on a writer's modernist discourse. Born in 1945 in northern Lebanon, al-Daif moved to Beirut in 1974 and began teaching literature at the Lebanese University, which, at the time, constituted a platform for the vanguard of the Lebanese left. Al-Daif soon joined the Lebanese Communist Party and remained throughout the war in West Beirut, the predominantly Muslim, leftist and pro-Palestinian area of the capital. In the 1980s, militant factions engaged in increasingly sectarian turf wars, which al-Daif perceived as a moment of awakening. He realised that the modernist, secular and socialist agenda that he had espoused in his writings had been, in fact, defeated. Al-Daif remembers how the war ushered in

> the end of politics and the demise of concepts. Political parties collapsed. Violence led to violence, breakdown to breakdown, and madness to hallucination. We all became victims of our illusion, the illusion that we were all autonomous subjects ... Politics spilled more blood. But my characters rejected this fate. They were against politics but at the same time, they articulated an ethical question. They were outside politics but never outside ethics. They bore witness to mainstream ethics and began searching for a new morality that does not turn the individual into coal wood on the fire of history and grand causes.[4]

The senselessness of the civil war and the demise of ideological justifications for militancy destabilised all salutary hopes for al-Daif and engendered a severe sense of disenchantment among the protagonists of his novels. The time was opportune to revisit the notion of political commitment and question the role of the militant intellectual in both narrative and practice. Thus, while al-Daif narrated the demise of the post-war intellectual, he repeatedly declared that he identified himself neither as a man of letters (*adīb*), nor as an intellectual (*muthaqqaf*).[5] As a result, he eschewed cultural practices – petitions, op-eds, solidarity campaigns – that interpellated him as an intellectual. Instead, he modelled an alternative concept of literary engagement around a populist understanding of writing, one that does not carry the teleological and positivistic characteristics of commitment and obligation (*risāla*), but is merely a vocation (*mihna*).[6] Al-Daif identifies himself as a writer who 'hopes' to write novels that are 'accessible to the illiterates, the workers, and the philosophers.'[7]

Al-Daif's novels and characters best articulate his disavowal of the archetype of the intellectual and anxiety about the fractured Lebanese modernity.
The recurring protagonist in almost all of his novels is a middle-aged intellectual overpowered by the multiple setbacks to his political and intellectual
trajectory. Boustani argues that the early severance of primordial ties constitutes the first stage of the tripartite trajectory of al-Daif's characters.[8] The
fictional intellectual debuts his leap into modernity by cutting the umbilical
cord with what he describes as premodern tribal structures and engages in a
process of self-distinction from his traditional, often illiterate, tribal and rural
milieu. From the rural and the tribal, al-Daif's self-fashioned subject delves
into the modern cultural and political community of the nation's capital.
Beirut was indeed the urban centre for emancipation, personal and collective. Yet it was also the stage for the senseless violence that began in 1975.
Al-Daif's *Dear Mr. Kawabata* (1999; English trans. 2000) best illustrates
his protagonists' second stage. In the form of a long letter addressed to the
Japanese novelist and Nobel Prize laureate Yasunari Kawabata (1899–1972),
the novel stages the disenchantment and mea culpa of a militant intellectual
beset by war-induced ideological ruptures and psychological trauma.[9] The
violence of the war transformed not only those who endured it, but also
the very ideological framework that had defined a generation of politically
committed intellectuals. The protagonist of *Kawabata* admits: 'one day, at
the beginning of the war – our war – in 1975, I realized that my mouth was
full of ants, that my lips were stitched together like a deep wound sewn up
with strong thread.'[10] After having broken his ties with what he had identified as premodern structures of identification and realising the shortcomings
of his vision of militant Marxism, the narrator of *Dear Mr. Kawabata* finds
himself in limbo, a space of ideological rupture and unconsumed desires for
the modern. The horrors that he witnessed reveal the unspeakable realisation
about the senselessness of speech and the futility of the written word. The
violence of this placelessness drives both the protagonist and the author who
conceived of him to abandon their previous unqualified attachments to crude
modernism in favour of alternative structures of identification and modes of
expression. At the third and last stage, al-Daif's protagonist arranges a shy
reconciliation with the familiar, tribal and rural structures, against which
he began his self-fashioning. Boustani observes how 'the protagonist exhits

bitterness when he realizes the depth of the rift that separates the idealism of his objectives and the conformity of the results. This regression appears on the personal, ideological, political, religious, and social levels.'[11] In *Who's Afraid of Meryl Streep* (2001; English trans. 2014), al-Daif illustrates that discursive regression and portrays a disillusioned protagonist who reverts to a retrograde, patriarchal, tribal and premodern ethos in the form of unrequited anxiety about his wife's sexual past. In *Dear Mr. Kawabata*, al-Daif stages the dramatic moment of disillusionment with the modernist discourse of militant Marxism that a generation of Lebanese intellectuals had embraced; in *Who's Afraid of Meryl Streep*, he fleshes out the subsequent moment of regression to a premodern state of primordial attachments. I will show how in *Tablit al-Bahr* (Paving the sea, 2011), al-Daif conceptualises the very first stage of this tripartite trajectory: the genesis of the modern intellectual, the original moment of radical self-fashioning that dictates a severe rupture with tradition and an unlimited embrace of the modern.[12] This embrace, as we shall see, is not without struggle and paradox and later on, disenchantment.

Read within this framework, *Paving the Sea* is the last instalment and the prequel to al-Daif's trilogy, his project of deconstructing the troubled path toward Lebanese modernity. As he weaves a hybrid narrative that borrows motifs from diverse genres such as historical fiction, biographies and travel literature, all construed at the turn of the nineteenth century, al-Daif reconfigures the historical narratives that imagined and reified Lebanese modernity. More specifically, al-Daif deconstructs the self-fashioning of the intellectual and his construction of an unwavering understanding of modernity, the collapse of which he subsequently endured. His novel, as Tarek el-Ariss rightly noted, 'stages modernity through symptoms and affects that require diagnosis and interpretation, thereby questioning modernity's association with the political and cultural project of Arab Enlightenment starting in the nineteenth century.'[13] Tapping into historical events and the narrative technique and language of Jurji Zaidan, one of the most popular luminaries of the *nahḍa*, al-Daif fictionalises the troubled journey of Zaidan and his friend Faris al-Hashim toward the modern. But, first, what is Zaidan doing in a contemporary Lebanese novel?

Jurji Zaidan Refigured

The year 2014 marked the centennial of the death of Jurji Zaidan. The Ottoman litterateur (*adīb*) was born in Beirut, where he attended Protestant missionary schools, and later moved to Cairo and became an established publisher, linguist, translator, novelist, historian and a leading ideologue of the *nahḍa*.[14] A writer of multidisciplinary interests, Zaidan positioned himself in the Egyptian literary scene as a *kātib ʿāmm*, a generalist or writer of the common and the vernacular. This variant of the *adīb*, as Anne-Laure Dupont notes, is a nonspecialised writer and media man, one who attended to the common reader that constituted the new literary classes that thrived on the school reforms in the Ottoman Empire and Egypt.[15] Zaidan believed in popularising Islamic history by making it pertinent to Arabs beyond the exclusivity of scriptures and religious scholars. As Marwa Elshakry argues, 'for Zaidan, it was only through novel genealogies of their past that the Arabs could thus map the future.'[16] In so doing, the *nahḍa* historian developed new literary genres, such as serialised historical novels in which he promoted his vision of what constituted Arab and Islamic identity at the turn of the nineteenth-century Ottoman Empire. On the pages of *al-Hilal*, the literary journal he founded in 1892 and that continues to appear in Egypt, Zaidan narrated the struggles of Muslim caliphs and princesses as they navigated worldly matters, such as coups, wars and conspiracies.[17] In addition, Zaidan understood that the unification of Arab identity is commensurate with the ability of Arabic to absorb the pressures of the two linguistic and political spaces of the time: the Ottomanised public sphere on the one hand, and the Anglophone and Francophone colonial educational institutions on the other. Zaidan referred in his writings, Kamran Rastegar writes, to the emerging concept of a 'civilizational heritage' and suggested an approach to modernisation that is both endogenous and organic to his readerships. As he introduced new literary genres or, more precisely, reworked traditional genres in secularised religious narratives, Zaidan envisioned the tenets of Arab identity and ultimately situated himself at the vanguard of Arab modernity.[18]

In the last decade, there has been a renewed interest in the *nahḍa*. Numerous studies in intellectual history and literary criticism have looked back at the *nahḍa* not merely as a historical juncture, but as a living and evolving tradition that continues to shape and inform contemporary debates in the Arab world and beyond. Since 2011, Zaidan's writings have returned in full force to Europe and North America. Leading scholars in the field of Arabic literature have translated six of Zaidan's twenty-two historical novels into English.[19] In 2012, the growing interest in Zaidan's historiographic and literary repertoire culminated in a colloquium at the United States Library of Congress, where critics and historians discussed the timeliness of his thought, particularly in the context of an Arab world refiguring notions such as secularism, nationalism and equality.[20] Zaidan, however, remains controversial among Islamic scholars who have deplored his Orientalist historiography, most apparent in his tripartite periodisation of Islamic history.[21] Furthermore, critics have denounced Zaidan's iconoclastic portrayal of Muslim figures and have condemned his reliance on Orientalist historical narratives that ultimately desacralise Islamic history and neutralise its figures.[22] Zaidan was not only the subject of criticism and praise; he also appears in fiction as a protagonist in al-Daif's historical novel *Paving the Sea*.

In the context of this contemporary celebration and condemnation of Zaidan, it is important to ask what exactly drives this contemporary retrieval of the *nahḍa* intellectual in literature and criticism. What is at stake in recuperating Zaidan more than one century after he began conceiving of what constitutes Arab modernity? One way to approach this question is by examining al-Daif's contemporary depiction of Zaidan in relation to the paradoxes inherent in the translatability, or lack thereof, of the concept of modernity in the Lebanese context. While this chapter does not aim to contribute to the rich critical corpus pertaining to Zaidan's *oeuvre*, it nevertheless focuses on the significance of invoking Zaidan in a contemporary moment of ambivalence, the kind al-Daif depicts in *Paving the Sea*. Al-Daif returns to the celebrated *nahḍa* intellectual Jurji Zaidan and his fictional friend Faris al-Hashim in a historical metafiction about a nineteenth-century Syrian intellectual and his troubled encounter with Western modernity. As I explore al-Daif's contemporary refiguring of the East/West and modernity/tradition binaries that framed the critical discourse of the *nahḍa* intellectual, I reveal his contemporary ambivalence toward hegemonic historical narratives that are constitutive of Zaidan's secular, nationalist and modernist legacy.

The *Nahḍawī* Self-fashioned

The story of Faris al-Hashim begins at the intersection of two historical moments that transformed Greater Syria: the civil war of 1860 on the one hand and the increasingly visible British and French colonial interference in the Levant on the other.[23] Faris is conceived in Beirut, in a missionary school that shelters his parents following the 1860 massacres of Mount Lebanon. He is born on 14 December 1861, the day British ships in the port of Beirut commemorate the death of Prince Albert, Queen Victoria's Prince Consort. On that day is also born a certain Jurji Zaidan, who will later become Faris's neighbour, friend, colleague and accomplice.[24] Dispelling the reader's doubts, the narrator announces from the outset that 'the Jurji Zaidan intended here is none other than the Jurji Zaidan whose fame as one of the greatest luminaries of the *nahḍa* is unmatched among the Arabs.'[25] By attributing facts from Zaidan's memoirs to the fictional characters Jurji and Faris, the narrator deploys metafictional strategies of manipulating and rerouting what he alleges is a factual historical narrative. Al-Daif begins by drawing a complex portrait of Zaidan, in which he appears not only as the silent creation of intertwined colonialism and civil war, but also as an Ottoman effendi, deeply engaged in the construction of a modern and modernising Syrian subjectivity.

Al-Daif portrays Faris and Jurji as the embodiment and the precursors of modernity in Greater Syria. Their fathers had attended the same Protestant missionary schools in Beirut, where they learned from British and American missionaries how to reclaim wholesome traditions from alleged ignorance and superstitions. At school, the young men also learned to eschew ancient Eastern superstitions about the perils of depicting human figures and were later rewarded for perfecting their drawings of the human anatomy. They had believed this was the first step toward understanding modern medicine and sciences (*ᶜilm*). The first time Faris's father hears the Arabic word for myth (*khurāfa*; pl. *khurāfāt*) is from the mouth of an American Protestant missionary. 'So our entire lives are superstitions then?' Faris's father wonders.[26] The missionaries' classification of Syrian customs as unfounded myths and their promotion of binaries such as myth/truth, tradition/modernity and customs/science are an early injunction to discourse that prompted the young boys to begin imagining the modern by situating themselves and their traditions in relation to Western modernity, if not in opposition to it. So begins a long spiritual and material journey through an imagined and reconstructed West that will ultimately transform the Syrians' 'perceptions of the Self and Other', to use Rasheed el-Enany's terms.[27]

A generation later, Faris and Jurji complete their secondary education at renowned missionary schools in Beirut and attend the medical school of the Syrian Protestant College (present-day American University of Beirut). Founded in Beirut in 1866 by the American Protestant missionary Daniel Bliss (1823–1916), the college began attracting the sons of the growing class of Christian *effendiyya* hailing from different Ottoman-Syrian cities.[28] Soon after its establishment, the college's leading medical school became a gateway for young Syrians who aimed to practice medicine across the Ottoman Empire. As students in the self-professed beacon of modern sciences and liberal education, Faris and Jurji believe that they have a patriotic duty (*wājib watanī*) to heal Syrians not only from their physical illnesses, but also from the chains of backwardness and ignorance.[29]

The object of their fantasy, the new Syrian nation, will be free from poverty, need and illiteracy.[30] Syrians will have to eschew despicable habits and uncivilised traits such as lying, cheating and lethargy and transform their premodern and irrational worldviews. Syrians, as the missionaries repeatedly say, are naturally predisposed to lie and deceive others. Dr Post, one of the most influential professors of the college, regularly complains about how 'lying is a biological need for Syrians, just as water and air are.'[31] As students in the college, Faris and Jurji are taught that the faithful (Protestant) Christian is a truthful and honest citizen. The two students concur. They, too, begin complaining about the dishonesty of their fellow Syrians and their unfulfilled promises.[32] This uncivilised trait, they insist, was the original sin that hampered the Syrians' ascent to the Eden of civilisation.[33] The pair's representation of the Syrian self in relation to the imagined Western civilisation channels Jurji Zaidan's writings in *Rihla ila Uruba* (A journey to Europe). At the end of his account of his trip to France, Switzerland and Britain, Zaidan writes a list of injunctions and prohibitions that value time, labour and honesty. As el-Enany remarks, however, Zaidan's infatuation with Europe was checked by a 'reactionary' hesitation toward wholeheartedly accepting the emancipation of women and the excess of freedom, an ambivalence that the fictional Zaidan does not convey.[34]

The modernisation of the new Syrian subject was organically tied to the modernisation of his language. At the core of Faris's and Jurji's Enlightenment discourse is a shared anxiety about whether Arabic will be able to withstand the deep shock of Syria's encounter with modern sciences, technology and educational institutions. Faris and Jurji channel the concern of other *nahḍa* literati as they wonder if Arabic, the language of the rising nation, will ever be able to subdue lethargy, idleness and neglect, which have shackled it for five centuries. They also ponder about whether their native tongue will rise to the challenge posed by the semiotic and conceptual richness of Western civilisations. The two friends are eager to find answers:

> What register [*mustawā*] shall we embrace?[35] What kind of lexicon? What syntax? In what style? Arabic has been idling in books for centuries. If it weren't for the influence of the Quran on Christians and Muslims alike, Arabic would have vanished and been replaced by Turkish, the language of the Ottomans.[36]

The linguistic debate about the standardisation of Arabic and the formal dismissal of local dialects, which had already begun preoccupying Arab Ottoman scholars, informs the two *nahḍa* intellectuals. The standardisation of Arabic has been Zaidan's concern, indeed. The real Jurji Zaidan reverted to the rich Quranic legacy as a means to standardise modern Arabic and create one unified language community (*ummat al-lugha*), as Marwa Elshakry argues.[37] Questions pertaining to the future of Arabic not only as language, but also as a common unifying force among Arabs, were the main concern of Zaidan, both the historical figure and the character in al-Daif's fiction.[38]

The two friends believe that the modernisation of Syrians and their idiom is conditional on embracing modern sciences, which have the capacity to silence the irrational and demystify the sacred. The medical career that Faris and Jurji choose is thus fundamental to their modernising mission. As medical students, they repeatedly flirt with the abject and reject irrational attachments to the sacred. Together, they engage in a practice common in Beirut at the time, that of unearthing fresh corpses from local cemeteries in order to dissect them in the anatomy classes of medical schools.[39] Jurji and Faris conspire with an enlightened Ottoman officer to cover up their nightly raids on cemeteries.[40] The two friends' commitment to science and progress is tested twice. The first time is when Faris's colleagues are in desperate need of a corpse. Faris volunteers to donate the body of his dying aunt in an intricate operation that involves convincing the pastor to bury the sealed casket without taking a final look at the corpse, already dissected and discarded in Beirut. 'Medicine plays an essential role in the progress of the homeland ... It's for the sake of the nation', Faris assures himself.[41]

Later, Faris's and Jurji's faith in science and the value of progress and modernity is tested a second time. When medical students are frantically searching for a corpse to dissect in preparation for a critical anatomy exam, Faris's mother is on her deathbed. Torn between his primordial attachment to the family on the one hand, and his rational sensibilities on the other, Faris does not know what to do with his mother's potential corpse. He has to answer a question that defines the essence of the modern subject that he would like to become: what would a civilised man do? After deliberating with his friend Jurji, Faris favours reason over passion. From the narrator we learn that

> Composure and wisdom are qualities that students acquired from their foreign teachers. Students saw in this conduct a civilized virtue [ḥasana ḥaḍāriyya], which was necessary to create modern subjects. It's all for the sake of the nation ... But it's his mother ... His loyalty to his principles and his conviction about the importance of sacrificing that which one cherishes the most for the sake of his nation, overcame the customary [al-mawrūth] veneration of the dead. Cherishing the dead, he concluded, should not hinder the welfare of the nation. The respect for the dead is a virtue, indeed, but seeking the welfare of the nation is a higher virtue. If one was willing to sacrifice his life for the sake of his nation [taqdīm ḥayātihi ʿalā madhbaḥ al-waṭan], how can he refuse to surrender the corpse of his mother?[42]

The moral conundrum that Faris encounters at his mother's deathbed outlines the predicament of the personal and intellectual self-fashioning of the nahḍa intellectual. In that personal yet immensely political instance, Faris has to choose between faith and science, his loyalty to the clan and to the scientific community, his mother (*umm*) and his nation (*umma*) – between an authentic and a disingenuous enactment of *nahḍa* values. Faris's anxieties, as he faces this dramatic and existential moment, channel the perennial Shakespearian moment, albeit with a *nahḍa* twist: to be modern or not to be.

Not only is the modern subject ready to surrender his mother for the sake of the Syrian nation, he is also willing to challenge fundamental religious precepts such as Genesis. With their Christian faith intact, Faris and Jurji espouse the controversial tenets of Darwinism.[43] Around 1881, when Charles Darwin's social evolution theory was slowly gaining ground among American missionaries in Beirut, Faris and Jurji (both the person and the character) were involved in a real incident known as the 'Darwin Affair' at the Syrian Protestant College.[44] Unwilling to incorporate evolutionary theory in the college curriculum, the dean of the college in 1881 launches a campaign to expel students and faculty who promote Darwinism. Jurji and Faris mobilise the student body against the administration's prejudiced measures and lead the first student protest at the college.[45] After refusing to withdraw their statements, the two students are expelled from the college and are thus compelled, along with many others, to pursue their education in either Istanbul or Cairo. As they sail away from the port of Beirut, the two young students pledge in an elevated register of Arabic, purified from colloquialism: 'I swear by God Almighty that I shall return to my hallowed homeland, after receiving my degree, so that I may dedicate myself to its Rebirth, from mighty metropolis to humble hamlet.'[46] Faris has vowed to suffer for the sake of his nation and so, shall hold his tears. Tears, he thinks, undermine

> the rise of the new Syrian, a man who favours reason over his emotions and passions [*hawāh*], a new man who believes in the reawakening of the people and the right of the nation to exist. He shall struggle for a nation that withstands the clamour of the winds of change. The nation shall rise as a unified body in a sea of storms. It shall have a leading role in the race of nations toward glory [*al-majd*].[47]

Although Jurji and Faris both take to the sea, a rite of passage that ushers them into modernity, they embark on separate adventures. Whereas Jurji moves to Cairo and becomes a prominent figure of the *nahḍa* vanguard, as we all know, Faris boards on a long trip to the United States, the beacon of modernity and civilisation.

The Grandeur of Western Modernity

Faris al-Hashim is determined to shed his skin and become a modern man. Soon after disembarking at the port of Marseille, Faris realises that he has finally reached a civilised, modern and free country.[48] He decides, therefore, to replace his Ottoman tarboosh with a western hat and wear a clean and elegant suit that 'for some reason, made him proud of himself'.[49] In Paris, he speaks French, discusses the legacy of Robespierre, and admires the Paris Commune and its egalitarian values.[50] He impresses his interlocutors by the sophistication of his French and is in turn impressed by French urban infrastructure and technology.[51] As he admires the elegant street lamps of Paris, Faris wonders: 'When will Beirut glow with the light of knowledge and progress? When will light replace darkness?'[52] Even trains, which he compares to steel rooms and magnificent snakes, signal to him the quantum leap to modernity the Western world has accomplished. Faris interprets train exhaust as a sign that reason has prevailed over tradition and mimesis (*taqlīd*): 'Train exhaust occupied the skies in the form of a smile and a sign of victory signalling that hope is alive and that the future is clear.'[53]

Faris's journey to the American modern, however, is rigged with rejection. Faris buys a first-class ticket on a boat appropriately called 'grandeur' (*al-ʿaẓama*), which carries him from Le Havre to New York. Faris is proud to be the first Syrian to travel first class. 'Never again!' he exclaims, 'Never again shall Syrians be forced to travel in third class compartments!'[54] Refusing to allow Faris to travel among the gentry, a sailor escorts Faris out of his first-class cabin and into a filthy compartment carrying cattle. Although he is an educated, well-mannered polyglot, Faris is still a colonial subject, a man of colour banned from sitting alongside European travellers. When Faris resists, he is thrown into the sea. The thought of becoming the first martyr for the sake of the Syrian nation enthrals Faris. He sees in his inevitable death a lesson that other Syrians will learn about the hefty price one should be ready to pay in order to ensure the progress of the nation. Faris wants to tell the sailor who pushes him to his death: 'Do bury me in my homeland so that my blood fertilizes it, so it may grow red flowers every spring.'[55] Faris's fantasies of martyrdom are interrupted, however, when he is promptly rescued. He emerges dry, clean and even more determined to challenge Europeans – not by pointing to their racism, prejudice and failed Enlightenment principles of liberty, equality and fraternity but by showing them that Syrians are indeed as civilised as Europeans are.[56]

America, the land of the free and the home of the brave, does not welcome Faris either, because he is a man of colour. In New York, Faris becomes a street peddler, sleeping on sidewalks and selling silk scarves and cedar memorabilia to make ends meet.[57] After becoming romantically involved with the daughter of a reputable Protestant pastor, Faris falls prey to her brother's scheme. The brilliant student of the most prestigious medical school in Ottoman Syria ends up incarcerated in a cold American jail. The narrator describes the dramatic moment of Faris's incarceration: 'Although he swore to become an ideal citizen and travel to America to learn from its civilization that which suits his homeland, Faris now lies helplessly in prison.'[58] After a series of unfortunate events and implausible adventures that oscillate between tragedy and farce, Faris serves in the US Army as a soldier in the Spanish-American War (1898) and eventually graduates from medical school and starts his medical practice. This is Faris's way of proving to his fellow Americans that Syrians can and should indeed excel in modern professions. The trials of the young *nahḍa* intellectual in the West thwart neither his determination nor his infatuation with modernity. Against all odds, Faris succeeds in America and becomes a wealthy and reputable physician. Separated from the pastor's daughter whom he loves dearly, Faris settles with a Japanese prostitute he met in Cuba and decides to return with her to Syria. On their way to Beirut, Faris suddenly dies; his Japanese wife finds herself alone in a foreign Ottoman city with a baby in her womb and the corpse of her husband by her side. But what of Jurji Zaidan? Where is he in all this? Having travelled all the way from Cairo to greet Faris at the port of Beirut, Jurji is appalled to learn that his friend, his twin, has died – and worse, that his casket has been stolen from the docks by science-hungry medical students.

The Remains of the *Nahḍawī*

The two *nahḍawī* intellectuals, Faris and Jurji, navigate the political and social complexities of Ottoman Syria following a strict interpretation of the tradition/modernity nexus within the concordant triangulation of past, present and future. They are pained by how Syrians have been weighed down by traditions, so they take it upon themselves to enlighten, modernise and rescue their compatriots from the shackles of tribalism and mimesis. Their world is bound by two possibilities: one might be either traditional or modern, and modern is what Faris and Jurji aspire to be. Without posing the false question about author intentionality, one cannot help but wonder what exactly al-Daif is doing in *Paving the Sea*. Is al-Daif serious in his melodramatic requiem for the *nahḍa* archetype? Or are the readers the laughing stock of this seemingly solemn yet banal account of two *nahḍa* intellectuals? One wonders why the author of *Paving the Sea* has returned to the now-tired, rags-to-riches genre of the Syrian travel narrative. Furthermore, why is the character of Faris al-Hashim so naïve? And why is the narrative voice so simplistic? In other words, the reader doubts whether the novel's contemporary narrator, who shamelessly espouses a crude self-Orientalising discourse, is familiar with the critique of Orientalism. Much less does this narrator appear to be familiar with the early twentieth-century Arab literary corpus that already problematised East/West relations.[59]

The answer to these disconcerting questions may be somewhere in between reality and fantasy, history and fiction, deference and play. At the core of this sombre show of respect, homage and unabashed nostalgia toward the heroism of Faris al-Hashim and Jurji Zaidan lies historiographic metafiction. This literary genre, mostly associated with postmodern fiction, draws on the historical novel on the one hand and on postmodern narrative techniques on the other. At the intersection of historiography and irony, *Paving the Sea* reassesses historical subjectivity by portraying Faris and Jurji as historical subjects who double as sites of irony and paradox. But what exactly distinguishes historiographic metafiction from ideological novels? How are readers expected to interpret truth claims in historiographic metafiction? Authors of historical novels, David Cowart writes, probe 'the past to account for a present that grows increasingly chaotic'.[60] But postmodern narrative techniques build an additional layer of doubt on the historical novel. Susan Suleiman argues that historical metafiction does not aim 'through the vehicle of fiction, to persuade their readers of the "correctness" of a particular way of interpreting the world'.[61] On the contrary, it makes demands on their readers to question and destabilise the dominant and hegemonic interpretation of history. Because of the destabilising potential of historiographic metafiction, Linda Hutcheon reminds us, 'all the various critically sanctioned modes of talking about subjectivity whether it's character, narrator, writer, textual voice fail to offer any stable anchor. They are used, inscribed, entrenched, yes, but they are also abused, subverted, undermined.'[62] As it conveys a seemingly unequivocal reading of history, historical metafiction toys with the bizarre and the ironic and thereby exposes the hegemonic nature of historical narrative.[63] Historiographic metafiction or irony consecrates power – in our case that of Jurji and Faris – and simultaneously contests it. It centres the *nahḍawī* in order to decentre him. It elevates him high enough to shame him later. This contradictory doubleness – or the act and its undoing, the word and its oxymoron, the hero and the hero's fall – permeates the narrative. But how exactly does al-Daif articulate this duplicity?

First, al-Daif parodies the prose, the wordiness, of the *nahḍa* intellectual. The struggle of the Arabic language facing the radical changes that began transforming its speakers is, as we saw earlier, the main concern of both Jurji and Faris. Despite Faris's travels in the United States and his mastery of French and English, his native Arabic, particularly that in which he expresses his patriotism, remains ornamental at best. For instance, as he reflects on the inevitability of his immigration, Faris compares his journey to that of great men 'who lead the nation into the roads of struggle and herald its flags on the hills of glory'.[64] These self-conscious, florid soliloquies are adorned with an endless reservoir of superlatives: 'Man's sacrifice for the sake of his wretched people is a high noble purpose [*ghāya nabīla quṣwā*]!'[65] The semantic field on which Faris draws abounds with beauty, wholesomeness and honour and taps into standard Arabic (*fuṣḥā*) to establish solemnity and authority.

Faris is, however, not alone in the nationalist celebration of the Arabic language. The narrator frequently joins him in this baroque parade of rhymed prose, alliteration, assonance and formulaic expressions such as 'Resplendent Mount Lebanon: enchantress of prophets and pontiffs, of conquerors and conspirators; seductress of shepherds, ascetics, and passersby since the beginning of time ... The Lebanon of snow-brushed summits and hills nestled in springtime's embrace.'[66] The narrator's language conveys Jurji's and Faris's budding nationalism on the one hand and the contemporary narrator's own nostalgia for that bygone discourse on the other. But this language, which indeed recalls the nineteenth-century narrative language of the real-life Zaidan, works simultaneously to subvert it. Al-Daif's manipulation of the idiom of both the protagonists and the narrator ultimately exposes the hollow, inefficient and inflexible usage of Arabic. The question that had always haunted Faris and Jurji, about whether Arabic would be able to withstand and embrace change, has been answered through an ironic and playful contemporary appropriation of Arabic.[67]

Typical of postmodern historiographic metafiction, the narrator of *Paving the Sea* hovers consistently over the text. The narrator interferes, relates, comments and evaluates. He is everywhere. His frequent usage of the first-person plural in statements such as 'Nasim was surprised by the ways of this man, which were foreign to *our traditions* [ʿādātinā]'[68] or 'In *our* culture people believe in superstitions because they are ignorant and lack faith.'[69] The unabashed deployment of the first-person plural leaves the reader wondering about the narrator's imagined community. Does the narrator's first-person plural work to create a sense of solidarity and complicity between the contemporary reader and the *nahḍa* protagonists? Are Arab readers of the twenty-first century expected to sympathise with a protagonist still baffled by his first encounter with Parisian street lamps? Have the traditions of this imagined community (ʿādātinā) really remained intact since the nineteenth century? This injunction to identification and unity, I suggest, is the author's way of exposing the thin ideological fabric at the centre of the emerging Syrian nation.

The narrator's interventions are not restricted to language but extend to storytelling as well. The narrator haunts his own text and colours it with anachronisms. In between critical historical events, the narrator adds contemporary references that carry the reader from the pristine nineteenth century to the troubled present and back. For instance, in a narrative time set in 1860, the narrator invokes the vernacular poetry of Asʿad al-Sabʿali (1910–98) that was performed by Wadiʿ al-Safi (1921–2013) a century later.[70] In one such anachronistic gesture, the narrator parenthetically states '(No one anticipated all the disasters that will later befall this country and the suffering and sorrow that will wear its people down.)'.[71]

The omniscient narrator is, indeed, a man of his times. He makes sure to remind the reader that this narrative is told from a contemporary perspective. As he describes the sexual practices of nineteenth-century Syrian men, he states that 'Condoms weren't as popular as they are today' and then proceeds to describe the sexual practices of nineteenth-century prostitutes.[72] In parentheses again, the narrator subtly comments on the increasing influence of the United States in the world:

(The thought that carbohydrates were the leading cause for obesity was unknown then because America was not as visible as it is today in Beirut and around the world. Back then, millions of Americans did not suffer from obesity like they do today.)[73]

The narrator's numerous interventions operate as a reminder of the two precepts of the metafictional narrative at hand: first, that this historical narrative is undoubtedly contemporary; and second, that all alleged historical facts are artificial and constructed, a function of the narrator's contemporary sensibilities.

Al-Daif's parody appears not only in his narrative language and metafictional strategies, but also in his representation of the *nahḍawī*. The character of Faris conveys both bravery and ridicule. For instance, the enlightened intellectual battles Syrian ignorance and superstition in the most unlikely places: the brothels of Beirut. Faris explains to his favourite prostitute that her resistance to performing a certain sexual act stems from the ignorance and superstition of the Syrians. And it is only by agreeing to perform it that she will contribute to freeing not only her clients but also her entire nation (*umma*) from the shackles of backwardness and primitive myths.[74] Realising the importance of her role in this solemn historical moment, the prostitute obliges. 'And so', we are told, 'historians observed that this sexual act became common first in towns and villages and then across Syria and all Ottoman provinces. Married men began spending more time at home and crime rates dropped considerably. Faris was proud that he contributed to this grand transformation.'[75] What do readers, entrusted with decoding postmodern irony, make of this? How do we read Faris's sexual potency? How do we interpret the *nahḍa* hero's responsibility for public history and great social transformations not only in Syria but also in the entire Ottoman Empire? By elevating narcissism and megalomania, and doing so in a sombre historiographic narrative tone, al-Daif comments on our contemporary understanding of what constitutes a historical fact, a historical subject, and most importantly, modernisation and emancipation – even when they are staged, embodied and reenacted by a prominent *nahḍawī*.

Not only is Faris's contribution to history ironic, but so is his end. Let us remember the pledge that Faris and Jurji Zaidan recited as they took the sea: 'I swear by God Almighty that I shall return to my hallowed homeland, after receiving my degree, so that I may dedicate myself to its Rebirth, from mighty metropolis to humble hamlet.'[76] These were the last words of Faris as he bid Beirut farewell. Years later, upon his homecoming and moments before his sudden death, Faris confessed to his Japanese wife his longing for Syrian dishes such as the raw meat dish *kibbeh nayyeh* and the parsley-based salad tabbouleh.[77] The *nahḍawī*'s last words were thus a nostalgic yearning, not for the modern and the cooked, but for the traditional and the raw. By recalling the essence of the Syrian culinary tradition, instead of the grand nationalist and modernist paradigms, the returning *nahḍa* intellectual may have undone his original oath to modernise and change; he has neutralised it and perhaps ridiculed it.

But the ridicule of the *nahḍawī* continues post-mortem. Upon arriving in Beirut, Faris's body is stolen by medical students. History repeats itself, we are told, but the second time as farce. Dressed in drag as a foreign *khawājā* with a cigar and a western hat, Faris's body is smuggled to the Syrian Protestant College's medical school, where it is dissected and discarded.[78] The body of Faris, his private parts, which were once entrusted with the modernisation of the Syrian people, cannot remain whole. They are stolen, violated, mocked, cut and scrutinised by Syrian medical students enacting the same modernist project that he had initiated and because of which he had to embark to the United States. Al-Daif's flirtation with the grotesque, between the glorious beginning of Faris and his disgraceful cigar-smoking corpse, between his youth as a member of the Ottoman vanguard and his finale as a mere collection of bones, is a doubleness that al-Daif articulates throughout the novel and continues to the end. 'And so', the narrator concludes, 'this was the end of Faris al-Hashim's journey to the world.'[79] To the modern, I would add.

Our *nahḍa* hero is thus both the embodiment of ideology and the stage of its disintegration, dissection and mockery. But what becomes of his quest to modernise the Syrian nation? What can we say about this uphill struggle to capture the modern, tame it and domesticate it? What happens to the teleology of the prism of past/present/future that is intrinsic to the prophecy of the *nahḍa* intellectual? The answer may be in the ambivalence inherent in the novel's title, *Tablit al-Bahr*, which literally translates into 'paving the sea'. The controlling narrator historicises the Lebanese vernacular expression *tablīṭ al-baḥr*. He tells us that upon seeing the sea for the first time, rural Syrians thought it was so vast that no one could possibly pave it. And in his usual authoritative and didactic tone, the narrator explains: 'This is the origin of the expression "paving the sea", meaning that one is unable to respond to a challenge.'[80]

In Lebanese vernacular, the expression indicates impossibility as well as an act of defiance of an external force. In the command form, *rūḥ balliṭ al-baḥr!* (Pave the sea!), the expression signals a vociferous rejection of an imposed order, the English equivalent of 'Go to hell!' The tension between the purposeful and the futile, between the push and the pull, the domestic and the wild, the desired and the imposed, is at the centre of al-Daif's displacement of the past. The rite of passage to the modern becomes both the quest for the impossible and the rejection of that which is forcefully imposed. In the title, *tablīṭ al-baḥr*, one can also read the return of the vernacular and the traditional. As the vehicle of modernist ideology, standard Arabic (*fuṣḥā*), which had been central to the *nahḍawī*'s prophecy, is celebrated in the narrative but defeated in the title. It becomes solely the stage for the expression of void, archaic and formulaic expressions manipulated to undermine the *nahḍa* hero. As such, after reciting his oath, Faris al-Hashim appears in *Paving the Sea* as a historical hero, indeed, but also as a contemporary joke.

But I would like to extend my reading further. Contrary to what the narrator claims, Faris's story does not end at the dissection and disintegration of his body. Toward the end of the novel, al-Daif stages a captivating fast-forward, skips a few generations, and takes us all the way to Faris's great-grandson, Juan, born in 1951 in historical Syria that later became modern-day Lebanon. Twenty years after the end of the most recent Lebanese civil war, Juan exclaims: 'I'm tired of living in a country made up of Sunnis, Shiᶜia, Druze, Maronites, Orthodox Christians and others, a country bordering a

Jewish state.'[81] The descendant of the great secular patriot, the prominent *nahda* intellectual with an undeniable faith in modernism and the reawakening of the Greater Syrian nation, cannot fathom Lebanese sectarianism and announces: 'I would like to rip out my roots and plant them anywhere but here.'[82] This is the true end of Faris al-Hashim's story; not at the moment of his lacklustre return from America, but when his great-grandson gives up on the nation that his great-grandfather had idealised, thereby putting his forebear's memorable oath to rest. Such is the predicament of the future that Jurji and Faris had anticipated as they sailed away from nineteenth-century Beirut.

Between the death of Faris in 1900 and the emigration of his great-grandson in 2000, we witness the splintering of Greater Syria and rise and fall of Lebanese modernity in discourse. At stake are not only the stillbirth of the Lebanese state and the trauma of the civil war, but also the collapse of Jurji Zaidan's non-sectarian Arab unity project. The civil war, which al-Daif peculiarly omits from the novel, is the indescribable, the unspeakable; a moment of aporia that instigates the fall, the dissection and the multiple burials of the *nahda* intellectual's future prophecy. Al-Daif's recuperation of Jurji Zaidan, Faris al-Hashim's twin, self and other, is replete with irony that parodies, destabilises and eventually subverts the representation of the *nahdawi* and the modernism he embodies. Al-Daif's retrospection cannot be read as a nostalgic desire to recapture or learn lessons from a romanticised past. On the contrary, it is by deploying irony and parody that al-Daif narratively centres and subsequently decentres the archetypical *nahda* intellectual and his modern and modernising prophecy. 'But the critique of its irony is double-edged', as Hutcheon reminds us. 'The past and the present are judged in each other's light.'[83] Al-Daif's contemporary deconstruction of the *nahda* archetype conveys an individual as well as collective ambivalence toward the present, following the trauma of the civil war. But the most astounding element of Faris al-Hashim's end is not the dissection of his corpse, but the absence of Jurji Zaidan. Last seen at the port of Beirut frantically searching for the corpse of his friend, Zaidan disappears from *Paving the Sea*. He leaves no legacy or descendants, and his own story remains untold except through the disenchanted gaze of al-Daif.

In *Paving the Sea*, al-Daif reconstructs a portrait of Jurji Zaidan that channels his own. The postmodern narrative that combines contemporary stylistic experimentations and a self-reflexive recuperation of traditional genres such as the biography, the travelogue and the historical novel appeals both to popular and specialised audiences. In other words, even if al-Daif's straightforward, earnest, troublesome and naïve prose astounds critics, it nevertheless draws in a nonspecialised reader. Al-Daif's simplistic rendering of an otherwise complex theme speaks to Zaidan's *nahda* fantasy about literary accessibility as the ethos of the modern writer. Al-Daif's recurrent rejection of the symbolic capital of the *muthaqqaf* and the *adib* and his desire to write novels that are 'accessible', let us remember, 'to the illiterate, the worker, and the philosopher', invokes Zaidan's self-identification as a generalist, a *kātib ʿāmm*.[84] Are we, thus, in the presence of a twenty-first century generalist?

Al-Daif's overt infatuation with literary accessibility, universalism and the subservience of literature parodies Zaidan's persona and thereby reveals the author's ambivalence toward his precursor, a combination of admiration and cynicism toward Zaidan's project. Al-Daif's contemporary revival of Zaidan pays tribute to the *kātib ʿāmm* and simultaneously articulates a critique of the humanist ethos that is central to Zaidan's *nahda* discourse – an ethos that has failed to resonate with al-Daif's contemporary disenchanted world.

Notes

1. Seigneurie, 'Introduction: A Survival Aesthetic', p. 13.
2. My translation from the original French. Boustani, 'Le héros chez Rashid Ad-daʿif', p. 55.
3. Seigneurie, *Standing by the Ruins*, p. 35.
4. My translation from the original Arabic. Al-Amir and al-Daif, 'Hiwar', p. 82.
5. In an interview with the Lebanese daily *al-Akhbar*, al-Daif states: 'I am not talented. I just have a job, and it's about writing novels ... I am not a man of letters [*adib*], or more precisely, I no longer wish to be one. Men of letters write beautifully and work on aesthetics in literature. I am beyond this question and I believe that novels should also transcend this question.' Bin Hamza, 'Rashid al-Daif'. In another interview, al-Daif discusses his return to writing as a means to challenge the senselessness of the civil war. See Anonymous, 'Al-Riwaʾi Rashid al-Daif'.
6. Ghosn (ed.), *Rachid el-Daïf*.
7. Bin Hamza, 'Rashid al-Daif'.
8. Boustani, 'Le héros chez Rashid', p. 48.
9. For an analysis of the modernity/tradition nexus in *Dear Mr. Kawabata*, see

Aghacy, 'Contemporary Lebanese Fiction'. Ken Seigneurie approaches the novel by searching for humanist poetic discourse in war and post-war literature. Seigneurie, *Standing by the Ruins*, pp. 61–70.

10. Al-Daif, *Dear Mr. Kawabata*, p. 6.
11. My translation from the original French. Boustani, 'Le héros chez Rashid', p. 49.
12. Al-Daif, *Tablit al-Bahr*. The novel is hereafter referred to as *Paving the Sea* for ease of reading, although the complete novel has not been published in English as of this writing. All translations from the original Arabic are my own.
13. El-Ariss, *Trials of Arab Modernity*, p. 2.
14. See Zaidan, *The Autobiography of Jurji Zaidan*. For the two extensive biographies of Zaidan, see Philipp and Zaydān, *Gurgi Zaidan*; Dupont, *Gurgi Zaydan*.
15. Dupont, 'What is a *kātib ʿāmm*?', p. 171.
16. Elshakry, 'Between Enlightenment and Evolution', p. 144.
17. Zaidan named the journal *al-Hilal* (Arabic for 'the crescent') in homage to the crescent of the Ottoman flag. On the significance of *al-Hilal* in the *nahḍa*, see Khuri-Makdisi, 'Inscribing Socialism into the Nahda'. The archive of the first fifty years of *al-Hilal* is now available on the Zaidan Foundation official website: Zaidan Foundation, 'First Fifty Years of al-Hilal'.
18. Rastegar, 'Literary Modernity between Arabic and Persian Prose', p. 370.
19. I second Rastegar's caution against the facile use of the term *novel* as a direct equivalent to the term *riwāya/riwāyāt*. Rastegar rightly observes that it was not until the 1940s that the two terms were accepted as equivalent. See ibid. p. 362.
20. Entitled 'Jurji Zaydan: His Contribution to Modern Arab Thought and Literature', the colloquium was held at the Library of Congress on 5 June 2012. The colloquium proceedings were later published by the Zaidan Foundation. See Philipp and Zaidan (eds), *Jurji Zaidan's Contributions to Modern Arab Thought and Literature*.
21. Zaidan was influenced by the Orientalist historians of his time. But as Anne-Laure Dupont observes, he had reservations about the ways in which Orientalist historians depicted Islam. Zaidan was keen on presenting an alternative depiction of Islam in his historiographies and historical novels. See Dupont, 'How Should History Be Written?'.
22. Critics of Zaidan's historiography included Rashid Rida (1865–1935); Shibli al-Nuhmani (1858–1914) in his *Book of the Critique of the History of Islamic Civilization* (1912); and Luis Shaykho (1859–1927), who objected to Zaidan's evolutionary worldview. Contemporary Islamist scholars have reacted to the

renewed interest in Zaidan within academic circles and have deplored Zaidan's historiographical methodology and condemned it for what they argue is an Orientalist tripartite periodisation of Islamic history.

23. Born in present-day Lebanon, Faris al-Hashim and Jurji Zaidan were identified as Syrians in the *fin-de-siècle* Ottoman Empire. Greater Syria (*bilād al-shām*) was a geographic but also proto-nationalist designation for the eastern Mediterranean Ottoman provinces that included Lebanon, Jordan, Palestine and Syria. With the surge of nationalist sentiments during the *nahḍa*, Ottoman subjects who originated from that area self-identified as Syrians (*sūriyyūn* or *shawām*). After the independence of Lebanon, Jordan and Syria, and the emergence of Palestinian nationalism, the designation went out of style and became a referent to citizens of the present-day Syrian Arab Republic only.

24. The circumstances of Faris's birth correspond exactly to those of Jurji Zaidan. See Zaidan, *The Autobiography of Jurji Zaidan*, p. 131.

25. Al-Daif, *Tablit*, p. 26.

26. Ibid. pp. 14–15.

27. El-Enany, 'Theme and Identity in Postcolonial Arabic Writing', p. 34.

28. See Betty Anderson's account of the missionary colonial role in the establishment of the Syrian Protestant College. Anderson, *The American University of Beirut*.

29. Al-Daif, *Tablit*, p. 46.

30. Ibid. p. 41.

31. Ibid. p. 101.

32. Ibid. p. 101.

33. Indeed, Jurji Zaidan placed high value on honesty in his writings: 'We pretend to have reached the heights of the civilization – and this is accurate in many ways, but not for "honesty in speech," because we are still lacking in this regard. And this itself has two sides: the first is honesty in opinion and advice, and the second is honesty in transactions ... The best, most refined, bravest, and most cultured behavior is honesty in speech.' Zaidan, 'Honesty in Speech as a Form of Superior Conduct', pp. 281–9.

34. El-Enany, *Arab Representations of the Occident*, p. 39.

35. Register (*mustawā*) refers to Arabic diglossia or the culturally and politically charged interchange between the use of standard Arabic and local dialects among Arabic speakers.

36. Al-Daif, *Tablit*, p. 98.

37. Marwa Elshakry discusses Zaidan's conception of the Arabic language and

observes that 'the influence of an evolutionary worldview on his theories of the origin of language was highly apparent in his work.' See Elshakry, 'Between Enlightenment and Evolution', p. 125.

38. See, for instance, Philipp, 'Language, History, and Arab National Consciousness in the Thought of Jurjî Zaidân (1861–1914)'; and Elshakry, 'Between Enlightenment and Evolution'.

39. Zaidan hints in his memoirs that he and his colleagues secretly engaged in this practice. He recalls his unease upon realising that the corpse of the little boy that they stole and dissected had been in fact the son of his father's friend. Zaidan, *Autobiography of Jurji Zaidan*, pp. 173–4.

40. Al-Daif, *Tablit*, p. 65.

41. Ibid. p. 65.

42. Ibid. pp. 91–2.

43. On the influence of Darwinism on the social and epistemological landscape of the Arab literati, see Elshakry, *Reading Darwin in Arabic*. On how Darwinism effected a redefinition of theological and exegetical approaches on the nineteenth-century Syrian thinker Husayn al-Jisr, see Elshakry, 'Muslim Hermeneutics'.

44. On the 1881 'Darwin Affair', see Jeha, *Darwin and the Crisis of 1882*; Anderson, *American University of Beirut*.

45. Jurji Zaidan discussed in his memoirs the details of his role in the 'Darwin Affair', the student body's negotiations with the administration and the college's subsequent crackdown on student protestors. Zaidan, *Autobiography of Jurji Zaidan*, pp. 180–202.

46. I am grateful to Benjamin Koerber for his eloquent translation of the original Arabic text that reads:

أقسم بالله العظيم أنني سأعود إلى بلادي المقدسة، بعد نيلي شهادتي، لأعمل فيها على نهضتها، في مدنها قاطبةً، وفي كلّ قراها الطاهرة.

Al-Daif, *Tablit*, p. 103.

47. Ibid. p. 111.

48. Ibid. p. 116.

49. Ibid. pp. 113–16.

50. Ibid. p. 118.

51. Ibid. p. 117.

52. Ibid. p. 113.

53. Ibid. p. 115.

54. Ibid. p. 118.

55. Ibid. p. 119.

56. Ibid. pp. 119–20.
57. Ibid. pp. 130–2.
58. Ibid. p. 141.
59. See, for instance, el-Enany's analysis of Tawfiq al-Hakim's and Alfred Faraj's plays depicting the East/West encounter in el-Enany, 'The Quest for Justice'; and 'Tawfiq al-Hakim and the West'.
60. Quoted in Allen, 'Rewriting Literary History', p. 255.
61. Suleiman, *Authoritarian Fictions*, p. 1.
62. Hutcheon, *A Poetics of Postmodernism*, p. 189.
63. Hutcheon, *Narcissistic Narrative*, p. 26.
64. The original Arabic text reads:

يزرعون راياتها فوق الذرى والمجد.

Al-Daif, *Tablit*, p. 20.
65. Ibid. p. 45.
66. I am grateful to Benjamin Koerber for his eloquent translation of the original Arabic text that reads:

جبل لبنان الحالم، جبل لبنان الذي سحر الأنبياء والغزاة على السواء، والرعاة والنسّاك والعابرين على مدى الأزمنة. لبنان القمم المكلّلة بالثلج والروابي الملتحفة بالربيع.

Ibid. p. 22.
67. See for instance, al-Daif's *Learning English*, which portrays the narrator's identity crisis following the mysterious death of his father. The narrator engages in a fascinating process of self-doubt coupled with deep anxiety about whether Arabic will be able to withstand the shockwaves of the postmodern era. Al-Daif, *Learning English*.
68. Emphasis added. Al-Daif, *Tablit*, p. 18.
69. Emphasis added. Ibid. p. 14.
70. The vernacular *zajal* poet Asᶜad al-Sabᶜali wrote numerous songs for the Lebanese folk singer and composer Wadiᶜ al-Safi whose songs are patriotic and nostalgic, if not overly romantic.
71. Al-Daif, *Tablit*, p. 193.
72. Ibid. p. 51.
73. Ibid. p. 72.
74. Ibid. p. 59.
75. Ibid. p. 61.
76. Ibid. p. 103.
77. *Kibbeh nayyeh* is a Levantine delicacy of minced lamb meat with parsley, bulgur wheat, onions and spices served uncooked.

78. Al-Daif, *Tablit*, pp. 199–200.
79. Ibid. p. 202.
80. Ibid. p. 97.
81. Ibid. p. 204.
82. Ibid. p. 204.
83. Hutcheon, *Poetics of Postmodernism*, p. 39.
84. Bin Hamza, 'Rashid al-Daif'.

2

Elegy for the Intellectual

Beirut, our image.

Mahmoud Darwish, 'In Praise of the Tall Shadow'

In the first few years following the end of the civil war, the Lebanese cultural scene lost two prominent intellectuals. In 1993, Maroun Baghdadi (1950–93), the director of more than sixteen films and documentaries about the war, fell to his death under mysterious circumstances in the elevator shaft of his Beirut apartment. Two years later, Ralph Rizqallah (1950–95), a professor of psychology at the Lebanese University and a regular contributor to *al-Mulhaq*, the cultural supplement published by the daily *al-Nahar*,[1] committed suicide by jumping into the sea right in front of Raouche Rock, Beirut's most iconic landmark.[2] The deaths of the two intellectuals were intimately linked to the political juncture that defined post-war Lebanon. In the early years following the end of the civil war, the state began implementing urban reconstruction projects that critics condemned for silencing war traumas and erasing Beirut's pre-war identity and social fabric. Leading figures in Lebanese literary circles interpreted the deaths of both Rizqallah and Baghdadi as an allegory of the post-war politics of erasure that the Lebanese state began enforcing. The suicide of the post-war intellectual was thus perceived as an act of protest against the city's enduring appetite for violence and its endemic propensity to silence and forget its war traumas.

In *Ralph Rizqallah fi-l-mir'at* (Ralph Rizqallah through the looking glass), Rabee Jaber fictionalises the suicide of Ralph Rizqallah and tackles the Lebanese post-war memory and collective amnesia discourse, especially as Elias Khoury conceives of it in his novels and op-eds.[3] I explore in this chapter the ways in which Jaber simultaneously engages and subverts the dominant narrative framework of post-war novelists in order to propose an alternative literary representation of the Lebanese intellectual. Drawing on intertextuality in his frequent references to Rizqallah's original writings and Lewis Carroll's novels, Jaber displaces Rizqallah from the dominant interpretation of his suicide as an act of protest. Specifically, Jaber returns to text and conducts a close reading of Rizqallah's writings, which reveal a melancholic intellectual suffering from personal angst and alienation. In his novel, Jaber departs from the objectification of the intellectual as the embodiment of his generation's collective memory and thereby challenges the literary discourse that had ideologically codified the intellectual in the early years of the post-war era.

The Writer and the City

As the urban centre that embraces multiple cultural and ideological imaginaries, Beirut has figured extensively in Lebanese literature, not only as a geographical space, but also as a reflection of the paradoxes that intellectuals have navigated since the country's independence in 1943. Following the 1967 war and the collective feeling of loss and defeat experienced by Arab writers, Halim Barakat (b. 1936) conceived of Beirut in *Days of Dust* (1969; English trans. 1974) as a complex space that simultaneously liberates its free-spirited intellectuals and reaffirms their despair facing the gravity of the political and military defeat. Tawfiq Yusuf Awwad (1911–89) anticipated the civil war in his 1972 novel *Death in Beirut* (1972; English trans. 1976), which portrays the city as a mirror of troubled Lebanese modernity on the verge of war. Awwad's Beirut also nurtured politically engaged intellectuals committed to social justice and the Palestinian cause. In the iconic poem 'In Praise of the Tall Shadow' (1983) Mahmoud Darwish writes, 'Beirut, our fortress, Beirut, our tear ... Beirut, our image.'[4]

Beginning in 1975 and throughout the civil war, Beirut became a recurrent, if not the most central, motif in the Lebanese war novel. The impact of the civil war on Lebanese literature is akin to that of the 1967 defeat, which introduced to Arabic literature what Edwar al-Kharrat called the 'new literary sensibility' (*al-ḥasāsiyya al-jadīda*), which marked a break with social realism that had hitherto pervaded Arabic literature. Lebanese novelists who wrote about the war tackled the violent dispositions of the city represented as both victim and victimiser. Beirut appears in Hanan al-Shaykh's (b. 1945) *The Story of Zahra* (1989; English trans. 1994) as a space that simultaneously embraces war and endures its destruction while turning its inhabitants into amnesiac and aimless spectres.[5] Elias Khoury's war-torn Beirut in *White Masks* (1986; English trans. 2010) and *The Journey of Little Gandhi* (1989; English trans. 1994) are doubly violent. Not only does it abduct its citizens, the city silences their memory and condemns them to eternal oblivion. The recollection of the city's torn social and architectural fabric is central to Hassan Daoud's *The House of Mathilde* (1989; English trans. 1999), which transforms the literary text into an archive of the vanishing cityscape. As they place Beirut at the centre of multivocal diachronic narratives, these novels illustrate the novelists' mistrust of both reality and the modern narrative structures that represent it. The war novel's depiction of the dismemberment of Beirut, its dislocation and violence, was the outcome of a deep aesthetic and discursive rupture that was nurtured and sustained in the post-war era.

The Lebanese civil war ended in 1990 with the Taef Agreement, a regionally sponsored peace treaty that stipulated the immediate suspension of armed conflict and the restoration of post-war national unity by reestablishing state authority and institutions. In the early years of the post-war era, two controversial laws shaped the ways in which intellectuals conceived of their roles. In 1991, the parliament ratified a law that granted amnesty for crimes committed before 1990. In accordance with the law, no war crime investigations ever occurred, and the fate of thousands of citizens who disappeared during the war remains unknown.[6] In 1994, the parliament voted on a bill to establish SOLIDERE, a private real estate group entrusted with rebuilding Beirut's ravaged downtown.[7] The project's advertisement portrayed the heart of the city (*qalb al-madina*)[8] as a meeting place for all sectarian communities that would heal the wounded national body and achieve social reconciliation.[9]

The master plan implemented by SOLIDERE conceived of downtown Beirut as a gentrified space built on the ruins of popular pre-war venues such as markets, cafés, shops and theatres. In line with Beirut's desire to project the image of a modern and global city, all physical reminders of the civil war were either destroyed or masked through what miriam cooke calls 'a politics of innocence', which 'flattened, homogenized, and aestheticized the traces of war'.[10] Architects, economists and social scientists were critical of the new project, as they foresaw the erasure of the city's historical and archaeological identity on the one hand and the silencing of alternative historical narratives, on the other.

The general amnesty law and the reconstruction of downtown Beirut became symptoms of institutionalised amnesia and 'dis-memory', which Norman Saadi Nikro identifies as the state's resistance to acknowledging and commemorating war losses while promoting an image of downtown Beirut as the throbbing heart of the city.[11] Less concerned with the heart of the city, critics drew attention to the city's memory (*dhākirat al-madīna*), without which, they argued, Beirut's post-war work of mourning will remain incomplete, which will in turn nurture the city's violent dispositions. Historians rewrote the history of Beirut and that of the civil war in order to recover the suppressed layers of the city's memory.[12] This concern was equally voiced in art, cinema and literature, all of which approached post-war Lebanon through the themes of trauma, memory and mourning. Commenting on the Lebanese war and post-war literary scene, Angelika Neuwirth and Andreas Pflitsch note that 'virtually all the Lebanese literature written during and after the civil war is a work of processing memory.'[13] As such, safeguarding the national community's collective memory became the defining ethos and the main master narrative of the post-war novels of Hoda Barakat, Rashid al-Daif and Hassan Daoud.[14]

The most prominent critic of post-war collective amnesia was Elias Khoury. His novels, articles, essays and play address the perils of cultural erasure and Beirut's inability to reckon with its losses and thus complete its work of mourning. Not only has Khoury been interested in post-war reconstruction policies, he has also invested in narrating the city's history as told by those who loved it and endured its violence. Placing the city at the core of his early literary and political project, Khoury is 'a writer *on* and *of* the city', as Dalia Mostafa rightly observed.[15] Like many intellectuals of his generation, Khoury's literary career began while he was working for cultural institutions affiliated with the Palestinian Liberation Organization (PLO) and the Lebanese left at the height of the civil war.[16] Between 1992 and 2009, Khoury was the editor-in-chief of *al-Nahar*'s weekly cultural supplement, *al-Mulhaq*. Like Khoury, the majority of writers associated with *al-Mulhaq* at the time were French-educated scholars from the Lebanese University, all endowed with cultural capital that drew on their training at the hand of prominent French thinkers in the 1960s.

The legacy of the civil war ushered in a new understanding of political commitment. In the wake of the 1967 defeat followed by the civil war, both of which had exposed the fault lines of socialist and Arab nationalist ideologies, Khoury as well as writers in *al-Mulhaq* negotiated the ethos of political commitment that Suhayl Idris (1925–2008) had initially promoted in *al-Adab*. Since he began writing in the 1970s, Khoury has been careful about wholeheartedly appropriating the notion of *iltizām* that compels him, as writer, 'to serve a cause', a position that seemingly advances a monolithic understanding of critical and literary engagements.[17] By articulating a nuanced reading of the notion of *iltizām*, Khoury has advanced a conception of the writer as a 'committed citizen and a public intellectual', one who upholds 'the values of freedom and justice'.[18] As such, he and other public intellectuals of the post-war era questioned their wartime militancy in a collective act of introspection that ushered in a revisionist historiography of the civil war and a re-examination of power and hegemonic practices. Hence, writers at *al-Mulhaq* argued for the necessity of exposing the symbolic acts of repression that the post-war state had been tacitly practicing. Under Khoury's guidance, *al-Mulhaq* became a platform for sociologists, economists, poets, writers, cartoonists, activists, social psychologists and playwrights – all critical of the state's post-war urban, cultural and economic politics of erasure. Memory, erasure and collective mourning became thus the loci of the post-war literary discourse.

In 'Memory of the City' Khoury describes the city's centre as 'an empty space, a placeless space, a hole in memory',[19] and proceeds to describe the city's amnesiac state:

> Beirut today can be understood both as a mythological prototype of the city torn by civil war, disheveled by death, dismembered by destruction, and as a former Roman and Phoenician city, a city with a past built on ruins of the past ... The city remains unstable, if temporarily sedated by the peace pact signed in 1989 – which is, in itself, a myth the city may smother at birth ... The huge machine that is reconstructing and regenerating the city is already wiping out the memory of old Beirut, relentlessly tossing the rubble of the old city into the sea.[20]

Khoury's lament of post-war Beirut draws on an anthropomorphic representation of the city as a war victim whose physical paralysis and mental breakdown are reinforced by policies that mask rather than heal her wounds. Beirut emerges as a dismembered, sedated and amnesiac mother whose unresolved war traumas will eventually drive her again to infanticide. In the midst of his city's interrupted and incomplete work of mourning, Khoury wonders:

> How are we to preserve the memory of this place in the face of such frightening architectural amnesia? *In this city systematically ravaged by civil war, the only space left for memory is literature.*[21] Indeed, in any attempt to analyze the destiny of a city's myth, it is crucial to understand the difference between the role of the architect and that of the novelist. Although both architects and novelists imagine places, cities, houses, and create them, the architect's media are building blocks and construction materials and the writer's are symbols in language.[22]

For Khoury, the remaining space for the preservation of memory is the literary text. He conceives of the post-war politically committed writer as a prophetic figure, one who reads 'the present as if it is the past, thus giving his/her text the distance and capacity to criticize, identify, destroy, rebuild and heal the wounds at the same time.'[23] Thus, the post-war writer is a prophetic figure, one who has to assume the role of an omniscient and omnipotent critic, capable of reading and reacting to tragedy across different temporalities, and at the same time articulating grief and leading the collective work of mourning. The intellectual-prophet that Khoury envisions is also a guardian of the city's memory and myths. Inasmuch as the architect rebuilds the city with stones and marble, the writer refigures the city in the literary text, which he conceives as a site of memory. The site of memory, or what Pierre Nora identifies as *lieu de mémoire*, is 'any significant entity, whether material or non-material in nature, which by dint of human will or the work of time has become a symbolic element of the memorial heritage of any community.'[24] For Nora, such spaces are the sites in which 'cultural memory crystallizes and secretes itself'.[25] The purpose of the sites of memory for Nora is 'to stop time, to block the work of forgetting'.[26] Khoury retrieves Nora's understanding of *lieu de mémoire* and thus attributes to the writer the power of transforming the literary text into a site of memory that safeguards the collectivity from erasure and shields the city from its own violent impulses.[27]

By entrusting the post-war writer with responsibility for rescuing the community from forced erasure, Khoury conceives of the intellectual as an ethical subject. As guardians of collective memory, writers occupy the idealised ethical position of agents who simultaneously embody their community's losses and incorporate those losses in their writings. Khoury's conceptualisation of the intellectual as the crucible of a community's losses channels Jacques Derrida's understanding of the work of mourning (*travail de mémoire*) as an ethical imperative. In *The Work of Mourning*, a collection of elegiac texts in commemoration of friends and public intellectuals, Derrida argues that the fusional relationship between the mourner and the mourned and the collapse of boundaries between them protects the mourned from oblivion and is thus the best sign of loyalty toward them. Derrida argues that it is only in the mourner that the dead may speak, and that it is only by speaking of or as the dead that the mourner can keep them alive.[28] Hence, the public intellectual that Elias Khoury imagined in the post-war context is engaged in a multilayered literary, critical and political project that is fundamentally an ethical one. The post-war intellectual is expected to lead the community away from its silenced, incomplete and interrupted work of mourning in both theory and praxis. The intellectual's political commitment draws therefore on literary and critical incorporation of the community's anxieties, the ultimate evidence of loyalty to a national community scarred by its troubled past.

Inasmuch as the writer's life was associated with the city's memory, the writer's death was symptomatic of the city's demise. In November 1995, or forty days after his suicide, *al-Mulhaq* published Ralph Rizqallah's unfinished article, 'Madkhal ila al-Taʿasa' (Introduction to misery), as well as several elegiac essays by his friends and colleagues.[29] The introduction of *al-Mulhaq*'s special issue read: 'Ralph Rizqallah died. As if he was, through his protest death, announcing the suicide of hope facing misery, hatred, degeneration [*inhitāt*], and banality.'[30] This succinct statement sets the framework in which *al-Mulhaq* and its readers will interpret the suicide: Rizqallah committed suicide in protest of the collective state of cultural and moral demise that has prevailed in post-war Beirut. In his obituary of Rizqallah entitled 'Al-Ihtihaj Intiharan' (Protest as suicide), Elias Khoury laments the sudden loss of his friend and links it to that of the director Maroun Baghdadi: 'Everybody was at the funeral. I shall not name them because you know who they are. Maroun Baghdadi was of course absent because he was the first to fall into the abyss of the city's darkness.'[31] Beirut, which Khoury holds accountable for the death of his two friends, is paradoxically the culprit and the victim, the deceased and mourner. Khoury then proceeds to lament the generation to which both he and Rizqallah belonged:

> Is this a generation of curses and disappointments, a generation of death and war, a generation of despair and madness, a generation of dreams and nightmares, a generation of ruins [*jīl al-kharāb*]? Are we the generation of ruins? Has Beirut deceived us? Beirut said she would be a city but turned into a grave. She said she would be a dream but turned into a nightmare. She said she would be the revolution but turned into an illusion. She said she would be the sea but turned into a desert ... Are you the innocent paying for a crime he has not committed? *Are you the sacrifice in the name of a generation, the sacrifice of a generation, and the sacrifice for the sake of a generation?*[32] I am torn by these questions, my dear. You see, I do not write an elegy because you dislike elegies. I write about our scandal [*faḍīḥatinā*] that our death unveils.[33]

In his elegy for Rizqallah, Elias Khoury politicises the tragic deaths of Rizqallah and Baghdadi by attributing them to Beirut's troubled binaries (city/grave; sea/desert), the artifice of its political engagement (revolution/illusion) and its traumatic history of violence (dream/nightmare). All of the city's contradictions and appetite for violence have scarred Khoury's generation, a construct that continues to be essential to the ways in which Khoury and other intellectuals reflect on their past and present. Khoury conceives of himself and his departed friends as members of an entire generation of post-war intellectuals (*jīl al-kharāb*) shamed by the scandal of defeat, relapse and the collective pain of confronting the banality of post-war Beirut. Just as those who have died before him, Rizqallah rises from Khoury's bleak lament as a human sacrifice (*aḍḥiya*) that salvages his community from the cardinal sin of forgetting. As he signifies the suicide of Rizqallah in a register that draws on the value of self-sacrifice and salvation, Khoury imagines the deceased intellectual as the expression of an ethos that transforms the narcissism of suicide into an unqualified altruistic act. This Derridian injunction to mourn, or the expectation that the post-war writer embodies both physically and intellectually his community's sufferings, is precisely the position that Rabee Jaber challenges in *Ralph Rizqallah*. By subverting the dominant ethos of the post-war critical discourse, Jaber presents a different approach to mourning the intellectual.

Ralph Through the Looking Glass

When Rabee Jaber wrote his first novel *Sayyid al-ʿAtma* (Lord of darkness) in 1992, he was twenty years old and a student of physics at the American University of Beirut. Between 1992 and 1999, he published seven novels, including *Ralph Rizqallah* and *Al-Bayt al-Akhir* (The last house; 1996), in which he retraced the last days of the director Maroun Baghdadi before his mysterious death. In these two novels, Jaber refigures the shocking death of Baghdadi and Rizqallah in intertextual narratives that weave biographical facts with references to novels by Youssef Habshi al-Ashqar (1929–92),[34] Baghdadi's films and children's literature, among other texts. Jaber's ability to publish a novel every year without compromising the quality of his prose or the complexity of his themes puzzled critics. They realised that they knew nothing about him, except that he was a young writer living in self-imposed seclusion at the margins of the cultural scene. Always shying away from promoting his work, Jaber continues to refuse to give interviews or public talks, which may explain the small number of reviews his novels received in the 1990s.[35] But what is most pertinent here is that Jaber disengaged from the Lebanese cultural scene at a time when intellectuals were addressing the problematic reconstruction of Beirut. His resistance to participating in the most important debate that marked Beirut in the 1990s seemed at odds with his position as a writer at *al-Mulhaq*. Some critics argued that Jaber identified with a new generation of writers who had not been engaged in the civil war and were thus searching for new modes of expression and looking inwards: inspecting the self, the psyche and personal memory.[36] Shortly after the publication of *Ralph Rizqallah*, Jaber left *al-Mulhaq* and in 2001 became the editor of *Afaq*, the cultural supplement issues by *al-Hayat* daily.

Jaber's literary trajectory witnessed a turning point with the publication of the historical novels *Yusuf al-Inglizi* (Yusuf, the Englishman; 1999) and

Rihlat al-Ghirnati (The journey of the Grenadian; 2002), which Lebanese critics welcomed with great interest. Jaber reinvented the historical novel, a literary genre that posed a new set of thematic and stylistic questions in the post-war literary scene. With the publication of the trilogy *Beirut: Madinat al-ᶜAlam* (Beirut: City of the world; 2003–7), the poet and critic Abbas Baydoun (b. 1945) and the historian Kamal Salibi (1929–2011)[37] lauded Jaber's work and declared him the master of the postmodern historical novel that weaves intertextuality and metafiction into historical documentation.[38] It is only after *Amirka* (America; 2009) was nominated for the 2010 International Prize for Arabic Fiction (IPAF/the Arabic Booker) that Jaber, hitherto known for his dense and experimental novels, became popular beyond Lebanon. After winning the IPAF for *Duruz Belgrad* (The Druze of Belgrade; 2011) in 2012, Jaber was long-listed again in 2013 for the same award for *Tuyur al-Holiday Inn* (The birds of the Holiday Inn; 2011), Jaber's second war novel after *Confessions* (2008; English trans. 2016), both of which appeared interestingly late in his literary trajectory. Although acknowledged as one of the most influential Lebanese novelists, only a few of Jaber's novels have been translated. Despite Jaber's prominence in contemporary Lebanese literature, his reclusive personality still occupies critics. Commenting on Jaber's self-positioning in the Lebanese literary scene, Abbas Baydoun writes:

> The image that Rabee Jaber wants for himself is unrelated to his life, his personal choices, his moods, or his physical appearance. The image that Jaber promotes of himself is that of a paper author [*muᵓallif waraqi*]. He is only a writer, an author, and all that remains are details that he would like to keep to himself.[39]

Jaber's self-fashioning as an intellectual and his distance from the public debates that marked the early post-war years may shed light on the significance of his early novels, particularly *Ralph Rizqallah*. When Jaber began writing *Ralph Rizqallah*, he was still working at *al-Mulhaq*, which provided writers with a platform to expose the ways in which state policies systematically erased war memories and hence impeded the collective work of mourning. Critical reviews of *Ralph Rizqallah* have associated the novel with that discourse. Not only do critics tie the novel to the debate about collective memory, but they also see in *Ralph Rizqallah* a reiteration of the literary discourse critical of post-war amnesia. Faysal Darraj, for instance, classifies *Ralph Rizqallah* within the 'literature of defeat' (*adab al-hazima*) and argues that Jaber commemorates the death of his peer in protest of the systematic voiding of meaning that occurred in post-war Lebanon.[40] Addressing specifically the notion of memory, Youmna el-Eid understands the expansive novels of Jaber as a contribution to the memory discourse.[41] Dalia Mostafa presents a similar reading of Jaber in an article comparing Khoury's *White Masks* to *Ralph Rizqallah* and argues that both novels are indeed 'trauma novels', in which the protagonists suffer from the consequences of a severe war shock. Mostafa maintains that although revealing itself psychologically, this traumatic event is far from personal. 'Through its representation of such traumatic experiences as depression, alienation, fear and nightmares, Jaber's novel offers important insights into our understanding of post-war Beirut and its inhabitants.'[42] Despite the lack of clear references to the civil war within the narrative, Mostafa sees the suicide of the intellectual in *Ralph Rizqallah* as a symptom of a social and psychological state triggered by a failed collective mourning process.[43]

The interpretations of Darraj, el-Eid and Mostafa, among others, illustrate the critical responses that have placed *Ralph Rizqallah* within the conceptual framework that has defined Lebanese post-war literary criticism since the 1990s. However, in the absence of clear textual references and clues about post-war collective memory discourse, such readings may be theoretical projections onto Jaber's narrative, which, as I argue, suggests an alternative portrayal of the post-war intellectual. Furthermore, interpreting Jaber's novel as a continuation of the literary and critical experience of precursors, such as Elias Khoury, runs the risk of overlooking Jaber's literary innovation. In this context, it is crucial to discuss the ways in which Jaber appropriates the narrative strategies and themes of his precursors in order to subvert them, thereby weaving an alternative poetics of commemorating the suicidal intellectual.

Jaber opens *Ralph Rizqallah* with the following lines. The intellectual parks his car in front of Beirut's most iconic landmark, opens his arms as a cross and jumps:

His name was Ralph Rizqallah.
On Saturday morning 28 October 1995, he stopped his green Toyota car parallel to the pavement, right in front of Dbaybo Café. He rushed out of

the car, climbed the parapet, and threw himself over the edge into space. Before jumping, he opened his arms as a cross. Behind him was Beirut, before him Raouche Rock. He was wearing his old blue jeans and his khaki shirt, which he bought two years ago. He was 45 years old. And he threw himself over. He fell from a height of 45 meters, hit the rocks, and then floated on the surface of the water. Everything came to a standstill.[44]

The diegetic narrator in the novel is called Rabee Jaber, a journalist struck by the suicide of his colleague, Ralph Rizqallah, who is a professor of psychology at the Lebanese University. Stretching the boundaries of his identity as a journalist, the narrator undertakes the role of a detective investigating the suicide in order to write a novel about Ralph. In a self-conscious tone that exposes the structure of the narrative process, the narrator announces: 'Now I know where to start my novel.'[45] In his investigation, Rabee identifies a few intellectuals that Ralph had known such as the scholar 'Mona F.',[46] the artist Jad,[47] the poet Bassam Hajjar[48] and the novelist and editor of *al-Mulhaq*, Elias Khoury, whose name appears several times in the narrative. Despite his interest in Ralph's intellectual circle, the narrator neither examines nor mentions the special issue that *al-Mulhaq* published after Ralph's death. Instead, he meets with Ralph's widow and elderly parents, reads his articles in *al-Mulhaq*, contemplates old and recent photographs of him, inspects his newspaper obituary, scrutinises the coronary and police reports, and finally draws a map of the site from which Ralph jumped. In the narrator's investigation of Ralph's intimate life, the reader learns about Ralph's struggle with depression and his reflections on his achievements and failures.

Intertextuality is an overarching narrative technique in *Ralph Rizqallah*. Jaber builds a multilayered narrative that remains close to Ralph's writings by borrowing from his original articles, which appeared in *al-Mulhaq* between 1992 and 1995. The narrative also alludes to Ralph's articles and books in Arabic and French, which range from studies about the Shiʿi religious ritual of ʿAshuraʾ to the representation of Dracula in contemporary culture. Jaber also makes multiple references to Lewis Carroll's *Alice in Wonderland* (1865) and *Through the Looking Glass* (1871), the latter being the referent to the title *Ralph Rizqallah Through the Looking Glass*.[49] The result of this expansive and elaborate metafiction and intertextuality is a hybrid and multilayered narrative that imagines Ralph and the narrator, both the searcher and the object of his search, as alienated characters suffering from an acute sense of personal loss and isolation.

In *Ralph Rizqallah*, Jaber simultaneously engages and dissents from the narrative discourse of his precursors through his systematic deployment of metafiction and intertextuality. The novel recalls several characteristics of the *mise en abîme* of metafiction, which Linda Hutcheon identifies as 'a fiction that includes within itself a commentary on its own narrative and/ or linguistic identity.'[50] Both the author and the narrator are called Rabee Jaber; both are journalists at *al-Mulhaq*; both are writing a novel about the suicide of Ralph Rizqallah; and both are acquainted with Elias Khoury. The self-reflexive, self-conscious and self-referential text in which the narrative and the authorial voices are enmeshed calls attention to the novel's nature as an artefact.

The manipulation of boundaries between the fictive and the real, the authentic and the artificial, the original and the replica is also a property of intertextuality, a defining feature of Jaber's novels and particularly *Ralph Rizqallah*. Commenting on the concept of intertextuality, Julia Kristeva notes that 'every text is from the outset under the jurisdiction of other discourses which impose a universe on it.'[51] Thus, the author's numerous references to his precursors are necessary elements of his writing process. Roland Barthes pushes that understanding further and argues that the 'intertext is the impossibility of living outside the living text'.[52] Texts originate from other texts that are the products of other texts, all of which constitute an infinite textual genealogy.

Jaber's awareness of the inescapability of lineage, whether textual or intellectual, is discernible not only in his novels, but also in his essays. In an article entitled 'Al-Katib wa-Aslafuh' (The writer and his precursors), Jaber wonders: 'Does the writer know his precursors [*asláf*]? Does the writer know who are the writers that have given him his vision, style, and outlook on language and the world? Literature is imitation and not invention. Literature is tradition.'[53] In his reflections on intellectual genealogy, Jaber uses the term *asláf*, which signifies both ancestors and precursors, a combination of genetic and intellectual heritage. His belief in the inevitability of channelling his precursors is manifest in his recurrent deployment of intertextuality. Jaber understands mimesis not as blind reproduction of the precursor's work. Rather, he defines it as the creation of a new text by rewriting the old, a creative process of parody that Hutcheon identifies as the

> exploration of difference and similarity; in metafiction it (parody) invites a more literary reading, a recognition of literary codes. But it is wrong to see the end of this process as mockery, ridicule, or mere destruction. Metafiction parodies and imitates as a way to a new form which is just as serious and valid, as a synthesis, as the form, it dialectically attempts to surpass. It does not necessarily involve a movement away from mimesis, however, unless by that term is meant only a rigid object-imitation or behavioristic-realistic motivation.[54]

Intertextual parody occurs on several levels in Jaber's *Ralph Rizqallah*. As he investigates the death of Ralph, the narrator simultaneously engages and comments on the very act of searching. Investigation, as a narrative theme, is common in Lebanese war novels, many of which revolve around a question, a riddle or the disappearance of a protagonist. The narrator in Rashid al-Daif's *Al-Mustabidd* (The despot), for instance, conducts an anxious search for a mysterious woman with whom he had a fleeting sexual encounter in the darkness of a Beirut war shelter. The search is also a dominant theme in Elias Khoury's work, particularly in *Journey of Little Gandhi* in which a narrator searches for Beirut's most famous shoe shiner.[55] Khoury also retrieves lost memories in *Gate of the Sun* (1998; English trans. 2005), a novel that portrays the Palestinians' experience of displacement following the 1948 *nakba*. Khoury based this novel on extensive interviews that he and a group of researchers had conducted in Palestinian refugee camps in Lebanon.[56] Appropriating the search as a theme and a narrative technique, the narrator in *Ralph Rizqallah* decides to investigate Ralph's suicide by interrogating at first his own reflection in the mirror:

> In June 1996, approximately eight months after his death, I decided to start looking for him. Just like that, on a whim, I found myself looking at the reflection of my face in the mirror and ignoring the black space that appears behind my ears, saying to myself: I will find him … I asked:
>   Where do you search for a dead man? I answered: Among his family, his acquaintances. I asked: Where else? I answered: In his pictures.

– And do you know of any other place to look for him?

– I do. In his writings.[57]

In one of his many dialogues with his own reflection in the mirror, the narrator reveals the nature of his investigation. Not only will he meet Ralph's family and friends, but he will also search for answers in texts that are either by or about the dead intellectual. In the first phase of his investigation, the narrator visits Ralph's widow and makes a revealing announcement: 'I told her that I wasn't looking for secrets and that I don't believe people commit suicide for a specific reason.'[58] With this statement, Jaber begins debunking the narrative theme of his precursors by a self-defeating declaration about the purpose of the search for knowledge and truth. Indeed, from the outset, the author dismisses the unveiling of secrets as a desired goal. More importantly, as he voids the intellectual's suicide from a preset meaning, the narrator begins his gradual disavowal of the post-war representation of the intellectual as a guardian of his community's collective memory. By subverting the act of unveiling secrets, which is at the core of his precursors' literary project, the narrator condemns interrogation as a narrative tool. After meeting with Ralph's widow, the narrator reports:

> I stared at her. Now I shall know. I did not say to her: tell me. I will never say that to anyone. The moment you start asking, you are no longer free. And without your freedom, your writing is dirt and deceit. I know that very well. And because I know it, I live underground.[59]

The narrator embraces the paradox of interrogating Ralph's widow without asking her a single question. Not only does the narrator shy away from asking, he also denounces the danger inherent in the process of asking: 'The moment you start asking, you are no longer free.' Speech solicitation, from his perspective, is 'dirt and deceit' and thus the most abhorrent form of search. Instead of asking, the narrator reads, decodes and interprets. The narrator shall learn the truth about Ralph's suicide just by staring at his widow, thereby replacing interrogation with physiognomy. As such, reading facial expressions becomes the interrogator's only valid search tool. The narrator, however, does not reject the value of the search entirely; he merely subverts it and searches for truth not in the spoken word, but in the silence inherent

in the widow's face. His simultaneous espousal and condemnation of the
interview as an investigation method operates in this context as a commentary on the themes of secrets, riddles and investigations, all of which have
dominated the works of his precursors. As he renounces the unearthing of
secrets as a narrative motif and the interview as the base for the narrative,
Rabee Jaber defines his ambivalence about the post-war novel. The new
narrative text that Jaber creates is a parody, which simultaneously engages
and dissents from the text of his precursors, or *aslāf*, which he attempts to
transcend.

Not only does Jaber parody the themes of the search and the uncovering
of secrets, but he also deconstructs the very purpose of intellectual interventions, or political commitment as defined by post-war intellectuals. Instead
of speech, Jaber promotes silence as a discursive framework. He summons
Ralph to the narrative by citing one of his posthumous articles entitled,
'Balaghat al-Sukut' (The eloquence of silence) in which Ralph writes:

> You did not listen, you who have written to the echoes of the void within
> you …[…] All you have to do is sit still … Keep silent. Do not write …
> For writing, as I have stated, is not revealing … Arabs have said: Eloquence
> lies in pithiness. I believe it is more accurate to say that eloquence lies in
> silence. Have you not read the Talmud? If speech is silver, then silence is
> gold. Eloquence is in silence, as Blaise Pascal once said.[60]

The narrator is struck by Ralph's unfinished article, in which the latter advo-
cates silence (*sukūt*), or the suspension of speech, as the ideal intellectual position: 'For writing is not revealing' (*lā tunbiʾ*). Ralph's use of the unusual verb
tunbiʾ (from *anbaʾ*) recalls Abu Tammam's (805–45) famous verse, in which
the Abbasid poet favours the sword over the written word: '*Al-sayf aṣdaq
inbāʾan min al-kutub*' (Swords reveal truth more than books). Capturing the
poet's fleeting moment of anxiety about the written word, Rizqallah stages an
intertextual homage to the poetic canon and pushes Abu Tammam's anxiety
toward nihilism and an overarching indictment of the book, the word, and
even the very act of writing. Just as Ralph uses intertextuality in order to challenge the power of the written word and prophesy discursive silence, so does
Rabee Jaber the author. In his reference to Ralph's fertile and multilayered
text, Jaber adds additional layers to his own narrative. As he weaves Ralph's

denunciation of speech and the written word into his text, Jaber comments on the value of silence in his own intellectual environment. By undermining speech and writing, Jaber addresses precursors such as Elias Khoury, who have written extensively on political commitment that draws on the power of the writer, the written word and the literary text.

The multilayered sabotage of the wisdom of his precursors, whether contemporary or ancient, is by no means an act of mockery, ridicule or erasure. Instead, it is a new model, which is just as legitimate and vital as the form it dialectically transcends. By separating the process of the search from its meaning and promoting discursive silence, Jaber detaches his novel from the prevalent interpretation of suicide as an act of protest. For Jaber, the suicide of the intellectual is no longer inscribed in his precursors' ideological framework, which had imagined him as an articulate and moral subject who embodied his community's post-war anxieties. Inasmuch as Jaber codifies the intellectual beyond speech and ideology, the diegetic narrator searches for truth not in ideology, but in Ralph's articulation of an existential and nihilistic angst. In order to capture Ralph's state of mind before his suicide, the narrator reverts to texts such as articles and photographs, which, he believes, are intimate and accurate reflections of the dead intellectual.

Reflections of Ralph

As the narrator conducts his unconventional investigation into Ralph's death, he delves into Ralph's past by exploring pictures and essays that the intellectual left behind. The narrator learns that Ralph's adolescence was shaken by the suicide of his young aunt, and he pursued a degree in psychology in order to understand the reasons why individuals end their lives.[61] The narrator gradually realises that the subject of his search was a melancholic man deeply unsettled by existential angst. In the official police report, Ralph's brother states that Ralph, who had been drinking heavily and talking constantly about death, committed suicide for personal reasons (*nājimah ʿan shakhṣihi huwa*), thereby signalling Ralph's personal and emotional anguish.[62] As he examines Ralph's contributions to *al-Mulhaq*, the narrator finds an article in which Ralph shares with his readers a startling discovery. Ralph's quoted passage reads:

You suddenly realize – one day, just like that, simply, without warning – that you have reached forty. This was the first of many discoveries. [...] I discovered, for instance, that anyone over forty has to be tested for cholesterol, diabetes, etc. in his blood. I also learned that the increase of cholesterol level might eventually clot arteries, which may lead to a heart attack and death. Unfortunately, however, one can foresee that problem and adjourn death by conducting an open-heart surgery in which the clotted artery is replaced by another vein etched from the leg. [...] In the United States, however, surgeons prefer to replace the clotted artery that feeds the muscles with that of a pig ... [...] The scene has also become so dull after I suddenly realized that life has ejected [*lafaẓat*] my generation [*abnāʾ jīlī*] to the city's seashore ... to the Manara Corniche.[63] At dawn, I run into them – the un-dead [*al-lā-mayyitīn*] – jogging, or so we all think ... They remembered that humans have bodies that shrivel ... They suddenly realized the thickness of the flesh that pulls them down and the unbearable heaviness of being [*thiqal al-kāʾin al-ladhī lā yuḥtamal*].[64]

In this passage, Ralph returns to the theme of blood that had fascinated him in his earlier studies about ʿAshuraʾ and Bram Stoker's *Dracula* (1897). In the Shiʿi ritual of the holy month of Muharram, in which some believers practice self-flagellation as a means to reenact the suffering of Imam Hussein, the gushing blood is cathartic and a means to regenerate life in a body worn down by sin and pain. Blood is also vital in the legend of Dracula, the vampire who sucks the blood of his victims to rejuvenate and prolong his life. At forty, however, Ralph is shaken by the realisation that blood, which once was equivalent to life, catharsis and a mythical exercise of power, now heralds illness, poison and death. Because of their illnesses and collapsing bodies, men and women of Ralph's generation have been expelled to the Corniche, the city's coastal periphery. Two meanings are associated with the verb eject (*lafaẓ*) in Arabic: whereas the first refers to the act of spitting, the second pertains to utterance and pronunciation. Thus, Ralph believes that life has not only physically ejected him to the city's peripheries, but it has also pronounced him and his generation dead. The human sacrifice (*adḥiya*) that Khoury will later lament in his elegy of Ralph Rizqallah had already been stripped of its powers. Ralph identifies his sudden awareness of his eventual yet slow death as the 'unbearable heaviness of being' (*thiqal al-kāʾ in al-ladhī lā yuḥtamal*), a double reference to the Nietzschean 'heaviness of being' and Milan Kundera's parody of the notion later in *The Unbearable Lightness of Being*.[65]

Ralph's association of the term 'my generation' (*abnāʾ jīlī*) with the neologism 'un-dead' (*al-lā-mayyitīn*) is an eerie reference to *The Un-Dead*, the title Bram Stoker had originally chosen for *Dracula*. Deploying textual parody, Ralph strips members of his generation from significant political identities such as the '1960s generation' (*jīl al-sittīnāt*) with which his peers identify. Ralph's understanding of his generation is also strikingly different from the 'generation of ruins' (*jīl al-kharāb*), the generation of urban and ideological demise featured in Khoury's elegy of Rizqallah. By linking members of his generation to the un-dead, predictable illnesses, abject pigs and mindless jogging rituals, Ralph draws a new profile of the post-war generation of intellectuals and thus resignifies the notion of generation from a political to a biological category. De-politicised and de-historicised, Ralph's generation is no longer a political referent that signals political commitment and a critical standpoint against the state of collective amnesia in post-war Beirut. Instead, it represents merely an indiscriminate group of random people from Beirut united simply by a collective fixation on ageing and dying.

Ralph's anxiety about his physical demise overlaps with an acute sense of isolation. In his conversations with Ralph's widow, the narrator discovers that before his suicide, Ralph had begun a gradual fall into depression. The world, according to Ralph, 'was a forest full of evil people', in which 'he no longer saw one familiar face'.[66] Ralph's estrangement had reached its peak when he began seeing only strangers around him. Friends, colleagues, family members – all became strangers in the eyes of the depressed writer. In the absence of companionship, Ralph fell into loneliness and a savage sociality only found in the wild. As he inspects a picture in which Ralph poses next to a polar bear in a zoo, the narrator becomes curious about bears and about Ralph's interest in them. In order to decipher Ralph's mysterious affinity with bears, the narrator turns to animal encyclopaedias and learns about the bears' poor and primitive faculty of expression. The narrator discovers that polar bears live in utmost loneliness and do not connect with other bears except in fights.[67] When the narrator examines Ralph's picture with the polar bear, he sees two faces of the same savage and lonely creature. Ralph had mentally exited his world, the 'forest full of evil people', and joined a new sociality in the wild. Just like the polar bear, Ralph had been unable to communicate to the world his emotional state and was thus banished into nihilism and exile. In such an environment, where emotion and speech are muted, what becomes of writing and intellectual interventions?

One week before his suicide, the narrator explains, Ralph conveyed his disillusionment about writing:

> During Ralph's last visit to *al-Mulhaq*, Bassam Hajjar asked him if he was going to send them an article, i.e. to *al-Mulhaq*. Like a child, Ralph waved his hand and said that all of this was meaningless. He mumbled a few words and left in a rush.[68]

Similar to the polar bear that cannot express itself to the outer world, Ralph makes unintelligible gestures about his apathy toward writing, an exercise that had become neither valid nor credible. Having lost the faculty of speech and the ability to express himself, the nihilistic writer avoids *al-Mulhaq*, the post-war critical space that attributes to the word – particularly to the written word – the power of rescuing the memory of the national community. Toward the end of his search, the narrator reaches the following conclusion about the site from which Ralph committed suicide: ' "Raouche Rock is not too far", I say to myself. We only need a bit of disappointment. And a bit of loneliness. And a little headache.'[69] Ralph's suicide, the narrator concludes, is neither an act of protest nor a symptom of a post-war collective psychic condition. Not secretive or mystical, the intellectual's suicide is merely an incident caused by the intertwinement of personal alienation, physical ailments and a nihilistic perception of the role of the intellectual. If Ralph Rizqallah, the writer at *al-Mulhaq*, committed suicide because of an overarching existential angst, what is the profile of the post-war intellectual that the narrator reveals?

The Writer Through the Looking Glass

The narrator's motives for conducting his unconventional search remain unclear throughout the novel. Early on in his search, the narrator announces that he is not looking for secrets and that he does not believe people commit suicide for a reason. Furthermore, the narrator and his object of search had not been friends, but merely acquaintances who had met a few times at *al-Mulhaq*. The narrator remembers his last awkward encounter with Ralph: 'Ralph died before I read any of his articles. This is probably why I looked down when we last met at the entrance of *al-Nahar*.'[70] Not only had the narrator not known Ralph as a friend, he had not known or read him as an intellectual. If neither *al-Mulhaq* nor the intellectual circle that surrounds it unites the narrator and Ralph, what is the nature of the narrator's identification with Ralph? It becomes gradually clear to the reader that the narrator identifies with Ralph not by means of their intellectual association but through texts, particularly English children's literature such as Lewis Carroll's *Alice in Wonderland* and *Through the Looking Glass*.

Upon reading 'Madkhal ila al-Taʿasa', Ralph's posthumous article in *al-Mulhaq*, the narrator is struck by Ralph's numerous references to *Alice in Wonderland*. An avid reader of Carroll, the narrator exclaims: 'If only I knew that Ralph liked Alice in Wonderland! If only!'[71] The narrator begins identifying with Ralph the moment he realises the influence of Lewis Carroll's novels on Ralph's writings. From that moment, the mirror appears more than fifty times in *Ralph Rizqallah* and emerges as the novel's principal metaphor. In a close and comparative reading of *Ralph Rizqallah* and Carroll's novels, Sobhi Boustani rightly observes that the narrator deploys the mirror metaphorically in order to establish a parallel between three journeys: that of Alice, that of the narrator in search of Ralph, and that of the latter – through his suicide – in search of an exit from life.[72] The narrator reflects on the function of the mirror:

> In his first novel, Carroll invented a secret underground world, a world of wonders to which Alice arrived only after she fell into a rabbit's hole. In the second novel, however, we do not access this world through a hole in the ground but through a glass surface that resembles water. Because we see ourselves in glass. In water too.[73]

As such, the mirror that led Alice to the underworld is similar to the bathroom mirror in which the narrator contemplates himself. Both mirrors are equivalent to the mirror-like water into which Ralph jumped. Thus, the mirror emerges as the only space that unites the narrator with his object of search. The narrator stretches the boundaries of identification, almost fusing with Ralph. When the narrator looks at himself in the mirror, he sees Ralph; when he looks at Ralph's pictures, he sees himself. In a moment of fusion between Ralph and the narrator, the polar bear – Ralph's alter ego – emerges: 'And now, bear facing bear. As if facing a mirror. I wore my sandals. I left the book open on the table. I walked outside. In a white desert, a polar bear walks in sandals.'[74] One could also read in the centrality of the motif of the mirror a gesture to the mirror in Khoury's *Journey of Little Gandhi*, a narrative of lost memory that begins and ends with the search for the story of Gandhi, a shoe shiner who vanished from the the war-torn streets of Beirut. Addressing the narrator, Alice describes Gandhi as 'something else. He was a man … but somehow not a man … man as if, how can I put it, as if you yourself are standing in front of a mirror.'[75] In this instance, just as the diegetic narrator in *Journey* recognises the object of his search, Gandhi, in the mirror, so does the diegetic narrator in *Ralph Rizqallah*, who looks in the mirror and sees Ralph.

The narrator, however, pushes his identification with Ralph further and uses it as a means not only to learn more about his object of search, but also to resignify him and appropriate him entirely. As he identifies with Ralph, the narrator exposes himself to the reader through his self-portrayal as a marginal intellectual living in utmost destitution and isolation. He articulates his marginality by deploring his weak health, social seclusion and lack of intellectual interlocutors. The narrator struggles with many illnesses, such as migraines and ulcers, prompted by his intolerance to light and certain foods and his inability to navigate the social world.[76] As a remedy to his physical weaknesses, the narrator consumes painkillers and tranquillisers. The sickly character admits: 'I was born in 1972. But I have an old head hanging over my shoulders. I think that in the last ten years, I have taken enough Aspirin pills to kill a blue whale.'[77] The narrator's self-identification in these terms echoes Ralph's own anxiety over his ageing body and the deterioration of his blood, which was the subject of Ralph's article about his un-dead generation. Both Ralph and the narrator represent the intellectual in a register that is strikingly dissimilar to the ways in which the intellectual had been imagined. Indeed, the sickly intellectual that Ralph and the narrator embody contra-dicts the powerful figure that Elias Khoury evokes in his elegy for Ralph

Rizqallah, particularly when he asks 'Are you the sacrifice in the name of a generation?' No longer the human sacrifice that redeems a generation from its sins, the intellectual that both Jaber and Rizqallah imagine is frail, mortal and socially disengaged.

The narrator's living conditions contribute to his portrayal as a journalist and a novelist living in self-imposed social isolation. Recalling the habitat of a polar bear, the narrator lives in a 'cave',[78] which is 'seven steps underground' in a small windowless storage room of a residential building.[79] The dark and humid rented room is fit for one person only with one light bulb, one bed and one chair. The narrator has a sink with a small mirror in which he speaks to his reflection and to that of Ralph. The narrator does not own a car and takes the bus, the cheapest public transportation in Lebanon. Every time he senses the danger of being drawn into conversation with another passenger, the narrator breaks into song:

> Humpty Dumpty sat on a wall,
> Humpty Dumpty had a great fall.
> All the king's horses and all the king's men
> Couldn't put Humpty on his place again.[80]

In the original Arabic text, Jaber quotes the lyrics of the rhyme in English but changes the final wording from the original 'Couldn't put Humpty together again' to 'Couldn't put Humpty on his place again'. In the context of my analysis, Jaber's rewording of the rhyme reiterates recurrent questions about the place of the intellectual, the displacement, banishment and alienation that the narrator evokes in all instances of his self-identification. Indeed, as he performs this lullaby borrowed from English nursery rhymes, the narrator exhibits a deep mistrust of his sociality. This moment of anxiety forces him to regress to childhood, an earlier state of intellectual development where song and virtual companions sheltered him from the disillusionment and deceit of social and intellectual exchanges. The narrator's enactment of strangeness, if not madness, mimics Ralph's last days when he became reclusive, incongruous and stranger to his friends, family and colleagues. All were baffled by his childlike behaviour. As such, the narrator's nihilism and disdain for reason and the spoken word echoes that of Ralph, who distanced himself from post-war intellectual cacophony and celebrated silence in his writings.

Furthermore, the narrator's cultural capital is different from that of the writers who contribute to *al-Mulhaq*. Unlike Elias Khoury and his peers, the narrator holds a degree in science from the American University of Beirut and is therefore not French-educated like his peers. In order to understand Ralph's writings in French, the narrator engages another text, the French-Arabic dictionary, and thus exhibits another sign of marginality from the intellectual circles that he navigates.[81] When asked about his work at *al-Mulhaq*, the narrator admits that it is by mere chance (*innahā al-ṣudfa*) that he works there. By refusing to attribute any importance to his contributions to *al-Mulhaq*, the narrator demystifies *al-Mulhaq* not only as an institution, but also as a platform for the project that Elias Khoury upholds in his articles. The narrator's demystification of *al-Mulhaq* announces his contempt for criticism and writing altogether, as he compares writing to prostitution: 'Then I decided not to write for newspapers much. Just as a spoiled whore who decides one day to welcome only the most handsome of men.'[82] Not only does the narrator equate writing to prostitution, he also denounces the futility of critical interventions, as Ralph did in 'Balaghat al-sukut'. In a recurring moment in which he fuses fantasy with reality, the narrator imagines the following scene:

> One day my landlord will walk into my room and realize that I have turned into a giant fungus. At least fungi do not suffer from migraines. Why not, I wonder. Maybe because they do not have heads.[83]

The headless fungus-like character at the core of the narrator's fantasy differs from the post-war intellectual. Indeed, unlike the writer whose written word induces change by safeguarding collective memory, the new intellectual that emerges from the narrator's reappropriation of Ralph is unsettling. The young intellectual lives in complete social and intellectual isolation. In self-imposed exile, the intellectual appears as a lone sickly figure both alienating and alienated by sociality. In the absence of interlocutors, the lone figure disengages from the dominant discourse that defines the intellectual scene and replaces the cultivation of collective memory by an intimate examination of the emotional state of a dead peer.

The portrait of the new intellectual that emerges from the narrator's search for Ralph is strikingly different from the intellectual that post-war writers had imagined in their literary and critical writings. Jaber redefines

Ralph not as a human sacrifice entrusted with the responsibility of embody-ing his community's grief, but as a melancholic, marginal and nihilistic writer disengaged from the burdens of the dominant literary discourse that he was expected to carry. Jaber therefore refrains from objectifying the intellectual as a site of memory. Instead, he humanises his peer as an individual consumed by a personal narrative of loss and disillusionment. Furthermore, in his depic-tion of Ralph, Jaber also formulates a critique of Ralph's generation, which Khoury had defined as the 'generation of ruins'. As he replaces the 'genera-tion of ruins' with the generation of the 'un-dead', Jaber voids the concept of generation of its historical and ideological associations and restores its exis-tential meaning as a group of individuals who merely reach an age threshold and share a concern about illness and death.

By refiguring the experience of loss, Jaber formulates a parallel critique of the post-war intellectual. Less interested in the mytheme that Khoury had deployed to explain Rizqallah's death as protest, Jaber reconstructs Rizqallah's suicide as a dim yet strikingly ordinary story. Moving away from the post-war discursive focus on collective memory to an ordinary post-war story, Jaber deconstructs and makes banal the question of authorship, which perme-ates our understanding of the post-war novel. The new author that emerges from Jaber's thorough critique is not an omniscient and omnipresent author but merely an investigator, a collector, a pastiche artist who demystifies the elevated status associated with authorship.

The post-war novelist, however, is not the sole object of Jaber's criticism. It is also *al-Mulhaq*, the cultural institution that constituted a platform for the expression of critical discourse, which attributed to the post-war intellectual the ability to achieve collective salvation. The narrator commemorates Ralph not by publishing eulogies in *al-Mulhaq*, but by reverting to original texts drawn from pictures, articles, encyclopaedias, police reports and dictionaries that the narrator believes are more accurate reflections of Ralph's emotional state. In other words, Jaber closely reads the deceased intellectual's writings and reflects on his angst and nihilism in order to neutralise the violence of ideological projections onto the suicide of Ralph Rizqallah. Jaber's subversion of the narrative and critical discourse of his precursors not only undermines the status of the writer, it also disentangles political engagement from the narrative text. As he deconstructs the portrait of the post-war intellectual,

Jaber eschews the subjugation of the literary to the ideological by returning to text as the only source for knowledge and meaning. In *Ralph Rizqallah*, Jaber also reifies his own identity as a *muʾallif waraqī* or a writer living only in text.

Rabee Jaber's *Ralph Rizqallah* appeared at a historical and critical juncture preoccupied with the exploration of collective amnesia in post-war Lebanon. In an environment that attributes to the intellectual-prophet the power of change through discourse, the suicide of Ralph Rizqallah was interpreted as a protest against post-war cultural erasure. In *Ralph Rizqallah*, Jaber cleverly deploys intertextuality, particularly parody, in order to present a narrative that simultaneously channels and transgresses that of his precursors. Jaber builds his novel on the theme of the search, which he subsequently deconstructs and redefines. As he undermines the search for truth as a valuable narrative technique, Jaber detaches his novel from the dominant discourse that reads the suicide of the intellectual as an altruistic act of protest. Instead, he resignifies the intellectual's suicide as the narcissistic act of an individual unable to reconcile with insurmountable personal grief. Jaber's literary approach suggests that Ralph did not jump from Beirut's most iconic landmark in protest of the city's post-war state of collective amnesia, but rather for reasons that pertain only to his physical and emotional vulnerability, on the one hand, and his unmatched social and intellectual isolation on the other. In other words, unlike the poet-prophet standing on Mount Nebo overlooking and haunting the Promised Land, the suicidal intellectual of Jaber stands over Raouche Rock turning his back to Beirut and, in so doing, embraces finitude.

Notes

1. Although the supplement is formally known as *Mulhaq al-Nahar*, I refer to its abridged version, *al-Mulhaq*.
2. The rock is also called Pigeon Rock, Pigeon Grotto and Death Rock due to the number of people who have committed suicide there.
3. Hereafter I refer to the novel as *Ralph Rizqallah* for ease of reading. The complete novel has not been published in English at the time of writing and so all translations are my own, unless otherwise stated.
4. Darwish, *al-Aʿmal al-Ula*, pp. 331–92.
5. In her study about women and the Lebanese war novel, miriam cooke coins

the term 'Beirut de-centrists' to describe women writers who intervened in the Lebanese literary scene by simultaneously voicing a moral critique of sectarianism, patriarchy and war within the discursive void that the latter had created. See cooke, *War's Other Voices*.

6. The thousands of Lebanese citizens who disappeared during the civil war have figured extensively in novels and plays. For a review of Lebanese fiction pertaining to the disappeared, see Zeina G. Halabi, 'The Bereaved and the Disappeared – and Beirut Makes Three'.

7. Following Rafic Hariri's assassination in 2005, his family inherited his SOLIDERE shares. His son Saad Hariri was the head of a large parliament group and prime minister between 2009 and 2011. Hariri's assassination transformed the collective memory debate as it had been conceived in the 1990s and shifted the attention of Lebanese intellectuals to the political turmoil that Lebanon has witnessed since 2005. See Sune Haugbolle's social and political analysis of the Lebanese post-war memory debates from the early 1990s to 2005, particularly the reverberations of Hariri's assassination, in Haugbolle, *War and Memory in Lebanon*.

8. The irony lies in the double meaning of *qalb*. As a noun, *qalb* means 'heart' and as a verbal noun [*maṣdar*], it indicates the act of turning something on its head.

9. Makdisi argues that SOLIDERE rebuilt downtown Beirut following a neoliberal postmodern urban model that transformed the site into a socially disconnected and synthetic space. Makdisi, 'Laying Claim to Beirut'.

10. cooke, 'Beirut Reborn', p. 409.

11. Norman Saadi Nikro argues that 'dis-memory encompasses the glaring absence of any state initiatives to engage a public inquiry into the war, as well as state supported museums, memorials or commemorative practices that could be studied as contested sites of memorialisation.' Nikro, *The Fragmenting Force of Memory*, p. 1.

12. See Kassir, *La guerre du Liban*; and *Beirut*.

13. Cited in Nikro, *Fragmenting Force of Memory*, p. 4.

14. Ken Seigneurie examines the humanistic undertones of novels by Hoda Barakat, Rashid al-Daif and Hassan Daoud who drew on memory and the *aṭlāl* motif as a framework for the refiguring of distorted humanist values. Seigneurie, 'Anointing with Rubble', p. 57.

15. Italics are integral to the text. Mostafa, 'Re-Cycling the Flâneur', p. 96.

16. Elias Khoury reflects on his intellectual trajectory and concept of modernity and cultural heritage in Khoury and Mejcher, 'Interview with Elias Khoury'.

17. Khoury, 'Beyond Commitment', p. 80.
18. Ibid. p. 80.
19. Khoury, 'Memory of the City', p. 139.
20. Ibid. pp. 137–8.
21. My emphasis.
22. Khoury, 'Memory of the City', p. 139.
23. Khoury, 'Beyond Commitment', p. 85.
24. Nora, *Realms of Memory*, p. vii.
25. Nora, 'Between Memory and History', p. 7.
26. Ibid. p. 19.
27. Khoury also comments on the necessity of forgetting: 'It is a human necessity to forget. People have to forget. If I do not forget my friends who died in the civil war I cannot live, I cannot drink and eat … The question is what to forget and what to remember. It can be an ideological choice. In literature it is very complicated because literature deals with a lot of details.' Khoury and Mejcher, 'Interview with Elias Khoury'.
28. Derrida, *The Work of Mourning*, p. 39.
29. Rizqallah, 'Madkhal ila al-Taᶜasa', p. 4.
30. Khoury, 'Ralph Rizqallah', p. 4.
31. Khoury, 'Risala ila Ralph Rizqallah', p. 19.
32. My emphasis. The original Arabic reads:

هل أنت أضحية باسم جيل؟ وعن جيل؟ ومن أجل جيل؟

33. Khoury, 'Risala ila Ralph Rizqallah', p. 19.
34. Youssef Habshi al-Ashqar is one of the earliest and least recognised novelists who have written about the civil war. See al-Ashqar, *Al-Zill wa-l-Sada*; and *La Tanbut Judhur fi al-Samaᵓ*.
35. Abbas Baydoun relates the critical blackout on Jaber's 1990s novels to Jaber's young age, his withdrawal from the literary scene, and his proliferate and complex writings that overwhelm critics and readers alike. Baydoun, 'Man Yaqraᵓ Rabee Jabir?', p. 18.
36. Iskandar Najjar made a similar claim in Najjar, 'ᶜAn Shay Aswad', p. 14.
37. See Kamal Salibi's reading of Jaber's trilogy. Salibi, *Beirut wa-l-Zaman*.
38. Shawqi Bzih (Shawqī Bzīᶜ) writes about how Jaber's trilogy rescues collective memory from oblivion. Bzih, 'Beirut Madinat al-ᶜAlam', p. 10. Ghenwa Hayek makes a similar argument in her analysis of the trilogy: 'What Jabir's novels set out to do is to construct the map of downtown Beirut for the new generation. They re-historicize the city space by delving into its distant past, and moving

forward in time into its contemporary present.' Hayek, 'Rabi Jaber's Bayrut Trilogy', p. 186.

39. Abbas Baydoun explains: 'We hardly know anything about Rabee Jaber except his novels. This author does not leave his text, allow interviews, or engage critical debates. Nor does he talk about himself or circulate his photographs. Even when found, these photographs are unauthorized.' Baydoun, 'Bukir Rabee Jaber', p. 1.

40. Darraj, Al-Dhakira al-Qawmiyya fi-l-Riwaya al-ᶜArabiyya.

41. Al-Eid, 'Rabee Jaber la Yudawwin al-Tarikh Bal Wujud al-Insan'.

42. Mostafa, 'Literary Representations of Trauma, Memory, and Identity', p. 213.

43. Ibid. p. 212.

44. I owe the translation of this passage to Mostafa, 'Literary Representations of Trauma, Memory, and Identity', p. 213. All other translations from the novel are my own.

45. Jaber, Ralph Rizqallah, p. 165.

46. 'Mona F.' is likely a reference to Mona Fayyad, Ralph's colleague at the Lebanese University. Fayyad has written extensively on mental disabilities, correctional institutions and gender in the Lebanese context. She also contributed to the special commemoration of Ralph Rizqallah in al-Mulhaq. Fayyad, 'Lam Naᶜud bi-Manʾaʾ'.

47. Known as Jad, Georges Khoury is an animation and Claymation artist whose depiction of traditional characters and neighbourhoods in Beirut is humorous and nostalgic.

48. Bassam Hajjar was Ralph's colleague at al-Mulhaq. In his poetry, Hajjar wrote about death, internal exile and existential angst in an innovative and experimental language. He also wrote an article about Ralph in al-Mulhaq's special issue. Hajjar, 'Al-Taᶜasa Huna', p. 6.

49. The original Arabic title 'Ralph Rizqallah fi al-mirʾāt' has been translated literally to 'Ralph Rizqallah in the mirror' in previous studies pertaining to the novel. I believe that my translation of the Arabic title into 'Ralph Rizqallah through the looking glass' is a more accurate reflection of the intertextuality that Jaber establishes with Carroll's Through the Looking Glass. See Jaber, Ralph Rizqallah, p. 30.

50. Hutcheon, Narcissistic Narrative, p. 1.

51. Kristeva, Desire in Language, p. 1.

52. Barthes, S/Z, p. 36.

53. Jaber, 'Al-Katib wa-Aslafuh', p. 25.

54. Hutcheon, Narcissistic Narrative, 25.

55. In Journey of Little Gandhi, the narrator sets himself on a mission to find out

what really happened to Beirut's beloved shoe shiner Abd al-Karim al-Mughayri, nicknamed Ghandi al-Saghir. Khoury conducts a series of extensive interviews with marginal characters and narrates Ghandi's untold story. See how Khoury understands his role in the novel in Aghacy, 'Elias Khoury's *The Journey of Little Gandhi*. Also see Dalia Mostafa's interpretation of the character of Ghandi al-Saghir as Walter Benjamin's *'flâneur'*; Mostafa, 'Re-Cycling the Flâneur'.

56. In the novel's postscript, Khoury writes: 'This novel would not have been possible without dozens of men and women in the (Palestinian refugee) camps of Burj al-Barajneh, Shatila, Mar Ilyas, and Ayn al-Hilweh. All of them told me their stories and took me on a journey across their dreams and memories.' Khoury also thanks seven fieldworkers who assisted him in conducting these interviews. It is this interview-centred anthropological approach that Jaber arguably alludes to in his writing. See the postscript of Khoury, *Bab al-Shams*.

57. Jaber, *Ralph Rizqallah*, p. 37.

58. Ibid. p. 43.

59. Ibid. p. 81.

60. Ibid. p. 20.

61. Ibid. p. 72.

62. Ibid. p. 16.

63. Manara Corniche is Beirut's seashore walkway, a popular space for promenades and exercise. It is also a short walk from Raouche Rock, the site from which Ralph Rizqallah committed suicide.

64. Jaber, *Ralph Rizqallah*, pp. 27–8.

65. The title of Kundera's novel *The Unbearable Lightness of Being* is in dialogue with Friedrich Nietzsche's notion of 'eternal recurrence', or the idea that the universe has been and will always be in constant recurrence, which constitutes an insurmountable burden or heaviness on human beings. Kundera writes: 'If every second of our lives recurs an infinite number of times, we are nailed to eternity as Jesus Christ was nailed to the cross. It is a terrifying prospect. In the world of eternal return, the weight of unbearable responsibility lies heavy on every move we make. This is why Nietzsche called the eternal return the heaviest of burdens.' Kundera, *The Unbearable Lightness of Being*, p. 4. As such, Rizqallah establishes a double intertextual reference here by referring to Kundera who is in turn in dialogue with Nietzsche.

66. Jaber, *Ralph Rizqallah*, p. 175.

67. Ibid. pp. 119–24.

68. Ibid. p. 175.

69. Ibid. p. 152.
70. Ibid. p. 23.
71. Ibid. p. 23.
72. My translation from the original French. Boustani, 'Intertexte et mémoire', pp. 90–2.
73. Jaber, *Ralph Rizqallah*, p. 73.
74. Ibid. p. 126.
75. Khoury, *The Journey of Little Gandhi*, p. 16.
76. Jaber, *Ralph Rizqallah*, p. 33.
77. Ibid. p. 27.
78. Ibid. p. 64.
79. Ibid. p. 11.
80. Ibid. pp. 51–2.
81. Jaber, *Ralph Rizqallah*, p. 99.
82. Ibid. p. 24.
83. Ibid. p. 18.

3

The Banality of Exile

The margin is a window looking out on the world. You are neither in it, nor outside it. The margin is a cell without walls. The margin is a personal camera that selects the images it wants from the scene, so that the king is not the king and David's slingshot is nothing but Goliath's weapon.

Mahmoud Darwish, *In the Presence of Absence*

The Palestinian poet Rashid Hussein (1936–77) died twice, once in exile and again when his New York apartment caught fire. Soon after settling in the United States in 1973, Hussein descended into a cycle of addiction and depression. As he fell asleep one night, his cigarette butt, still hanging from his lips, ignited the collection of tapes on which he had recorded his poetry.[1] The image could not have been more tragic: Rashid Hussein choked on the poetry he had written in exile. 'But how do we read Rashid Hussein?' Elias Khoury wonders, 'Do we read him as an unfulfilled life or as poetry fulfilled by death?'[2] Mahmoud Darwish captures this same paradox in his elegy of Hussein entitled 'What Will Be Has Been' (1977). Reckoning with his friend's exile and his own, Darwish portrays New York as a perilous space that transforms exiles into anti-heroes embattled by alienation, poverty and demise:

> And he disappeared into Fifth Avenue or the gate of the Antarctic
> All I remember about his eyes are cities that come and go.
> And he withered ... and withered [*talāshā*].[3]

Twenty-five years later, Darwish confronts the death of another Palestinian friend in exile. In his elegy for Edward Said, 'Edward Said: A Contrapuntal Reading' (2005; English trans. 2007), Darwish again ponders on exile, this time though from the vantage point of a consecrated poet mourning another consecrated intellectual.[4] Darwish recounts Said's morning routine, which begins with Mozart and a tennis match and ends with reading, thinking and writing.[5] Captivated by Said's interstitial positioning, of an intellectual in between spaces, identities and languages, Darwish writes:

> He says: I am from there, I am from here,
> but I am neither there nor here.
> I have two names which meet and part ...
> I have two languages, but I have long forgotten
> which is the language of my dreams.[6]
> [...]
> So carry your homeland wherever you go, and be
> a narcissist if need be
> The outside world is exile,
> exile is the world inside.
> And what are you between the two?[7]

No longer a city of doom, Said's New York has morphed into a space of contradictions that encompasses alienation and empowerment, dislocation and privilege. If Rashid Hussein's exile silences and annihilates, Said's exile elevates and empowers. From the discursive space of the two elegies, the contours of the exilic intellectual emerge. Despite the pain and tragedy of exile – or because of them – exilic intellectuals are formed between homes and away from them, by national and personal identities and without them, between languages and at their intersection. This seemingly impossible mode of being is embedded in cultural capital that constructs and empowers exilic subjectivities and engenders discourse. Thus, as displaced Palestinian intellectuals, Darwish and Said represented exile, despite its tragic consequences, as an enabler of creativity and criticism. Said's conception of secular criticism channels that particular understanding of exile – as a state of displacement that is at once tragic and a catalyst for change.

This conception of exile, as a tragic yet formative state of displacement, was central to the writings of the Palestinian exilic intellectual Jabra Ibrahim Jabra. In his numerous essays, novels and poems, Jabra drew on the archetype of the Palestinian intellectual, an exilic modern subject in a modernising yet troubled Arab world. Specifically, Jabra's protagonists in *The Ship* (1970; English trans. 1985) and *The Journals of Sarab Affan* (1992; English trans. 2007) are exilic Palestinian intellectuals navigating an Arab world enchanted by the promises of modernity yet shackled by consecutive political setbacks. In *In Search of Walid Masoud* (1978; English trans. 2000), Jabra draws his mirror image and builds the archetype of the exilic intellectual as a modern and modernising force. That which unites Darwish, Said and Jabra in their respective exiles is their conception of intellectual displacement that draws on a word-centred episteme that enables and ultimately emancipates. The romantic portrayal of exile as a reluctant instrument for emancipation was subsequently displaced by Rawi Hage in *Cockroach* (2010) and Elia Suleiman in *Chronicle of a Disappearance* (1996). In this chapter, I stage this unlikely transnational, cross-generational and multidisciplinary conversation between Jabra and Said on the one hand and Suleiman and Hage on the other. I reveal the ways in which the two contemporary authors turn to metafiction, irony and play and in so doing demystify the secular modern intellectual in exile, which Jabra and his title-character Walid Masoud exemplify.[8]

Jabra, Said and Exile

Issa Boullata describes the Palestinian intellectual Jabra Ibrahim Jabra as 'a true Renaissance man [who] has been rightly considered a strong force for modernism in the Arab world in the second half of the twentieth century.'[9] Boullata recalls how, around the time Jabra settled in Iraq in the early 1950s, Baghdad was blooming with a new generation of Iraqi poets, artists and writers searching for alternative modes of expression. A leavening force in Iraqi arts and letters, Jabra became a prominent member of the Iraqi cultural vanguard, which 'propelled him further into creative modernism'.[10] The novelist Abdel Rahman Munif observes that this cultural boom would have been unimaginable without Jabra's influence and leadership. Munif recalls how Jabra was 'one of the most prominent Arab intellectuals since the 1950s', who 'contributed to the genesis of Iraqi culture [*takwīn al-thaqāfa*]' and to laying 'Iraq's cultural foundations [*al-taʾsīs al-thaqāfī*] by means of his translations, lectures, and theories on modern poetry'.[11] Here, Munif does not situate Jabra as a creation of the Iraqi cultural field, but rather historicises the Iraqi cultural field as a stop on Jabra's lifelong journey. Moreover, Munif points to

Jabra's transcendental power of cultural genesis (*takwīn al-thaqāfa*), Jabra's ability to conceive the Iraqi cultural scene and lay its foundations. Boullata's and Munif's recollection of Jabra as a germinator in the Iraqi cultural scene is aligned with Jabra's own vision of the exilic Palestinian – himself included – as a catalyst for change.

As a novelist, poet, artist, critic and translator, Jabra posed a set of critical questions: why did Arabs lose Palestine in 1948? Why were they defeated again in 1967? And what exactly is the responsibility of Palestinian exilic intellectuals toward Arab societies as they embrace modernisation? Jabra searched for answers to the first question in Arab culture, specifically in the question of modernity and tradition. He observed that the *nakba* was symptomatic of the multifaceted Arab defeat that was not only political and military, but also cultural and epistemological. If Arabs had lost Palestine, it was because they were 'cheated and betrayed by a thousand years of decay'.[12] Arabs, he thought, 'had confronted a ruthless modern force with an outmoded tradition'.[13] Put differently, the Arabs' retrograde political, cultural and scientific institutions were accountable for the loss. The problem was thus clear and so was the solution: Arabs had to embrace modernity by inventing 'a new way of looking at things. A new way of saying things. A new of way of approaching and portraying man and the world.'[14] Therefore, the moment of loss was also one of self-reflection and self-fashioning: what is the nature of the Palestinians' exile? In statist jargon and legal categories, what had become of Palestinian intellectuals? As members of a new stateless diaspora, what is their new role?

In a seminal autobiographical essay, 'The Palestinian Exile as Writer' (1979), Jabra reminisces on his displacement from Bethlehem following the partition of Palestine; the trials of his journey through Damascus, Amman and Beirut; and the opportunities that Baghdad offered him. Jabra's uprooting from Palestine triggered a sense of alienation, a 'malaise' that was simultaneously 'deeply collective and deeply personal'.[15] He describes exile as an unmatched sense of loss that splinters the self and disrupts it, a tragic state of displacement that had turned Palestinians into 'wanderers'.[16] But as thousands of Palestinian refugees fled to neighbouring countries, Jabra had to reflect not only on the nature of his displacement, but also on his new status and role as an educated Palestinian: 'If anyone used the word "refugee" with me, I was furious. I was not seeking refuge. None of my Palestinian co-wanderers were seeking refuge.'[17] To Jabra, 'refugee' was a politically charged term that portrays Palestinians as asylum seekers expected to relinquish their identity and origins in exchange for assistance and charity. The term, he thought, would ultimately de-politicise the tragedy of occupation and condemn the Palestinian people to oblivion.[18]

But, if Jabra and his Palestinian compatriots were not refugees, what were they? Jabra identified himself as a translator,[19] scholar, a man of letters and artist, exchanging his intellect for sustenance: 'We were offering whatever talent or knowledge we had, in return for a living, for survival, we were knowledge peddlers pausing at one more stop on our seemingly endless way.'[20] He describes the painful moment when an Iraqi customs officer addressed him as a refugee: 'I offered him a battered suitcase full of books and papers, a small box of paints and brushes, and half a dozen of paintings on plywood. I was not a refugee, and I was proud as hell.'[21] Jabra's reluctance to identify as a refugee evokes an ethos of dignity and autonomy not uncommon in the writings of exiles. Exiled from Germany, Hannah Arendt articulates a similar discomfort with the term, of being one of those *schnorrers* (beggars; parasites) living off the philanthropists of her time: 'If we are saved we feel humiliated and if we are helped we feel degraded.'[22]

Edward Said takes Jabra's visceral reaction to the term 'refugee' further. Said thinks of exile as a historical practice of banishment of individuals at odds with a social and political consensus, where 'once banished, the exile lives an anomalous and miserable life, with the stigma of being an outsider.'[23] And yet, 'exiled poets objectify and lend dignity to a condition designed to deny dignity', he says, thus channelling Arendt's and Jabra's anxieties toward their new status of displacement and their unwillingness to forego the remainder of a personal and collective sense of dignity.[24] Said considers refugees a modern political category that originated with the creation of the national borders of modern states. But what is at stake between the two types of displacement is the different positioning of refugees and exiles in their host countries. Refugees, in Said's understanding, suggest 'large herds of innocent and bewildered people requiring urgent international assistance', whereas the notion of exile evokes 'a touch of solitude and spirituality'.[25] This solitary and spiritual state, Said observes, drives exiles into professions and activities that draw on the intellect and typically require a minimal investment in material belongings and rootedness.[26]

The sense of solitude and spirituality, of which Said speaks, is precisely what tragically haunts and positively empowers Palestinian exiles. As he distinguishes between refugees and exiles, Jabra conceives of Palestinian displacement as a heartrending yet enabling condition. The tragedy of the *nakba* that caused the dispersal of an entire people and the loss of historic Palestine was, he thought, due to the inability of Arab traditions to withstand the thrust of modern colonising forces.[27] But that same tragedy was empowering because it scattered educated Palestinians throughout the Arab world and transformed them into a leavening force in their new host societies.[28] By means of their deracination and mobility, both physical and intellectual, exilic intellectuals became permanent inhabitants of the border, a liminal state of being neither in Palestine nor entirely in Iraq. Jabra saw in the exilic intellectuals' liminality an advantage that reinforces their critical sensibilities and enables them to lead the desired leap into the modern. Jabra identified himself and his educated peers not as refugees in need of assistance, but as an emerging community of educated mobile intellectuals, navigating smoothly across political and ideological borders. They are 'wanderers', 'knowledge peddlers', exchanging knowledge for survival, all at the service of their host societies.[29]

Jabra's description of this state of non-belonging caused by literal and metaphoric homelessness evokes Said's concept of secular criticism, a condition of intellectual displacement that paradoxically enables critical and creative power. Said observes how, as they inhabit at least two languages, spaces and nations, exiles acquire a plurality of vision and a layered awareness that is 'contrapuntal', fostering a multilayered worldview that stems from intellectual displacement.[30] Said's conception of exile as contrapuntal channels Adorno's vision of home as a set of prefabricated beliefs and morals. As secular critics, Said notes, exilic intellectuals embrace a paradigm that is 'life-enhancing and constitutively opposed to every form of tyranny, domination, and abuse; its social goals are non-coercive knowledge produced in the interest of human freedom.'[31] In both Jabra's and Said's notions of exile, displacement is not a privilege, but an alternative to primordial attachments and a state that allows the exile to 'cultivate a scrupulous (not indulgent or sulky) subjectivity' and 'a new way of seeing things'.[32] As exiles observe – in bitterness or nostalgia – their home from a distance, they develop a sense of

detachment from the complex structures of ideological and primordial identification that create and sustain consensus. As the exiles' home is a structure
of the past, the only space that breeds attachments and subjectivity is the
word.[33] Inhabiting a liminal space, exiles are the wandering souls who found
in the word their last home.

Exploring the genealogy of exile in the Euro-American tradition, particularly in the representations of European intellectuals such as Adorno and
Auerbach, Caren Kaplan builds on the Saidian archetype of the secular critic
and argues that contemporary conceptions of exile have drawn on the necessary intertwinement of three constructs: exile, intellectuals and modernity.
As such, in its celebration of singularity, solitude and alienation, the concept
of exile has defined modernist sensibilities and has been considered both the
precursor and the outcome of a distinctively modern subject position.[34] For
Said and Jabra, indeed, the distinctive power of exiles is their written word. In
this sense, exile signifies an elevated cultural capital, the holders of which are
in command of their fate and a force for change in the lives of others. Jabra
sees his Palestinian peers as a 'leavening force for a meaningful future for
Arabs everywhere'.[35] Palestinians 'were suddenly everywhere: writing, teaching, talking, doing things, influencing a whole Arab society in most unex-
pected ways. They were coping with their sense of loss, turning their exile into
a force, creating thereby a *mystique* of being Palestinian.'[36] Jabra explains the
bond that tied Palestinian exiles to the wider Arab world:

> Right from the start Palestinians had declared that their fate and the fate of
> the Arab nation were interlocked, were in fact one. Palestinians could not
> fail, except by the failure of the whole Arab nation. But they also knew that
> so much depended on themselves: on their efficacy as a leavening force for
> a meaningful future for Arabs everywhere.[37]

By virtue of their education and their displacement, which accelerated
their dissociation from parochial identities, Palestinian intellectuals emerged
as archetypical modern and humanist subjects. For Jabra, the exilic intellectuals' border position and critical abilities are not only the precursors of but also
the precondition for a modern and critical outlook on the world. Drawing
on their liminality and the critical sensibilities that flourish at the margins of
primordial identifications, Palestinians will usher Arab societies into moder-

nity. Such is the mystique of the Palestinian exiles: their unmatched power to transform the tragedy of dispossession into a mythical power of change that ultimately enables Arab modernity. Jabra and Said, thus, carefully draw a portrait of the exilic intellectual in an interstitial position between two worlds. Exiles are not refugees in need of sympathy and assistance. They are, rather, lone wanderers who eventually reconstitute themselves among a community of exiles. Exilic intellectuals in this sense are secular critics, dignified and autonomous; nomads, who turn their self-sustenance into an unmatched power to deeply transform their new host societies. By means of their physical and intellectual displacement and liminality, exilic intellectuals are catalysts for change. Fully committed to the causes of their age, they are the exilic prophets looking at the past and future. Jabra's character Walid Masoud embodies this vision, in both his mystique and tragedy.

Jabra/Walid Masoud, Exiles Extraordinaire

Jabra constructs his mirror image in *In Search of Walid Masoud*.[38] Walid is an established Palestinian intellectual who leaves Palestine in 1947 and later becomes a catalyst for change and innovation in Baghdad. Unlike Jabra, who remained in Baghdad until his death in 1994, Walid disappears a few years after the 1967 war in mysterious circumstances. Rebecca Carol Johnson writes that *Walid Masoud* is about a search that is both a process (*baḥth* as investigation) and an outcome (*baḥth* as research).[39] It 'brings into focus' she adds, 'both the product of intellectual inquiry and its process, as it takes as its object knowledge, the intellectual, and the very project of intellectual production itself.'[40] The search is revealed in a polyphonic, intertextual and disconnected narrative, in which the reader witnesses the disillusionment of a group of Iraqi intellectuals and their shared guilt regarding the tragic disappearance of their friend Walid in 1970s Baghdad. Walid's car is discovered on the border road that links the Iraqi and Syrian customs stations. In the abandoned car is found a tape, on which Walid has recorded what seems to be his last words: a stream-of-consciousness narrative recounting disconnected memories from his childhood in Palestine, his activities in the Palestinian resistance against the British mandate and his Iraqi exile. Puzzled by the content of the tape, his closest friends gather to make sense of their disconcerting discovery. Together they listen to Walid as he reflects on his relationships with lovers, friends and rivals and mourns his teenage son Marwan, a PLO fida'i who was killed in a military operation in Galilee. Each friend suggests a different hypothesis about Walid's disappearance. Right before his disappearance, Walid had been outspoken against the complaisance of Arab regimes with the occupation of Palestine, which leads his friend Jawad to believe that he was assassinated. Another friend, the psychiatrist Tariq, who treats Walid's female lovers, believes that Walid had been suffering from an acute bipolar disorder that may have driven him to commit suicide. However, Walid's lover Wisal, who is familiar with his latest underground political activities, has evidence, undisclosed to the readers, that Walid neither killed himself nor was killed. She claims that Walid has, in fact, staged his disappearance from Baghdad and joined the Palestinian resistance in Lebanon. In the absence of definitive answers, Walid's friends conduct an internal search for all the reasons, personal and political, that could be behind his disappearance. The incomplete narrative of Walid's disappearance, Samira Aghacy suggests, 'provides a sense of deferred meaning in that each attempt to speak of him is not seen as the ultimate truth but, rather, of yet another in a series of multifarious discourses.'[41] The disappearance of the Palestinian exile cannot be represented and shall remain coded in mystery.

The novel portrays a 1950s and 1960s Baghdad at the height of modernist trends in literature, architecture and the arts. It is a city where Western, particularly Anglophone, literature and philosophy are translated and debated by Walid's Iraqi friends, all members of a rising class of scholars, doctors, journalists, financiers, artists and bureaucrats who regularly challenge traditional values and celebrate their individualism. They form a circle of bourgeois intellectuals versed in the Western humanist tradition and driven by the need to build and perform what they believe is a modern Arab subjectivity. In their conversations, they debate the role of the intellectual in modern Arab societies, the importance of promoting vanguard art, and the aesthetic and ethical functions of modernist poetic trends.

Walid's friends remember him as the archetypal Renaissance man: a charismatic and wealthy Palestinian financier with an exquisite and eclectic cultural capital that materialises in his fine taste for Baroque music, contemporary English poetry and modern Iraqi art. His confidant Ibrahim declares that Walid's mission was to 'foster the new spirit based on knowledge, freedom, love, and a revolt against looking back – all this was a means of achieving the complete Arab revolution.'[42] In this sense, Walid is a transcendental figure who understands revolution as a moment of triumphalism adjourned to the future. The word of the exilic intellectual allows him, as Margaret Litvin notes, 'to embrace his own history and integrate it into that of his time', allowing him to 'become an integrated character' and also an effective political actor – to overcome the crisis of threatened identities and find a credible way 'to be'.[43] In addition to a collection of short stories and the first volume of an autobiography – incidentally bearing the same title as Jabra's autobiography[44] – Walid's friends speak of his groundbreaking philosophical treatise entitled 'Man and Civilization' (Al-insān wa-l-ḥaḍāra), in which he probes the essence of humanity, progress and civilisation.[45] Walid set his energies on building a 'new spirit', a budding Arab subjectivity that rejects the backward traditional and metaphysical structures impeding the progress of Arabs toward modernity. In this sense, Walid was a man of his time, channelling the anxieties of Arab thinkers and their debates on questions of authenticity, innovation and the delicate equilibrium that constitutes the modern. Walid is, thus, a Saidian secular critic, a liminal subject drawing on his mastery of the literary and philosophical word to induce change. 'He denies', Litvin writes, 'any simple opposition between words and deed',[46] yet concludes his trajectory by embracing political action as a last attempt at salvation, as I argue elsewhere.[47]

Both Jabra and Walid were depicted as Renaissance figures, and both espoused a humanist and modernist conception of the role of the writer. As Palestinian exiles in Baghdad, they were both celebrated as catalysts for change. Ibrahim situates Walid as 'one of those exiles' who 'shake the Arab world', establishing a causal relationship between the generation of Palestinian exilic intellectuals and Arab cultural innovation.[48] Furthermore, like Munif, who positioned Jabra at the core of the Iraqi cultural bloom of the 1950s, Ibrahim believes that:

> Walid was the kind of Palestinian who rejected, pioneered, built, and united (if my people can ever be united); he was a scholar, architect, technocrat, rebuilder, and violent goader of the Arab conscience. As I knew him, Walid would refuse to undertake any role he hadn't mastered. His most important

task was to foster the new spirit based on knowledge, freedom, love, and a revolt against looking back – all this was a means of achieving the complete Arab revolution ... I've come to realize he's one of those exiles who'll use that vantage point to shake the Arab world into reexamining everything it's ever thought or made, and to fill the whole world with the word *Arab*, whatever epithets may be attached to it by enemies with all their complexes ... Where you find outstanding achievement in science, finance, ideas, literature, or innovation, you'll come across that exile Palestinian: he'll be doing things, urging, theorizing, and achieving everything that's different. Wherever there's anything worthwhile, involving self-sacrifice, you'll find the Palestinian.[49]

When Munif remembers Jabra, as I have shown earlier, he associates him with genesis (*al-takwīn*), or the moment of conception of the modern Iraqi cultural scene. Similarly, when Ibrahim remembers Walid, he resorts to a semantic field that equally evokes creation and genesis. He imagines Walid as an 'architect', a 'rebuilder', a 'violent goader' and a source of 'innovation' and 'achievement'. Ibrahim also portrays Walid, as well as all exilic Palestinians, as messianic figures sacrificing themselves for the salvation of Arabs. Furthermore, Walid's mystique materialises in his portrayal as a forger of 'Arab conscience', a man who has given Arabs a sense of self by means of his writings. This is where Walid's portrait as an intellectual-prophet emerges: stranded in exile, he embraces self-sacrifice, allegorical at the beginning but ultimately literal, for the sake of the Arabs and their future. Walid, however, was not the only holder of power; he was a 'kind of Palestinian', or a member of a generation of modernist exilic Palestinians endowed with the power of genesis.

But it is precisely the intellectuals' lack of rootedness that points to their limitations. Kaplan argues that the defining yet problematic property of exile, as it appears in modernist literary traditions, is the fostering of theoretical constructs at the expense of engaging the material world. She notes that 'the modernist trope of exile works to remove itself from any political or historically specific instances in order to generate aesthetic categories and ahistorical values.'[50] Jabra's notion of the politically driven (Palestinian) intellectual enfolded tensions in the intellectual's word-centred episteme and its binary structure (e.g. theory and praxis, aesthetics and politics, intellectuals and refugees). Pondering on the collective despair surrounding him, Walid probes, for the last time, his role as an intellectual in exile after the *naksa*: 'Events have become so momentous that all our faculties have shrivelled up trying to cope with them. The disasters [*fawāji'unā*] we've suffered can't be dealt with in verbal form; all the words have been pulverized.'[51] The modern Arab subject that Walid had conceptually forged as a sublime figure driven by humanist and ethical sensibilities was suddenly dwarfed, humiliated and ridiculed. In the wake of the *naksa*, bereavements (*fawāji'*) – a term evoking disaster, the loss of loved ones and insurmountable pain – have become a collective and unspeakable loss, so immense that it renders those driven by the power of the word irrelevant. The tragedy of the exilic intellectual, Palestinian or otherwise, is recapitulated by Walid's friend:

> In the final analysis, this is what lies behind the tragedy in Walid Masoud's life. He wanted to be a saint in a world of political parties, an undogmatic dogmatist in a world of rigid primness. He wanted to talk in symbols whose semantic force he thought people would understand, but he forgot they aren't the same symbols that people carry around their necks like charms. He was amazed that (when all was said and done) only a few people really understood him, and those few were the ones who loved his ideas because they loved him personally, a love based on something that sprang from his eyes, his hands, and his voice.[52]

Walid's disappearance in 1971, a few months after the death of his son Marwan, differs from Jabra's own exilic narrative. Whereas Jabra withstood Saddam's repressive regime and remained in Baghdad until his death in 1994, his mirror image vanishes, reportedly to join the Palestinian resistance in Beirut. 'Similar to a black hole in which the novel's protagonist disappears together with the hopes and dreams attached to the role of the intellectual in the Arab world', as Sonja Mejcher-Atassi astutely observes, 'the border crossing, and more specifically the no man's land between borders, is the very opposite of the exile's idealized homeland.'[53] As such, in the context of ideological fissures and intellectual self-doubt, where did Walid go when he vanished? In Johnson's succinct words, it is unclear whether Walid dropped '*out* of the world or *into* it'.[54] What was more real, more urgent and more consequential? Was it the world of ideals or the world of militants and refugees into which the *naksa* had propelled Walid? To the underworld of refugees, Rawi Hage invites Jabra Ibrahim Jabra and Edward Said.

Rawi Hage and the Underground Intellectual

Tall, handsome, charismatic, his arms wide open and legs crossed, a man stands in a smart suit before his Columbia University office staring straight at the camera. Signed by the photographer and novelist Rawi Hage, the picture is simply titled 'Portrait of Edward Said'.[55] Hage and Said crossed paths in 2000 in New York, where Hage had moved from war-torn Beirut before permanently settling in Montreal and becoming a celebrated and award-winning Anglophone writer. Hage belongs to a generation of Lebanese writers who, as Syrine Hout writes, are into 'the debunking of two myths: the return to a golden age of a romanticized Lebanon and the slavish imitation of a supposedly superior Western lifestyle'.[56] 'Instead, cultural hybridity typifies this literature and manifests itself not only on the levels of languages, settings and themes', she adds, 'but most prominently in a state, or a predicament, of in-betweenness which reflects a complex consciousness characterized by mixed modes and moods, such as irony, parody, satire, nostalgia and sentimentality.'[57] Hage's interstitial position, precisely at the fault lines of the nationalist myth and the mystification of the West, suggests multiple readings of his representation of Edward Said. Whereas his visual image of Said is indeed an exquisite depiction of the Palestinian exile's intellect and cultural capital, Hage's discursive portrait of displacement and exile, which had become tantamount to Said, evokes cynicism and dissent.

Hage describes his literary project as 'a satire of nationalisms that range from the totalitarian versions that thrive at the expense of the general poverty which they neglect, to the democratic versions that are in fact exclusionary and economically exploitative in various ways.'[58] The authenticity of his characters, he adds, evokes 'a human vision' that portrays humanity's complexity in all its crudeness and violence.[59] Beyond the humanism that marks the legacy of the modernist literary tradition, Hage's writings centralise the human experience of displacement only to unsettle it later and point to its inherent imperfections. His ambivalence toward modernist canonical notions of displacement is clear in his appropriation of the term 'wandering', a key notion in Jabra's notion of exile. 'After a long journey of war, displacement and separation', Hage reckons, 'I certainly feel that I am one of the few wanderers privileged enough to have been rewarded, and for that I am very grateful.'[60] Although iterating Said's and Jabra's nomadism, Hage's conception of wandering is unlike Jabra's. Whereas Jabra's wandering is solitary and at the same time experienced collectively, a state of displacement that implicates an entire generation of Palestinian exiles, Hage's displacement is individual. In addition, whereas Jabra's and Said's wandering is existential and perpetual, Hage's is purposeful and transitory, reaching an end the moment it receives recognition.

If Hage distinguishes his project from the humanism of the modernist literary tradition and portrays the notion of wandering as a transient state of displacement, how does he conceive of the intellectual? Hage challenges the intertwinement of criticism and morality, the *sine qua non* of the intellectual's self-fashioning: 'Maybe intellectuals don't necessarily bring morality to the table', he states. 'I don't think having religion or education necessarily makes you a moral person. Maybe it makes you live a more meaningful life to examine your life. But the antidote to evil is not necessarily education.'[61] It is clear, here, that Hage channels Foucault's declaration that intellectuals who embody 'conscience, consciousness, and eloquence' are no longer viable; that they are the remainders of an *ancien régime* that ties collective salvation to the persona of the intellectual-prophet. This may explain Hage's fascination with 'the reader and the murderer' and his recurrent attention to uneducated yet cultivated characters whose ethical ambivalence exposes the fragility and duplicity of the overarching moral order.[62] Hage's characters in his first novel, *De Niro's Game* (2006), and his subsequent novels, *Cockroach* (2010) and *Carnival* (2014), roam a marginal world equipped only with a dubious sense of morality adapted to the hardships of a new world that alienates them and that they alienate in turn. Hage's infatuation with and subversion of the character of the exilic intellectual materialises clearly in his second novel, *Cockroach*, set in Montreal among a community of immigrants and refugees.

Cockroach begins and ends at the epitome of alienation, self-erasure and state power. The novel opens with a dramatic scene in which the police foil a suicide attempt in a Montreal park. The rescued yet ungrateful narrator is sentenced to psychiatric wards and compulsory therapy sessions that he navigates by inventing stories of past abuse and violence. Hout observes that the novel 'delivers a dark, anti-heroic narrative of an eccentric immigrant whose first-person narration cannot always be trusted. The protagonist provides perhaps the best reason for his story not being that of an immigrant's journey toward successful integration.'[63] The impossibility of integration is central to the narrative. Having escaped the Lebanese civil war, the narrator was granted asylum in Canada, where he struggles to cope with mental health clinics, social security bureaus and the guilt of having inadvertently caused his sister's death back home.

From the vantage point of the troubled narrator, the reader delves into the Canadian underworld – that of Iranian, Afghan and African asylum seekers living off welfare checks, small thefts and black-market jobs. In specific narrative moments that flirt with magic realism, the narrator transforms into a cockroach, thereby mirroring the abjection of displacement, poverty and alienation from which he suffers. As he exposes the fault lines of the immigration underworld, the narrator-cockroach wonders:

> Where am I? And what am I doing here? How did I end up trapped in a constantly shivering carcass, walking in a frozen city with wet cotton falling on me all the time? And on top of it all, I am hungry, impoverished, and have no one, no one.[64]

Cockroach thus chronicles the lives of marginal diasporic subjects, those carrying baggage not like Jabra's – of paint, canvases and translations of Shakespeare – but of political oppression, trauma and persecution. As it depicts the refugees' clever navigation of Canadian welfare institutions, the novel exposes 'western consumption of otherness' and puts an end to the myth of the morality of the welfare state coming to the rescue of immigrants. In this dystopic world, no one is righteous and innocent, neither the state nor the refugees.[65]

The theme of displacement that the novel poses introduces Hage's discursive probing of the notions of exile and refuge. But what exactly is the nature of Hage's imagination of exile and immigration? Are they one and the same? Hout argues that 'the unnamed Lebanese protagonist in Montreal is neither exilic in the sense of wishing to return home nor a travelling immigrant with a homing desire', that he is 'both an immigrant and an exile'.[66]

Whereas Hout sees a conflation between the two states of displacement, I will show how Hage makes a double move. First, he deromanticises the archetype of the refugee by delinking it from a discourse of innocence and charity. Second, as I will suggest below, he comments on the idealisation of exilic intellectuals, specifically on the ways in which Edward Said and Jabra Ibrahim Jabra portray them.

In the panoply of diverse yet similarly wretched diasporic subjects fleeing to the heart of Montreal from trauma of wars and persecutions of far-away lands, the Algerian journalist Youssef stands out. Self-fashioned along the lines of the idealised archetype of the French public intellectual of the 1960s generation, Youssef inhabits an imaginary world, disconnected from that of the immigrants and refugees, which earns him the name 'Le Professeur'. He spends his days at Artista Café reading Algerian newspapers aloud to an audience of downtrodden Iranian, Afghani and African refugees, who cannot speak a word of Arabic, or French for that matter. In his characteristic eloquence, the Professor flaunts his Parisian idiom as he reminisces on past conversations with the icons of the French intelligentsia of the 1960s. The Professor dazzles the café's patrons 'with his stories and grand theories', causing his listeners to flock around him like 'nostalgic souls'.[67] If his enactment of a Francophone Arab intellectual is not enough to impress his audience, the Professor self-identifies as an Algerian exile, a lone voice speaking truth to power, to both the Algerian military and Islamic fundamentalists, the two stakeholders in Algeria's civil war of the 1990s.[68] The Professor claims that he 'exposed the Algerian dictatorship for what it was, and also exposed the plan of the bearded ones for a theocratic state', and was thus forced into exile.[69] His enactment of prestige and exile before his makeshift audience elevates his position as a rebellious Foucauldian intellectual who is 'conscience, consciousness, and eloquence'.[70]

The Professor's mystique and stories of intellectual feats impress all but the cynical narrator, who remains sceptical of the Professor's narratives of heroism and distinction. The narrator, as Maude Lapierre observes, knows what the 'Professor fought *against* but not what he is fighting *for*'.[71] In other words, although the narrator is familiar with the Professor's past exploits, he is cynical about his present project, his vision for the future. The narrator is mystified by the Professor's ability to impress his audience all the while being 'a charlatan' who is 'in it for the free coffee and to bum cigarettes from those nostalgic souls'.[72] He observes this 'suave beggar' as he pauses his stories to ask a listener for coffee and a cigarette. The narrator thinks that the Professor is a

> lazy, pretentious, Algerian pseudo-French intellectual [who] always dresses up in gabardine suits with the same thin tie that had its glory in the seventies. He hides behind his sixties-era eyeglasses and emulates French thinkers by smoking his pipe in dimly lit spots. He sits all day in that café and talks about *révolution et littérature* ... Arrogant smile, existential questions ... The bastard plays Socrates every chance he gets. He always treated the rest of us like Athenian pupils lounging on the steps of the agora, and he never answers a question. He imagines he is a pseudo-socialist Berber journalist, but he is nothing but a latent clergyman always answering a question with another question.[73]

The narrator's portrait of the Professor evokes a meticulously described legacy, that of the politically committed Marxist/existential intellectual self-fashioned along the lines of the Parisian school of distinction. The Professor's gabardine suit, 1970s tie, 1960s glasses and pipe channel the iconography of Jean-Paul Sartre and his characteristic attire.

The narrator adds political content to the Professor's aesthetic self-fashioning by invoking Leon Trotsky's *Literature and Revolution* (1924), existentialism and the Socratic method. But the description of the Professor reeks with expired signifiers. Instead of the Paris of the 1960s and its legendary cafés, such as Les Deux Magots and Café de Flore, where Simone de Beauvoir and Jean-Paul Sartre regularly appeared, the Professor holds court in downtown Montreal in Artista Café – the home of 'a circle of smoke and welfare recipients and coffee breath'.[74] The anachronism that imbues the portrait of the Professor transforms him into a simulacrum, if not a parody, of the 1960s politically committed existentialist French intellectuals. The Professor conceals his ignorance by refracting questions to an audience who speaks neither French nor Arabic. Even the Professor's invocation of Trotsky in this context signifies the remainder of Trotsky's revolutionary prophecy: that 'the average human type will rise to the heights of an Aristotle, a Goethe, or a Marx. And above this ridge, new peaks will rise.'[75] The new portrait of the intellectual and, more significantly, the intellectual's audience, counters the literature with which the

Professor constantly aligns himself. Hardly reaching the height of an Aristotle, Goethe or Marx, the audience of the Professor's monologues includes nameless, dark-skinned, wretched refugees whose word cannot be heard. The narrator calls the Professor a 'crook', 'charlatan', 'bum', 'coffee beggar' and 'fake', precisely because he claims to be an exile, precisely because he identifies himself with the likes of Jabra Ibrahim Jabra, Mahmoud Darwish and Edward Said, in an attempt to elevate his status and set himself apart from other asylum seekers.

Just as he sees through the Professor's intricate performance of status and cultural capital, the narrator bursts through the pretence of distinction in the Professor's claims of superiority and intellect. On the first day of every month, the narrator collects his welfare allowance from the social security bureau. On one of these monthly visits, he encounters the Professor standing in line, just like any other asylum seeker, and surprises him with a question: 'Tough times ha?' The narrator proceeds to describe the encounter:

> The coffee beggar buried his face in a newspaper and pretended not to see me. 'Well no, no. I am here for a business meeting, a consultation job for the government.' ... I caught him on the defensive, when he was busy convincing himself that he really had an appointment with some government official. The officials, of course, would love to consult him on the distribution of wealth, equity, and the establishment of an egalitarian society. He is in total denial that he is just like me – the scum of the earth in this capitalist endeavor. I'll bet he thought that, coming from Algeria and having lived and studied in Paris, his *vocabulaire parisien* would open every door for him in this town ... It angered me that the socialist does not want to be identified as poor, a marginal impoverished welfare recipient like me. At least I am not a hypocrite about it. The bum of a professor often talks about his stay in Paris, and how he saw so-and-so sitting *dans le café*, and how he told her such-and-such and she told him such-and-such. But I'll bet the exile existed in one of those Parisian shitholes, washing his ass and cleaning his dishes in the same tub. I'll bet the asshole sought out a few well-off old ladies and discussed Balzac while he stuffed himself with food and wine. I know his type. He does not fool me.[76]

Under the levelling gaze of the Canadian welfare system, the narrator unsettles the Professor's resistance to embrace his refugee status. Busted and embarrassed as he collects his monthly welfare check, the Professor struggles to stretch his bluff. He explains that, in fact, considering his outstanding record in upholding social justice, the Canadian state needs his vision and expertise to design egalitarian social policies. By confronting the Professor, the narrator neutralises his claim to class and status. The Professor, as it turns out, is just another wretched and deprived soul. The narrator's suspicions are finally confirmed: 'gathering his belongings closer to his body, hugging his bag like a refugee on a crowded boat. He is in total denial that he is just like me – the scum of the earth in this capitalist endeavor.'[77]

Thus begins the narrator's obsessive pursuit of the Professor's secrets in order to expose his bluff further. The narrator morphs into a cockroach and breaks into the Professor's 'ground-hole', the 'dark and smelly' 'semi base-ment apartment'.[78] The cockroach-narrator notices how the Professor keeps the newspapers that he has stolen from Artista Café in chronological order near 'a few X-rays, an official letter of amnesty addressed to the Professor, and other documents in Arabic.'[79] The narrator finally realises that the Professor is, in fact, a cockroach just like him,[80] that he is 'Filth. Charlatan. Just like his new briefcase, he is an empty container made of skin-deep materials.'[81]

As he confronts the Professor with the reality that he is just another asylum seeker, the narrator destabilises the foundation of the notion of exile that we saw earlier in Jabra and Said, collapsing the hierarchical distinc-tion between exiles and refugees, between wandering and seeking asylum. More precisely, the narrator challenges the ethical distinction previously made between Walid Masoud, the precursor of Arab modernity, and the Professor, the disgraced recipient of Canadian welfare checks. Furthermore, unlike Walid Masoud's friends, readers and lovers who were members of the Iraqi cultural vanguard, the Professor's interlocutors are the wretched of the Canadian underworld. Navigating the darkness of the Canadian welfare system, Rawi Hage's exilic intellectual is a fake enactment of an ideal type. As an exilic intellectual, the Professor in *Cockroach* blurs the distinction between exile and refugee and becomes a financial burden but also a wel-come addition to a self-congratulating welfare state. As such, the Professor is precisely the opposite of what Walid Masoud represented for the Iraqi vanguard of the 1950s and 1960s. It becomes clear that the Professor is not a wanderer – a catalyst for change and progress – he simply has nowhere else to go. The archetype of the exilic Arab intellectual appears thus as a 1960s historical relic, a redundant laughable character voided of mystique. The image of the exilic intellectual as portrayed by Hage in *Cockroach* is further dislocated in the Palestinian director Elia Suleiman's film, *Chronicle of a Disappearance.*

Elia Suleiman and the Silenced Exile

Elia Suleiman is a reluctant icon of Palestinian cinema. His videos and feature films simultaneously espouse the Palestinian nationalist narrative and reject it. They channel the Palestinian experience of loss and occupation and coun-ter it, oppose it, undermine it, parody it, redefine it and code it anew. They reinvent the parameters of the new political under Israeli occupation, whether military or 'psychological', as Suleiman calls it.[82] Born in Nazareth, displaced to New York and living in Paris, Suleiman travels from centre to periphery and back in a cyclical process of departure and return that his diegetic films depict so well. Suleiman's idiosyncratic style is perhaps fostered by his lack of formal cinematic training and his distance from the legacy of Arab film auteurs, from Youssef Chahine to Michel Khleifi. Instead, Suleiman searches for inspiration at the intersections of the dramatic and the ordinary, where Jacques Tati and Hou Hsiao-Hsien intersect and diverge.

Suleiman owes his cinematic sensibility to literature. 'I work very much like a writer and usually start with a series of notebooks', he says. 'But I keep reading novels and try to think of ideas.'[83] His library includes Walter Benjamin, Primo Levi and Maurice Blanchot in addition to biographies, essays and interviews of film directors such as Jean-Luc Godard. In reading, he searches for a field of meaning that will later frame his image.[84] Reading is for Suleiman a salutary experience that frees him from the confines of a strict nationalist aesthetic discourse and allows him to realise that he is 'not alone, that there are people out there who have similar feelings and resentments concerning the usual mode of expression, and that there is an alternative.'[85] The alternative for Suleiman is iconoclasm, a mode of engagement that he advances in a kind of cinematic manifesto:

Ridicule the images that we produce of ourselves and cancel out their power. Constitute new ones to avoid the danger of one clotted truth. A one truth is a stagnant truth. Real as it can get, it becomes our only reality and we become its prisoners.[86]

That which hovers over Suleiman's *oeuvre* is a continuous reflection on dislocation, displacement, estrangement, alienation and the futility of return. Here, his debt to Jabra Ibrahim Jabra and Edward Said and their conception of exile is significant. Likening the Jews' diasporic condition to that of the Palestinians, Suleiman reiterates earlier observations by Jabra and Said about how the diasporic people – whose experience of dislocation has irreversibly informed and transformed their worldview – have, in turn, become responsible for the exile of Palestinians:

Israel came and handed us their Jewishness and off we went. The Israelis became racist tribalists, and we became the diasporic people. And now we are the ones who are feeding on non-centred cultures, on resisting power structures. We are feeding on cultures that do not automatically assume for themselves a dominance of some kind. We are the ones who are doing the interesting culture, the interesting cinema. And for me – for a few of us, the very privileged among us – there is this luxury, the privilege of living this kind of transgressive life, if you will. To be able to consume different cultures, different othernesses, to have the exoticism of being in another place, to be able to feel at home in quite a few territories, and that you can be the perfect stranger, and that in fact life is a lot richer than just creating a binary opposition and always thinking of yourself as what the other does not have. So, I mean, all this is very Palestinian.[87]

Like the Saidian secular critic that has severed ties to structures of identification such as the tribe and the nation, Suleiman revels at the margin, at the interstitial place where he can observe without being drawn into political and aesthetic conformism that binds his creative project. On being a constant outsider, Suleiman writes that Palestine is

a concept, not a country. It's not an *at home*. I am not *at home*. In other words, I have no sense of what we mean by anchored. In my film, there is no center … In a sense, it was so tempting for me to be the perfect stranger, to disconnect myself from any sense of belonging to Palestine.[88]

Suleiman is thus the Saidian secular critic that relishes his estrangement; he is the Walid Masoud who locates his word at the margin. And yet, in a typical move of embrace and rejection, Suleiman dissents from that very archetype. Renouncing what he perceives as a tendency to romanticise exile, Suleiman disjoins exile from memory, or from the perception of exile as a safeguard of memory. Exile is

> a permanent transgression of the self [*transgression en soi*], one that traverses borders, and integrates traversed cultures ... True exile, to me, is in fact to be in Palestine – this Palestine that is being politically, socially constructed, where even the very notion of Palestine is being construed thereby putting an end to the fantasy of return.[89]

As such, Suleiman's position is doubly dissident: first, because it stands in opposition to primordial structures of identity; and second, because it challenges the romanticisation of the (Palestinian) intellectual – reified, objectified and consecrated by exile – and condemns him to silence, or the loss of the prophetic word.

Silence is a recurrent motif in Palestinian cinema. 'It channels', as Tom Hill observes, 'a broader – but entirely compatible – argument for the staging of elective silences as contemporary language of Palestinian mimesis: elective as opposed to entirely imposed silences, or, say, articulation imposed in political rather than aesthetic terms.'[90] The silence of protagonists is revealed in laconic conversations and the celebration of mundane and insignificant actions. Silence works in this context to reverse, as Hill argues, 'the form of excess' that has come to characterise the representation of the Palestinian experience of displacement.[91] True to his iconoclasm regarding the fossilisation of national identity, Suleiman thinks of silence as a poetic tool. The absence of speech reveals the power of the poetic. But the poetic in this sense is not an act of avoiding the political. On the contrary, it is an inherently political act:

> Silence is a place where the poetic can reign. If there's anything the authorities hate, it is poets, because of poetry's potential for liberation. So obviously it's extremely political ... It tells the tension, the powerlessness, the potential of explosion. It tells a lot.[92]

From within this simultaneous engagement of and dissent from the secular critic emerges Suleiman's exilic intellectual. The intellectual, for Suleiman, is the vehicle of both heroism and defeat, the logic of truth and its futility, the safeguard of collective memory and its banality. In his third feature film, *The Time that Remains: Chronicle of the Present Absentee* (2009), Suleiman takes us back to the original moment of the loss of Palestine. Near the beginning of this film, a handsome Palestinian young man in thick glasses, with long hair and a tailored suit walks into a detention centre. He stands before his Israeli jailors, reaches for a piece of paper in his right pocket, unfolds it and reads aloud the Palestinian poet Abdel Rahim Mahmoud's (1913–48) iconic poem 'The Martyr'. He folds the paper back into his pocket and shoots himself in a dramatic scene that nevertheless leaves the jailors unfazed. The intellectual in Suleiman's films is also Taha Mohamad Ali (1931–2011) who makes a cameo appearance in *Chronicle of a Disappearance* in order to narrate, repeatedly, a non-story of non-bravery that he has heard numerous times from his grandfather who survived the Ottoman wars. But the problematic figure of the intellectual is exemplified by Elia Suleiman himself, who appears in *Chronicle* only to deconstruct the idealisation of the exilic intellectual by means of self-parody.

In the early 1990s, Palestine was at a crossroads: it was a moment of utmost invisibility for the Palestinian citizen of Israel, but also a moment of return for diasporic Palestinians as stipulated by the Oslo Accords of 1993. In sum, the buzzword was return, not in the meaning of return (*ᶜawda*) with which Palestinian revolutionary literature abounds, but the return of a select group of entrepreneurs, developers and public officials entrusted with building budding Palestinian state institutions that remain, nevertheless, paralysed by occupation. It is this context of ambivalence and restricted hope under military and psychological occupation that Suleiman's first feature film, *Chronicle of a Disappearance*, stages.

Chronicle is set between Nazareth, Jerusalem and Ramallah, all Palestinian cities with different narratives of displacement. The film begins at a conundrum: how does one hold record of that which is not there? How does one chronicle the experience of an event or of a people that have disappeared? The diegetic protagonist called Elia Suleiman or E. S. is a film director who returns to Palestine to write a film, only to face the difficulties of writing under psychological occupation, or writing the experience of being a present-absentee, an invisible Palestinian in the Israeli state.[93] The director E. S. chronicles his uneventful days on a computer without, however, reconstructing a meaningful narrative. E. S. observes his elderly parents, friends and neighbours as they lead dull lives and engage in meaningless conversations in Nazareth, an increasingly marginal city contained within the ideological parameters of the Israeli state. *Chronicle*, Suleiman observes, 'tries to be anti-nationalistic, anti-tribal'.[94] Indeed, the film demystifies the iconography of Palestinian nationalism, calling out the puerility of fetishising flags, nationalist icons and narratives. The object of Suleiman's critique is not only static nationalist iconography, but also the archetype of the Palestinian exilic intellectual, mystified and ideologically coded into stagnation. Suleiman's portrayal of the returning artist demystifies the exilic intellectual on multiple levels. It banalises the returning intellectual's interlocutors, stages his speechlessness and points to the indifference of the Israeli military to his return.

Chronicle depicts the senselessness of intellectual exchanges and critical interventions. E. S. meets old friends over drinks in a rundown café in Nazareth trapped in the 1960s, its walls painted with a Gauguin-like chipped landscape of women by waterfalls. While bad recordings of Asmahan's (1912–44) songs play in the background, the three friends drink and chain-smoke. The scene opens with a long minute of silence interrupted by one of E. S.'s friends who, in a tone that exudes ennui, initiates a conversation:

> Have you heard? A guy from Nazareth wrote a PhD dissertation on how men pee, they shake and shiver at the last drops. He concluded that men descend from animals, that they once had a tail ... which is now gone. Yet, they keep shaking their ass as if they still had one. Is this true? [silence] Welcome back. Cheers.

Just like it started, the scene ends with silence. This uneventful conversation between reunited friends parodies those that Walid Masoud and Jabra had in the cafés of Baghdad in the 1950s and 1960s. It brings to mind the nights they spent recalling verses of Yeats, listening to Bach and debating the latest modernist sculptures of Jawad Salim (1920–61) and the

Figure 3.1 E. S.'s friends discussing evolutionary urology in a Nazareth café in Elia Suleiman's *Chronicle of a Disappearance* (1996).

paintings of Faiq Hasan (1914–92). As it recalls these images, this scene subverts them. E. S.'s conversation with his friends takes place in a rundown Nazareth café where friends smoke and talk about nothing, or more precisely, about a collection of insignificant signifiers. Celebrating silence, E. S. sits and listens to the latest research on evolutionary urology without adding anything of substance to the discussion. Far from Walid Masoud and his debates on 'the new Arab spirit', his book entitled *Man and Civilization*, and his theories about the rise of the new Arab subject, the exilic Palestinian intellectual in *Chronicle* has lost his interlocutors and does not, cannot or will not speak.

But there are instances when the exiled intellectual is asked to speak, to share his vision about three intricate constructs: 'peace', 'film' and 'exile'. In a small, crowded lecture hall, E. S. is invited to the stage:

> With us today is the Palestinian director Elia Sleiman, who has returned from his voluntary exile in New York. He chose his homeland as the set for his new film about peace. We will ask him to speak about the film plot, his narrative techniques, and the cinematographic language he will be using. [applause][95]

Figure 3.2 E. S. attempting to deliver a lecture in Elia Suleiman's *Chronicle of a Disappearance* (1996).

Meanwhile in the hall, a baby cries and the audience hears the deafening sound of feedback coming from oversized amplifiers and a dysfunctional microphone. A phone rings and a man starts a conversation claiming that he is having dinner with friends, even inviting his caller to join him for dinner. The scene ends without Elia Suleiman ever uttering a word.

E. S.'s 'return from his voluntary exile' (*al-ʿāʾid min manfāh al-ikhtiyārī*) is striking. 'The idea of return that most Palestinian refugees hold on to dearly', Refqa Abu-Remaileh argues, 'creates a sense of cyclical time as opposed to linear time.'[96] It places its subjects outside the process of accumulation and sets a sense of closure that is strikingly absent from *Chronicle*. Constantly on the move between Palestinian cities under all forms of occupation, the director E. S. cannot settle and therefore cannot write. So has he really returned? The false sense of return raises an additional question about the paradox of its association with exile, a voluntary act, a choice. How exactly can we read this category of voluntary exile? What happened to the tragedy of Palestinian displacement and the violence of dispossession? Has Palestinian exile become voluntary or even a life choice? If exile, as Said reminds us, is not a political space but a state of intellectual homelessness, how can one return from it? According to the talk organisers, though, E. S. has returned and is invited to discuss his film about 'peace', a post-Oslo buzzword in the Palestinian cultural scene both in Israel and the occupied territories. But the impatient audience wants to hear none of it. They engage in conversations and answer calls as amplifiers make a deafening noise. Here, too, we witness the cynical recuperation of the spectres of Walid Masoud and his peers who attributed to the word, spoken and written, the power of achieving collective salvation. The absent interlocutors and the amplified silence, thus, neutralise all salutary hopes for the intellectual's word. The returning intellectual in *Chronicle* not only witnesses but is himself a testament to the communication breakdown and intellectual dissonance of post-Oslo Palestinian society. The intellectual-prophet has nothing to say. He returns, indeed, but returns to a vacuous intellectual community.

The tragedy of returning exilic intellectuals also lies in their invisibility to Israeli occupation. One day, as he strolls on a Jerusalem street, E. S. finds a police radio that an Israeli police officer had mistakenly left behind. As he struggles in his daily attempts to write, E. S. listens to the coded conversations of the police and reverses their gaze: the Palestinian present-absentee under surveillance is, in turn, the one eavesdropping on occupation. This reversal of hierarchical power culminates in one of the most memorable scenes in Elia Suleiman's *oeuvre*, one in which two officers raid his Jerusalem home. As Yma Sumac performs 'Cha Cha Gitano' in her five-octave voice, armed police officers barge into E. S.'s home in choreographed saccadic moves that transform the violent intrusion into a dance, of which E. S. is the spectator. E. S. is simultaneously present in the scene (E. S. the invaded) and absent from it (E. S. the spectator), a present-absentee who stands watching the ludicrous performance of the police, silently observing their every move. The raid completed, E. S. returns to his desk/dining table and begins slurping spaghetti as he listens to an officer (code name 'Crow') reporting to the police headquarters (code name 'One') about what they saw in the raid:

Crow: two front doors, four doors, four windows, a balcony, a fan, a phone,
a picture with a hen, four seats ...
One: Fast! Faster!
Crow: Old wooden chairs, a computer, a stereo, a desk, two wicker arm-
chairs, a Japanese textbook, a painting of tulips, a white painting,

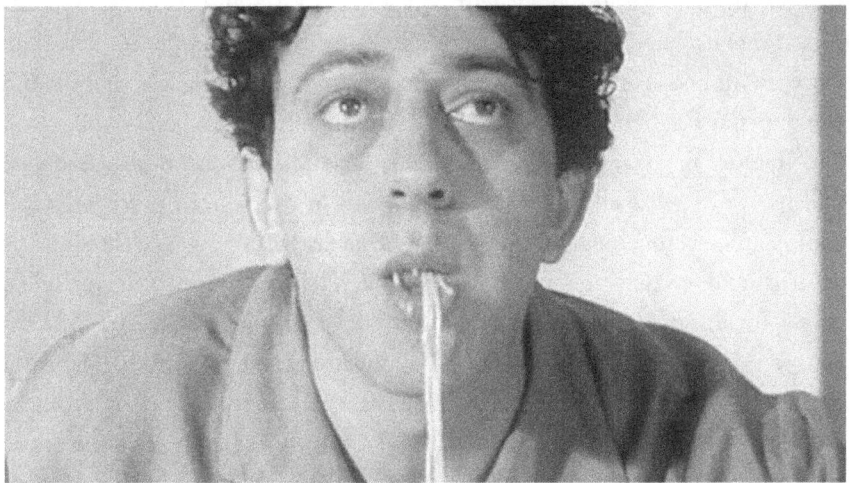

Figure 3.3 E. S. listening to Crow reporting to One about the raid on his home in Elia Suleiman's *Chronicle of a Disappearance* (1996).

> Sonallah Ibrahim … Carver, Karl Kraus, a fishing kit, Mustapha Qamar, Samira Said, Ragheb Alameh, nylon curtains, a guy in pajamas. Over.

The inventory of the returning exile's apartment is ordinary yet revealing. There is furniture, books by the Egyptian novelist Sonallah Ibrahim (Ṣunʿallāh Ibrāhīm; b. 1937), the American novelist and poet Raymond Carver (1938–88) and the Austrian satirist Karl Kraus (1874–1936). There is also a fishing kit and albums by the renowned 1990s Arab pop singers Mustapha Qamar, Samira Said and Ragheb Alameh. Last, perhaps also the least important, there is a guy idling in his pyjamas ungracefully slurping spaghetti, not even with sauce. The irony lies not in the raid itself or in the Palestinian intellectual being under surveillance, for surveillance reiterates significance and status. Irony materialises in the insignificance of what this surveillance reveals.

This scene operates, once more, as a parody of the self-fashioning of the exilic intellectual, particularly when compared to Jabra's memoirs of his first arrival in Baghdad. The personal belongings of both Jabra and E. S. are forcefully inspected by an authority suspicious of their arrival and in both instances their properties reveal who they are. Whereas Jabra is an aspiring painter, translator and scholar with a bag of canvases and paint, E. S. sends mixed signals. Israeli police confuse E. S.'s furniture with his cultural capital, between his books and his music; the canonical novelist Sonallah Ibrahim and the pop star Ragheb Alameh. To them, the furniture, the books, the music and the guy in pyjamas – both the object and the human, both the object and the word – are all under surveillance. From the police's perspective, all these signifiers are equally insignificant. Whereas Jabra's luggage casts him as an artist and a writer, it is unclear what Elia Suleiman's property reveals. We know, for instance, that he has a penchant for poetry and satire, that he likes Arabic pop and is learning Japanese. Rather than evoking any particularly literary or artistic sensibility, E. S.'s books and paintings are eclectic, ordinary and devoid of that mystique that imbues Jabra's aura. But the ridicule of the returning exile is sustained to the end, when E. S. listens to the summary of the report over the radio:

> One: What was in the house?
> Crow: A pilot.[97] Over. An airhead. Over. An intellectual.
> One: Problems?
> Crow: No. We forced him to land.

The summary of that police raid, or what the police deduced from the collection of books, albums and furniture, is that they were facing a man of letters, an intellectual. What the Israeli police see here is not a dangerous Palestinian exile, another Ghassan Kanafani or Kamal Nasser, both silenced by assassination. Instead, they see an inconsequential intellectual that they equate to an 'airhead'. Silenced and ridiculed, the archetype of the Palestinian exilic intellectual and his mystique are put to rest by his interlocutors, his audience and the ridiculous violence of occupation.

Ordinary Exile

We have seen how, in their works, both Rawi Hage and Elia Suleiman destabilise the notion of exile as it has been imagined by a previous generation of displaced Palestinian intellectuals, namely Jabra Ibrahim Jabra and Edward Said, but also Rashid Hussein and Mahmoud Darwish. So what do we make of these two distinct portrayals of the displaced intellectual? How can we understand the conceptual dissent that Suleiman and Hage stage in their works? What unites these two projects is a revisiting of the constitutive elements of exile: the power of marginality and liminality as conducive to change and an imagined national community awaiting salvation. But what is the predicament of speech and the imagined national community in these two works?

Not only is Elia Suleiman unable to represent himself, he is also unable to speak. Throughout the film, the returning exilic intellectual does not utter a word. He has lost his voice, which ceases to appeal to his audience and interlocutors. On the other hand, the Professor in *Cockroach* continuously speaks and lectures his audience about bygone days of glory. But here, too, speech is no longer credible as the narrator exposes the Professor's pretence revealed by his material and intellectual poverty. The Professor's audience comprises not the vanguard of Canadian culture but, rather, new immigrants and refugees who may or may not understand the eloquence of his French accent.

Hage and Suleiman articulate different notions of the political in their revised conception of exile. First, Hage steers away from the strict binary vision of exile as a transcendental, individualistic, romantic and ethical state of intellectual displacement toward a new vision that fuses exile and asylum seeking. Hage grounds exile back where it started: in wars, occupation, and political persecution. As he chronicles the lives of the new exiles, those refugees with individual and collective stories of displacement, Hage repoliticises the notion of exile. His political intervention lies precisely in rejecting the romantic and politically sterile representation of exile and giving exile a new sense of political urgency. Hage's scope of critique extends to Walid Masoud and his understanding of the new Arab subject, the forging of the new Arab spirit along modernist, progressive and teleological lines. As he chronicles the lives of asylum seekers in Canada, Hage revisits Walid Masoud's project and debunks the categories pertaining to progress, development and the promotion of a pan-Arab identity. The asylum seekers, or what the narrator calls 'the scum of the earth',[98] are those who were left out of this project, the lost sons and daughters of the prophecy of Walid Masoud whose modernisation project never saw the light. The Professor, in this sense, is a vestige of his generation's aborted project. While commenting on the same narrative, the political in Elia Suleiman's work lies elsewhere. In his film, Suleiman seems more self-reflexive, invested in deconstructing the iconography of the Palestinian exilic intellectual. By means of the absurd and systemic self-mockery, Suleiman destabilises the notions of return, home and speech. As he debunks the basic features of the identity of the exilic intellectual, Suleiman questions the mystique of the Palestinian in exile and perhaps also comments on the fate of Walid Masoud's prophecy of the 'complete Arab revolution'.[99]

The dissidence of both Suleiman and Hage materialises in their subversion of politically barren categories. Their works do not question the tragedy of displacement, dislocation and dispossession, but rather they articulate a contemporary disenchantment with the mystification of exile and its presumed humanism. Their dissent stems precisely from realising the discursive and political limits of the exilic intellectual. In so doing, Hage and Suleiman de-romanticise exile by reinscribing it in wider political and collective narratives of displacement told not only by intellectuals but also by disenfranchised diasporic subjects who are at once refugees and reluctant citizens of a settler-colonial state. As such, the two authors make a significant intervention by questioning the centrality of the written word as the main constituent of the mystique of exilic intellectuals. In their depiction of the intellectual in exile, Rawi Hage and Elia Suleiman are no longer searching for the vanished Walid Masoud and his unfulfilled prophecy. It seems that, now, they are reconciled with their disappearance.

Notes

1. Fluent in Hebrew, Rashid Hussein translated poems by the Hebrew poet Haim Bialik into Arabic and Palestinian folk songs into Hebrew. An active member of the Israeli Communist Party and a distinguished speaker and politician, Hussein was an advocate for Arab-Jewish dialogue, a political initiative that fellow Palestinian intellectuals, notably Mahmoud Darwish, severely criticised in the 1960s and 1970s. In New York, Hussein worked at the PLO office in the United Nations as he struggled with poverty and illness. A few years after his death, Kamal Boullata and Mirène Ghossein published a collection of eulogies of Hussein by Edward Said, Eqbal Ahmad and Halim Barakat, among others. See Boullata and Ghossein (eds), *The World of Rashid Hussein*.
2. Khoury, 'Rashid Hussein', p. 55.
3. My translation from the original Arabic. Darwish, *Aᶜras*, p. 23.

4. The elegy was first published in August 2004 in the London-based pan-Arab daily *al-Hayat*.

5. Darwish, 'Edward Said'.

6. Ibid. pp. 176–7.

7. Ibid. p. 177.

8. A version of the following section entitled 'Jabra/Walid Masoud, Exile Extraordinaire' appeared in Halabi, 'The Day the Wandering Dreamer Became a Fida'i'.

9. Boullata, 'Living with the Tigress and the Muses', p. 215.

10. Ibid. p. 215.

11. Munif (ed.), *Al-Qalaq*, p. 74.

12. Jabra, 'The Palestinian Exile as Writer', p. 82.

13. Ibid. p. 82.

14. Ibid. p. 82.

15. Ibid. p. 83.

16. Ibid. p. 83. This nomadic conception of Palestinian exiles as a community condemned to permanently roam an unjust world draws on the trope of the wandering Jew. Jabra interestingly ties the notion of wandering to the Jewish experience of displacement: 'Way back in 1952, I wrote about the Wandering Palestinian having replaced the Wandering Jew. A historical horror, which over the centuries had acquired the force of a myth, seemed after 1948 to come alive again. It was ironical that the new wanderers should be driven into the wilderness by the old wanderers themselves': Jabra, 'Palestinian Exile', p. 77. Edward Said later makes a similar comparison: 'It was ironical that the new wanderers should be driven into the wilderness by the old wanderers themselves.' Said, 'Reflections on Exile', p. 181.

17. Jabra, 'Palestinian Exile', p. 77.

18. Ibid. p. 78.

19. His translations of Shakespeare are particularly reflective of his generational angst. See Litvin, *Hamlet's Arab Journey*, pp. 29–33.

20. Jabra, 'Palestinian Exile', p. 77.

21. Ibid. p. 77.

22. Arendt, 'We the Refugees', p. 114.

23. Said, 'Reflections on Exile', p. 181.

24. Said, 'The Mind of Winter', p. 50.

25. Said, 'Reflections on Exile', p. 181.

26. Ibid. p. 181.

27. Jabra, 'Palestinian Exile', p. 85.

28. Ibid. p. 85.

29. Ibid. p. 77.

30. Said, 'Reflections on Exile', p. 186.

31. Said, *The World, the Text, and the Critic*, p. 29.

32. Said, 'Reflections on Exile', p. 184.

33. Ibid. p. 184.

34. Kaplan, *Questions of Travel*, p. 50.

35. Jabra, 'Palestinian Exile', p. 85.

36. Emphasis added. Ibid. p. 84.

37. Ibid. p. 85.

38. Jabra, *In Search of Walid Masoud*, p. 178. All quotes from *In Search of Walid Masoud* are from Allen's and Haydar's English translation. Specific Arabic key terms are from the original Arabic text.

39. Johnson, 'The Politics of Reading', p. 178.

40. Ibid. p. 178.

41. Aghacy, *Masculine Identity*, p. 60.

42. Jabra, *In Search of Walid Masoud*, p. 244.

43. Litvin, *Hamlet's Arab Journey*, p. 33.

44. Walid Masoud's biography is entitled *The Well (Al-Biʾr)*, which is also the title of Jabra's autobiography. *Al-Biʾr al-Ula: Fusul min Sira Dhatiyya* (1987) translated as *The First Well*. For an analysis of the biographical references in Jabra's novels, see al-Shaykh, 'Sirat Jabra Ibrahim Jabra'.

45. Jabra, *In Search of Walid Masoud*, 57.

46. Litvin, *Hamlet's Arab Journey*, 32.

47. I address the trajectory of Walid Masoud, and consequently of Jabra, from exile to militancy more closely in Halabi, 'The Day the Wandering Dreamer Became a Fida'i'.

48. Jabra, *In Search of Walid Masoud*, p. 244.

49. Ibid. p. 244.

50. Kaplan, *Questions of Travel*, p. 28.

51. Jabra, *In Search of Walid Masoud*, p. 274.

52. Ibid. p. 237.

53. Mejcher-Atassi, 'The Arabic Novel between Aesthetic Concerns and the Causes of Man', p. 150.

54. Emphasis added. Jabra, *In Search of Walid Masoud*, p. 186.

55. Hage, 'Portrait of Edward Said', p. 143.

56. Hout, *Post-War Anglophone Lebanese Fiction*, p. 9.
57. Ibid. p. 9.
58. Rita Sakr, 'Imaginative Migrations', p. 346.
59. Ibid. p. 348.
60. Hage, 'To Roam a Borderless World', sec. Comment.
61. Taras, 'Manichean Taxis and Murderous Readers', p. 16.
62. Ibid. p. 16.
63. Hout, *Post-War Anglophone Lebanese Fiction*, pp. 162–3.
64. Hage, *Cockroach*, p. 9.
65. Lapierre, 'Refugees and Global Violence', p. 561.
66. Hout, *Post-War Anglophone Lebanese Fiction*, p. 160.
67. Hage, *Cockroach*, p. 116.
68. Ibid. p. 116.
69. Ibid. p. 116.
70. Ibid. p. 117.
71. Emphasis added. Lapierre, 'Refugees and Global Violence', p. 563.
72. Hage, *Cockroach*, p. 117.
73. Ibid. p. 10.
74. Ibid. p. 8.
75. Trotsky, *Literature and Revolution*, p. 207.
76. Hage, *Cockroach*, pp. 121–3.
77. Ibid. p. 123.
78. Ibid. p. 149.
79. Ibid. p. 150.
80. Ibid. p. 125.
81. Ibid. pp. 272–3.
82. Suleiman, 'The Occupation (and Life)', p. 70.
83. Suleiman and Porton, 'Notes from the Palestinian Diaspora', p. 24.
84. Suleiman, 'Occupation (and Life)', p. 66.
85. Ibid. p. 66.
86. Suleiman, 'The Hidden Conscience of Estimated Palestine', p. 166.
87. Suleiman, 'Occupation (and Life)', p. 73.
88. Prokhoris and Wavelet, 'Entretien avec Elia Suleiman', pp. 67–8. My translation from the original French.
89. Ibid. p. 68.
90. Hill, 'Staging the Sublimation of Cliché', p. 80.
91. Ibid. p. 87.

92. Suleiman, 'Occupation (and Life)', p. 6.

93. 'Present-Absentee' is a denomination imposed by the state of Israel to refer to the Palestinians whose towns and cities fell within the newly created state in 1948 but whose homes were confiscated upon being declared vacant on a given day. They are present within the Israeli state but absent from their homes and therefore denied ownership.

94. Aufderheide, 'An Interview with Elia Suleiman', pp. 77–8.

95. My translation from the original Arabic.

96. Abu-Remaileh, 'Palestinian Anti-Narratives'.

97. In the Hebrew vernacular 'pilot' (*tayas*) means 'spaced-out', 'high' or 'airhead'.

98. Hage, *Cockroach*, p. 123.

99. Jabra, *In Search of Walid Masoud*, p. 244.

4

Ruins of Secular Nationalism

Were the night devoid of us, those hunting ghosts would have returned to their barracks empty-handed. Were the night devoid of them, we would have returned safely to our homes.

Mahmoud Darwish, *In the Presence of Absence*

The publication of Rajaa Alsanea's (Rajāʾ al-Ṣāniʿ; b. 1981) debut novel *Girls of Riyadh* in 2006 was a turning point for contemporary Arabic literature in general and, especially, for Saudi Arabian literature. The novel, in the form of emails sent to a wide-reaching listserv, chronicles the lives of four affluent women as they navigate two intersecting worlds. The first of those worlds is that of globalised identities and changing social norms in Saudi Arabia today, and the second is that of state-enforced restrictions on young women's mobility and sexuality. The numerous controversies surrounding the novel, far from decreasing its popularity in the Arab world, accelerated its translation into several languages. This international commercial success transformed Alsanea into an overnight celebrity and brought attention to numerous Arab and Saudi women writers who have published extensively in the last decade. Zaynab Hifni (b. 1965), Samar al-Muqrin (b. 1970?) and Seba al-Herz are a few of the many Saudi women writers who have contributed to the proliferation of the controversial Arabian 'chick-lit' genre.[1] 'What unites the novelists with their heroines', Madawi al-Rasheed writes, is the fact that they are 'young urban women who have emerged as a result of the increasing immersion of Saudi Arabia since the 1990s in late capitalism, frequent travel, globalization, consumer culture, privatization, and the neo-liberal market economy.'[2] They are also a product, al-Rasheed adds, of the changing power relationship between the Saudi state and 'the guardians of religious nationalism in favor of the former'.[3]

Despite their thematic complexity and stylistic diversity, novels by Saudi women writers have either been praised for facing segregation or denounced for destabilising prescribed gender roles. They have rarely been lauded for their literary merit. Arab literary critics have expressed views that range from dismissal to outright condemnation of these women writers for their allegedly cursory approach and poor narrative language. Critics have interpreted this literary genre as an outburst of impressionistic and amateurish writings that do not aspire to, let alone succeed in, intervening politically. A close reading of such responses reveals the prevalence of a dismissive critical lexicon that identifies this genre as a literary 'phenomenon' (ẓāhira), a paranormal incident, driven by a 'rash' (ṭafra). This reference to a sudden growth also evokes the clinical term for skin rash (ṭafra jildiyya).[4] This new wave of writings is 'fashionable' (mūḍa), described as an articulation of a feminised mode of sociality such as 'chatter' (tharthara), and perceived as affective and reactionary as in 'eruption' (fawra),[5] a clear reference to tantrums and feminised consumption patterns.[6] Some have even admitted their 'fear' and 'pain' at the sight of this 'literary looseness' (infilāt ᶜadadī),[7] a term that channels popular expressions of anxiety regarding security collapse (infilāt amnī) and moral decay (infilāt akhlāqī).[8] Allgedly, the inherent problem of this genre is its superficiality and singular focus on breaking taboos. It has been described as a 'small literary incident' (ḥadath), one that 'limits itself to portraying "domesticated" [mudajjana] feminine culture that indulges in mainstream music, prayer rituals, horoscopes, and "trivial perspectives" [qirāʾāt ṣaghīra]'.[9] The problem therefore, stems from this genre's self-indulgent, limited and shallow rendering of otherwise complex Arabian societies. The genre is interpreted as an inconsequential literary 'incident' and yet it is perceived as a forceful literary 'landing' (inzāl), a term that means both male ejaculation and military invasions.[10] Central to the outright dismissive reading of this genre, one senses a general critical discomfort toward classifying it as 'literature'. Comparing the proliferation of Arabian women's literature to male ejaculation and military onslaught conveys an anxiety toward its aggressive and daunting character and illuminates how critics imagine Arabic letters (adab) as an autonomous, elevated category whose order, conventions and unity are disturbed by the voice of such unruly women writers.

Despite this cautious and dismissive critical reception among Arab critical circles, this genre has received a different, more positive response in global literary markets. Marilyn Booth identifies a number of reasons for this enthusiastic reception. Booth connects the success of many Arabian women writers with a growing interest among Western audiences, who, especially after the events of 9/11, desire to peek into what is believed to be the occult world of Arab and Muslim women. Booth links the global attention to this genre to what she names 'Orientalist ethnographicism', which is

> a way of seeing and writing the Other that grounds authority in a written narrative of personal experience, 'capturing' a society through the I/eye; and furthermore, claiming the authority of graphing the text in a global (and globalizing) language of reception, which is today predominantly English.[11]

Moneera al-Ghadeer probes the agency of writers by examining their self-Orientalising techniques as she discusses *Girls of Riyadh*. Al-Ghadeer observes how Alsanea employs an increasingly globalised language, but also negotiates a local and even folkloric cultural scene that 'provokes the phantasm that ultimately intensifies the interest in gazing at *Girls of Riyadh*'.[12] Madawi al-Rasheed voices a similar concern about the self-Orientalising approach of Arabian women writers and notes that 'Saudi women themselves are the authors of their own orientalist fiction.'[13] Al-Rasheed makes a compelling point, though, as she assesses the depth of the genre's political critique by examining the ways in which the novels' protagonists engage in a subversive and resilient mode of criticism. She maintains that if resistance is comprised of actions that challenge and subvert existing unequal power structures, then this genre cannot be considered subversive. But if resistance, she adds, comprises a set 'of subtle utterances, practices, silences, gestures, and rituals, then the new Saudi novel is without a doubt a textual critique of society and religion, with the state remaining beyond criticism.'[14] Despite its Orientalist reception and self-Orientalising discourse, it is vital to read the Arab 'chick-lit' as a complex and subtle literary genre that compels us to search for new theoretical frameworks in order to understand the extent of its authors' political critique.

One of the most controversial so-called Arab chick-lit novels to appear in the last decade is Seba al-Herz's *The Others*. Despite the novel's political subtext, critics have been drawn exclusively to its scandalous portrayal of graphic sex and homosexuality within a tight-knit community of Saudi women. One such critic describes Seba al-Herz as an agent provocateur, set on scandalising Saudi society with homosexual sensationalist narratives in order to shake off Saudi social and religious conservatism.[15] *The Others*, he adds, 'penetrates the inner and hidden world of women in order to cause a social scandal' (*faḍīḥa ijtimāʿiyya*).[16] Even the Saudi writer al-Muqrin, whose *Women of Vice* (2008) was no less controversial, reads *The Others* in a framework that examines solely the novel's homoerotic tropes. She makes a functionalist argument stating that al-Herz demonstrates how Saudi women are prone to engage in homosexual practices as a reaction to gender segregation and social oppression, without ever commenting on the novel's aesthetic and political nuances.[17]

Upon its translation into English, *The Others* became a sensation in American popular media. A reviewer in *New York Magazine* writes: 'This Saudi novel, in which a closeted lesbian Shiʿi girl feverishly narrates her struggles and affairs, offers a rare personal glimpse into the repressive Kingdom.'[18] Feeding the collective infatuation with the secret world of the Saudi harem, another reviewer adds that the novel is 'a trance-like excursion into contemporary Saudi Arabian life ... The novel takes the mixing of ancient and modern cultures in the Muslim world and spotlights the contrast between the two.'[19] Such critical responses reduce *The Others* to either a pamphlet exposing the repression of women in Saudi Arabia or a self-Orientalising ethnography of sex and homosexuality that thrives on age-old Orientalist tropes. The binary critical reception of the novel, seeing it as either an articulation of an emancipation ethos or as an iteration of Orientalist rhetoric, fails to attend to the depth of the novel's political critique.

Building on the observations that Booth, al-Ghadeer and al-Rasheed have put forward, I suggest searching within Arabian chick-lit for modes of subversion by engaging what al-Rasheed describes as 'subtle utterances, practices, silences, gestures, and rituals'.[20] Specifically, I challenge the overarching interpretation of Saudi women's writing as an apolitical or explicitly antipolitical mode of writing by suggesting an alternative reading of Seba al-Herz's *The Others*. Although *The Others* – like many other contemporary

Saudi novels – does expose the rigidity of religious and patriarchal structures with graphic emphasis on a troubled and contained female sexuality, it nevertheless stands out for its potential to open itself up to readings that transcend the collective focus on sensationalism as a literary genre. I show how the novel stretches out far beyond the generic nomenclature of 'chick-lit' v. 'literature' (*adab*). I take issue with the inherently gendered critical appraisal of the novel and suggest a critical excavation that reads the novel not only as an account of Saudi religious nationalism, but also as a layered, covert and undeniably groundbreaking critique of secular nationalism and the secular-nationalist intellectual, which have hitherto framed the Arabic literary canon.

Writing

The Others appeared in Arabic in 2006 under the pseudonym 'Seba al-Herz'. In the 2009 English translation of the novel, the publisher preserved the anonymity of both the author and the translator and identified Seba al-Herz as 'the pseudonym of a twenty-six-year-old Saudi woman from al-Qatif in Saudi Arabia'.[21] Writing anonymously or pseudonymously is not uncommon in Arabic and particularly Gulf women's literature. The Saudis Samira Khashoggi (1935–86) and Sultana al-Sudayri (1940–2011), for instance, began publishing under pseudonyms in order to avoid social stigma and religious conservatism in the early and mid-twentieth century. That the author of *The Others* feels bound by the same constraints that prevented the preceding generations of women writers from publishing openly speaks to the political climate that Seba al-Herz must navigate not only as a woman, but also as a Shiʿi writer within Wahhabi nationalist cultural institutions.[22]

The Others is set in Qatif, a small and predominantly Shiʿi city in the eastern province of Sharqiyya, near the Saudi oil centre Dammam and Bahrain to the south, and Iran to the east. Qatif has been a significant indicator of the Sunni-Shiʿi rift in the Arabian Gulf and of the increasingly defensive practices of the Saudi police state in facing the area's far-reaching transnational and sectarian identities. Despite sporadic media coverage of the recent events in Qatif – branded 'incidents' (*aḥdāth*) – of 2011 and 2012, it is clear that both dissidence and repression have reached unprecedented levels.[23] Political repression is not new to Qatif, however. The city has been the epicentre of political dissent in Saudi Arabia since the establishment of the Wahhabi Saudi state. In 1930, the Saudi central state granted the Shiʿa of Saudi Arabia, specifically those of Qatif, nominal autonomy in religious practices. But the Shiʿi community of Qatif remained subject to strict regulations that curtailed the propagation of religious literature and the establishment of Shiʿi mosques and community centres (*ḥusayniyya*).[24] The *ḥusayniyyāt* of Saudi Arabia have been pivotal in challenging Saudi religious nationalism by promoting a transnational Shiʿi sectarian identity. As spaces for religious and social rituals such as condolences and religious commemoration ceremonies, they are the antithesis of Saudi state power and bureaucracy. Never intended to represent official state nationalism, the *ḥusayniyyāt* foster an enactment of religious identity that is neither statist, official nor centralised. They traverse state borders and reach out, through kinship structures and political allegiance and solidarity, to Shiʿi communities in neighbouring Iraq, Iran, Yemen and Lebanon. Because of their grassroot, transnational and unofficial nature, the *ḥusayniyyāt* of Saudi Arabia have most certainly been strictly controlled, but never co-opted.

The advent of the Iranian Islamic Revolution in 1979 radicalised the Saudi Shiʿi community, whose tension with the Saudi regime escalated into an uprising known as Intifadat Muharram 1400. The uprising of the Islamic month of Muharram of the year 1400 Hijri (the equivalent of November 1979) was a turning point in the history of the Qatif community. Drawing on Shiʿi religious and political motifs of martyrdom and historical oppression, the uprising was able to spread rapidly and attract young men empowered and mobilised by the success of the Islamic Revolution. The uprising intensified and turned into a direct confrontation with the Saudi military forces that retaliated using live ammunition. The violent repression of the Intifada was followed by a siege of Qatif. The state sealed all the roads leading to the city, interrupted phone lines and prevented news of the uprising from reaching local and international media.[25] Residents of Qatif also endured the detention, torture and disappearance of hundreds of young men who participated in the uprising. To this day, the details of the events of Intifadat Muharram 1400 in Qatif are shrouded in secrecy. The uprising has occupied, however, a particular position within the Saudi Shiʿi collective memory at which the narrative of *The Others* only hints. Although the novel presents vague and disjointed snippets of the incidents of 1979, it does not conceal their impact on the Shi°i community of Qatif, and particularly on the narrator, who dwells in a perpetual state of mourning.

In an anonymous interview, Seba al-Herz identified *The Others* as 'a narrative about severed, incomplete, unbalanced, sick, and troubled relationships.'[26] The narrative arc of *The Others* begins and ends with violence and loss. Driving the affective contour of the novel, mourning and loss have scarred the narrator's relationships, body and sense of subjectivity. Narrated in the first-person singular, the novel is centred on a young woman's *post-memories*, what Marianne Hirsch has described as 'one's everyday reality overshadowed by the memory of a much more significant past that one's parents lived through'.[27] Suffering from unlived yet experienced memories of political violence in Qatif, the anonymous narrator struggles, in a series of diary entries, with her troubled identity as a Saudi woman. In a lyrical and interrupted narrative, she describes the complexity of her subaltern position in Saudi Arabia. She is Shi°i in a predominantly Sunni national community; a woman in a gender-segregated society; a woman with homoerotic desires in a heteronormative patriarchal society; and an epileptic in a close-knit community that shames congenital illness.

Born into a pious Shi°i family, the narrator's mobility is restricted to her all-women college, the *husayniyya* of Qatif, and the homes of her female friends and cousin. Her limited mobility bounds her exclusively within Qatif's feminised spaces, which inadvertently sanction her sexual experimentations including, but not limited to, homosexual encounters and relationships that oscillate between deep emotional attachments and unfettered sexual experimentation often verging on violence. The narrator's social interactions and physical mobility are further constrained by frequent epileptic seizures that engender social stigma and dependence on medications and the care of her family. Living with her illness in shame and silence, the frail narrator likens her seizures to violent attacks and invasions that detach her from her surroundings and elevate her to a state of unconsciousness and fantasy, in which she remembers all those who have departed from her life.

As a young woman growing up in Qatif between the local *husayniyyāt* and enclosed domestic spaces, the narrator is alienated by an outdated political but also epistemic order that has yet to meet the needs of her generation. She is dissatisfied with the rigid Saudi educational institutions whose curricula have prevented her from learning about the history of her own Shi°i community and whose schools ban the commemoration of Shi°i holidays. But the Saudi state is not the only reason for the narrator's sense of rupture from her surrounding world; the older generation of Saudi Shi°i also contributes to this sense. The narrator is at odds with her parents' generation, whose identification structures are not remotely connected to her own. With strong ties to the wider Arab world, the narrator's parents, whose political awareness matured in the 1960s, have exhibited a pan-Arab sensibility – that ought to be distinguished from Arab nationalism – which the groundbreaking appeal of the Iranian revolution did not succeed in displacing. Their structure of identification is not sectarian or even religious, but one that draws on Arab cultural identity, stretching out to Egypt, the epicentre of pan-Arabism in the 1960s. Her parents' complex political and cultural structure of identification, one that encompasses history and highbrow and lowbrow culture alike, leaves the narrator unfazed:

> I never drew my nourishment from Egyptian culture as so many others did. When I was little, I did not follow the evening serials on the Egyptian TV channel, nor the Ramadan Riddles that the Egyptian stars Nelly and Sharihan performed, nor the puppets Buji and Tamtam. Omar Sharif's looks did not leave me a wreck, nor did I fall in love with the dreamy romantic voice of the famous Egyptian singer Abd al-Halim Hafiz. I was not corrupted by famous comedies of stage and screen like *The School for Troublemakers* and *The Kids Grew Up*. I had no idea what Café Fishawi was, or where the Cairo neighborhood of Hilmiyya could be found, even though I saw them in films made from the novels of Naguib Mahfouz. I didn't read loads of romantic novels by Yusuf al-Sibai or stories by Yusuf Idris and Naguib Mahfouz and Tawfiq al-Hakim – that famous Egyptian trio of mid-twentieth century writers. It was only very late in the game that I even heard of something called Arab nationalism and of individuals named Sadat and Nasser and Heikal and Sayyid Qutb, or a group called the Muslim Brotherhood, not to mention The Project of Arab Unity and the Camp David Accords.[28]

The narrator's rejection of all things Egyptian – from iconic soap operas, leaders, actors and singers to award-winning novelists and intellectuals

– enfolds ambivalence. The narrator indicates, if not parades, her factual knowledge of what has marked Egyptian and Arab culture since the 1960s, yet she shows little interest in it. Her rejection here stems not from ignoring the significance of such signposts but, rather, from recognising their significance, which leads her to point to their irrelevance in her world. In addition, by rejecting these cultural signs, the narrator also rejects the predominant modes of literary and visual engagement (cinema, literature, TV, etc.), which previous generations had embraced. Most importantly, perhaps, is that the narrator here expresses the voice of a youth with little interest in an 'Egyptian legacy of secular writing, film production, the cinema industry, writers' meeting sites, and the once dominating issue of Arabism and Islamism.'[29] As al-Musawi rightfully observes, the narrator's self-conscious distancing may be read as a 'deliberate countererosion of a legacy of acculturation and intertextuality, whereby authors used to demonstrate to readers the extent of their readings and cultural engagements, especially in the journey narratives that make up a substantial portion of the Nahda literature.'[30] Self-distancing here eschews that very mode of sociality and acculturation that makes her a pan-Arab citizen. Instead of appropriating the modernist pan-Arab cultural referents of her parents, the narrator strikes her roots in global culture. Fluent in English, the narrator and her peers are avid consumers of Western entertainment culture, from American popular sitcoms to feature films.[31] The narrator's multifaceted structure of identification encompasses Hollywood entertainment culture and French existentialist philosophy. The ongoing reference to 'the others' (al-ākharūn) in the novel, may be read at the intersection of the narrator's favourite Hollywood thriller, *The Others* (2001), on the one hand, and Sartre's unforgettable dictum, 'hell is other people' (al-jaḥīm huwa al-ākharūn), which serves as the novel's epigraph. The double reference to existentialist philosophy and mainstream culture acquires an additional layer of linguistic and political complexity when placed in line with the narrator's other interests as a volunteer in her *ḥusayniyya*.

The narrator works at her community's *ḥusayniyya*, where she prepares intensive summer courses in Islamic jurisprudence and writes for a pedagogic magazine dedicated to familiarising Shiʿi youth with their history and traditions.[32] She has lost faith in her parents' generation, not only for espousing a radically different identity structure, but also for having prevented her and her peers from learning about their past and cultivating an alternative sense of identity. The very epistemological model that her generation has inherited from previous generations is at fault, especially their conception of the power of the written word. For the disillusioned narrator writing political essays in the community's magazine, even writing as political practice has lost its power as a means to speak truth. It has become merely a process of reiterating obsolete ideological paradigms using outdated modes of expression:

> As a matter of fact, this writing that I was doing was really not writing. The style was basically a matter of forcing your writing skills into a format that was both simple and truly difficult at the same time, something I would label 'popular writing.' Writing that everyone would get. The most important thing was to harness your mind to a particular and well-defined set of possible and acceptable ideas. It was writing whose fee was paid as long as you followed the rules … How do the intellectuals and the wordsmiths put it? Ideology?[33] Ideological writing? That might be it.[34]

Thus, the narrator understands the significance of writing and, because she does, she knows that her writing has become meaningless. 'You cannot know the truth from books and TV programs', she writes, 'or from magazines or newspapers. Nor can you pick it up from those who are older than you and who believe their goal is to protect you from it.'[35] She has become alienated from the genre of short didactic essays and irritated by the ideological red lines that her essays should respect. Between the irrelevance of mainstream secular Arab cultural referents and the confines of her strict sectarian and ideological community, the narrator finds herself at a loss. If mainstream Arab culture and ideological modes of writing do not convey truth, where is the truth about her religious heritage and the traumatic experiences of her community to be found? The narrator turns to technology, to the Internet in particular, in an aimless search for alternative ways of discovering the truth. She is looking for narratives that fall outside not only the religious nationalist discourse of the Saudi state and the secular-nationalist discourse of her parents, but also the strict ideological boundaries of her *ḥusayniyya*. The narrator appropriates a technological lexicon borrowed from chat rooms and social media outlets in searching for truth. She resorts to global tools in order to recuperate local narratives that have been erased and silenced by the inadvertent alliance between three ideological constructs: Wahhabism, pan-Arabism, and Shi‘i political ideology. The question about what really happened in Qatif was simple, but the answer triggered more than what the narrator could carry.

Loss

The narrator is constantly moved by the loss, absence and death of loved ones. The reader witnesses the narrator's continuous mourning of her older brother Hassan, who died from leukaemia when she was still a child. During bouts of epileptic seizures, the narrator sees the spectre of Hassan in interrupted vignettes that maintain the novel's sombre mood. Hassan appears in her memories both as a source of emotional attachment and a model to emulate (*marja‘*) as she cultivates a religious identity and political consciousness. He transformed her outlook on the world by explaining to her the importance of two dates in the Islamic calendar: the ninth day of the month of Muharram (*al-tāsi‘ min muḥarram*) and Muharram 1400 AH. The first month of the Islamic year, Muharram is central to Shi‘i religious traditions. During this sacred month, Shi‘i communities across the Islamic world perform lamentation rituals in remembrance of Hussein, Prophet Muhammad's great-grandson who was killed in battle in the Iraqi city of Karbala in 61 AH (680). Outnumbered and besieged by soldiers loyal to Caliph Yazid bin Muawiya (647–83), Hussein bin Ali (626–80) was killed on ‘Ashura’, the tenth day of the month of Muharram. The tenth day of the month is critical to Shi‘i religious traditions, as it evokes martyrdom and collective humiliation at the hands of tyranny. Muharram commemoration rituals have taken different forms in the Muslim world but have retained the lamentation ritual that began as far back as seventh-century Baghdad when Zaynab bint Ali (626–82), the sister of Hussein, held the first lamentation gathering (*majlis ‘azā’*). In Shi‘i tradition, the yearly lamentation gatherings and the weeping for the martyrs of Karbala represent a cathartic ritual that has become a marker of a distinctive Shi‘i identity in a predominantly Sunni Muslim world. On the ninth day of Muharram, the eve of the yearly commemoration of the martyrdom of Hussein, the narrator experiences her first climax with her female lover Dai. That event, which is ostensibly a bodily and private experience of pleasure, branches out to the political. It announces to the reader that the boundaries between the communal and personal, the sensory and the abstract, the past and the present, the personal and the political are in constant motion in the narrative world of *The Others*. As the emotive and the political realms collapse and fuse, they are inscribed on the narrator's body and turn into psychosomatic possessions, a violent spectral haunting that scars the narrator's body and psyche.

The Others shows how spectres of past communal losses haunt the narrator. These spectres are the embodiment of the unspeakable secrets of past generations that inhabit the psyche of their haunted descendants and disrupt their lives. Generations, in this sense, are what David Scott calls 'temporal institutions' that 'successively frame and reframe the conditions of social remembering'.[36] Each generation exhibits a distinct experience of loss in relation to formative events.[37] As one generation endures an intense political experience – in this context, political violence – the following generation witnesses its silence, whereas the third and contemporary generation stands on the ruins of that which has been erased. The experience of the contemporary generation is thus 'temporally removed and intellectually and affectively mediated', where a particular heritage of loss is not, rather, cannot be experienced in discourse, for it has been stripped of all it referents.[38] Rather, it lives affectively, subconsciously and somatically.

The covert secrets, pain and traumas of generations of oppressed Shiᶜa constitute a spectral figure, the phantom, that returns to disturb the lives of descendants oblivious to their past. The phantom, for Abraham, is a formation of the unconscious that is transmitted from the parent's unconscious into that of the child.[39] This formation within the unconscious constitutes a moment of aporia, a gap, or what Abraham calls 'the unspeakable'.[40] These unspeakable spectral manifestations that possess the narrator, in Abraham's terms, 'rule an entire family's history and function as the token of its pitiable articulations.'[41] Phantoms, in this sense, are not the spirits of the dead but their unspoken secrets left to us to resolve. Transgenerational memory, which the disappeared of Qatif have bequeathed to the living, is an active heritage that takes on a life of its own in the memory of survivors. Similar to the Freudian death instinct, transgenerational memory is productive, says Derrida: 'whether it transforms or transforms itself, poses or decomposes itself: the spirit, "the spirit of the spirit" is *work*. A certain *power of transformation ... the spirit ... work.*'[42] Generational memory has all the characteristics of a spectre that comes back, a '*revenant*'. The spectre of Qatif that haunts via its non-presence embodies, thus, an absent or departed one who no longer belongs to the realm of knowledge and affect. As I quoted from Derrida before, the spectre 'looks at us/concerns us [*nous regarde*] without being seen.'[43]

In the context of the novel, phantoms are therefore not a literal evocation of loss, of the spirits of Hassan and the martyrs of Qatif. Rather, they are the taboos surrounding the martyrs' absence and the unspoken secrets of their death that have returned to haunt the oblivious narrator. Early in her disjointed narrative, the narrator reflects on the complexity of her 'heritage' (*irth*), which she carries both as an individual and a member of a historically subjugated Shiʿi community. The narrator feels the weight of her community's trauma even though she was born after Intifadat Muharram 1400. On the communal heritage of pain and mourning, the narrator confesses:

> Weeping is not one of my distinguishing features. But it is true as well that I have inherited a superabundance of weeping that goes back to an ancient era. Ever since [the Battle of] Karbala, ever since the death of that young man so long ago, we Shiʿa have been weeping, and our tears never have dried up. And since Karbala, we have come to understand our weeping as an ongoing, never-ending daily act, a deed that is always there … And so, I do hold inside of me a profuse reservoir, tears that exhaust me every night, but I do not cry.[44]

The narrator's use of the first-person singular *I* and the first-person plural *we* collapses the boundaries between herself as an individual and herself as a member of a traumatised collectivity. Does the first-person plural refer to all Shiʿa, from Egypt to Pakistan, or specifically to those of Qatif? Does *we* reach out to the bereaved women of Qatif or to those of Karbala? In both cases, the narrator's identification structures extend to multiple transgenerational, transnational and gendered communities. Just as the collective trauma is experienced intimately, the narrator's personal loss is historicised and connected to the losses that her community has endured.

Always fusing the political with the personal, the narrator likens the blood disease of her brother, Hassan, to poisoning – the affliction that killed a previous Hassan, the Prophet Mohamed's great-grandson and the brother of

Hussein. The narrator describes the loss of Hassan in a register that is evocative of both emotional and somatic pain:

> Hassan's leaving is the very peak of what I am capable of enduring. It is the high ceiling of pain beneath which all else is indifferent. His leaving is pain, bereavement, the ache of missing someone, rejection, emotional breakdown, the fissuring of the soul, the body's deterioration and collapse, the reign of absence that you cannot shake, the curse of fear, the savagery of the death endured by the bereaved who is sadly left behind.[45]

Once again, the narrator is equivocal about her loss. Is the Hassan she mourns her late brother or the Prophet's great-grandson? By merging the two losses, the narrator historicises and politicises her loss and attributes to it collective significance. The narrator experiences the death of Hassan as the epitome of spiritual torment and bodily pain that provoke an array of affective reactions such as fear, grief, isolation and spiritual collapse. The narrator portrays the unspeakable loss of Hassan as a spectre haunting a space that is neither earthly nor heavenly but phantasmatic, at the intersection of sanity and sickness, sobriety and stupor, mourning and denial. The narrator's lamentation of Hassan reveals the depth and significance of the brotherly/religious figure and sheds light on another kind of heritage that she negotiates. At an early age, the narrator had access to Hassan's vast library, in which she discovered a significant political treatise, one that continues to mobilise the Shiʿi community of Iraq and the Arabian Gulf:

> So long ago, back in the days when, standing on tiptoe, I could not even make myself come up to his shoulders, I took from his bookshelves a book called *Our Philosophy* by the martyr al-Sadr. It had a blue leatherette cover and the fact that it was cool to the touch even at the height of the summer was what made my fingers pull it off the shelf and take it from his library. He did not say that I would not understand it, that perhaps I would need two more years or even three, plus ten additional centimeters, that there were other books there more appropriate to my small brain. He smiled slightly and said: 'Tomorrow I want you to come and discuss what you read, do you understand?'[46]

The narrator's ostensibly arbitrary choice of books is revealing. *Our Philosophy* (Falsafatuna, 1968; English trans. 1989) is a collection of philosophical essays by Imam Baqir al-Sadr (1935–80), an Iraqi Twelver Shiʿi cleric and the ideological founder of the Islamic Daawa Party in Iraq. Al-Sadr claims lineage with the Prophet through the seventh Shiʿi Imam, Musa al-Qazim, one of the earliest and most influential political ideologues of Shiʿi Islam.[47] Alarmed by al-Sadr's influence within Shiʿi communities of Iraq and the Arabian Gulf, Saddam Hussein ordered his incarceration and later his execution along with his sister and companion in struggle, Amina al-Sadr, also known as Bint al-Huda (1938–80). An influential political and feminist activist in the Shiʿi city of Najaf, Amina al-Sadr organised mass rallies against Saddam Hussein's persecution of her brother before they were both arrested and executed.

At an early age, the narrator's political identity drew on the collective significance of the execution of Baqir and Amina al-Sadr, and it is through her experience of their violent deaths that the narrator's political subjectivity crystallises. The narrator's selection of books establishes a direct linkage between the transnational Shiʿi identity that she consciously practices in Qatif today and the unconscious transgenerational heritage that she inadvertently carries. As Hassan's younger sister reading *Our Philosophy*, the narrator channels the spirit of Amina al-Sadr, who, like the narrator, was her older brother's protégée and confidante. This transgenerational identification, however, transcends both Amina al-Sadr and the narrator and extends to the original moment of sisterly loss in Shiʿi collective memory. The pain suffered by Amina al-Sadr during the persecution of her brother in the 1980s evokes that of the Prophet's granddaughter Zaynab, who spent the remainder of her life commemorating the martyrdom of her two brothers Hassan and Hussein. Thus, the narrator unknowingly carries the same transgenerational heritage of mourning and torment as her ancestors, the grieving sisters Zaynab and Amina. *Our Philosophy* unveils the enmeshment of the narrator's consciousness as a Shiʿi woman in Saudi Arabia with a transhistorical and transnational identification as the sister of a Shiʿi martyr.

The unspeakable secrets of violence and persecution that tormented the narrator's ancestor Zaynab resurface in her unconscious attraction to *Our Philosophy* and, by association, to Amina's history of suffering. As the spectres of Zaynab and Amina occupy the narrator's unconscious, they scar her psyche. Unable to identify or verbalise the nature of this unconscious legacy, the narrator articulates deep anxiety: 'I am afraid of those who have granted me a meaning and a history. I am afraid because they grant me something that stays with me after they have departed.'[48] The narrator's transgenerational heritage of violence, which ties her to a historical community through sisterly modes of grief practiced by Zaynab and Amina, resurfaces in the form of spectres that not only haunt her memory but also paralyse her body.

Abjection

Haunting occupies a space both literally and figuratively. In the case of *The Others*, the body of the narrator represents the receptacle of transgenerational haunting. As it extends to the original moment of Shiꜥi loss, the narrator's heritage collapses temporal and spatial boundaries and haunts her as spectres that roam across her body. Like the phantom, whose movements and anxieties it mimics, transgenerational memory is inscribed in space. Whereas the phantom haunts derelict and abandoned spaces such as cemeteries and mansions, the transgenerational phantom of Qatif inhabits the body of the narrator and dictates her actions. In this sense, the phantom operates almost as a parasitical entity, revealing itself through the destructive traces it leaves on the narrator's body and psyche. For Abraham, the phantom 'pursues in silence its work of disarray', and scars the unconscious of the haunted and the possessed.[49] The spectres of past generations, which the narrator defines as 'the others', occupy her body:

> Other people become corpses that loiter within me and turn to rot. These others refuse to go away. These others refuse to leave me in peace … The nights are unbearable here – the screaming, the scratching and wrangling, the massing and piling of bodies. They redraw the borders of each one's dominion over the territories of my body. I would have preferred dust and cobwebs to rats chewing relentlessly at my heart, leaving splinters of wood behind. Splinters everywhere inside of me.[50]

'Other people', or the spectres that occupy her body, resurface as zombies who fight to mark the boundaries of the space they occupy within her. The violent imagery deepens as those spectres materialise into rodents slowly gnawing on her heart and violently competing over the space of her body. The struggle and competition that the narrator describes pertain to the different memories of loss and persecution that she and her religious community have suffered beginning from the Battle of Karbala to the recent events of Intifadat Muharram, ending with the death of her brother Hassan. The 'splinters of wood' that the departed leave behind are precisely the subconscious heritage that the narrator relives through her seizures.

The unspeakable secrets of her Shiʿi ancestors and those of her brother Hassan have returned to haunt the narrator and occupy her body through epileptic seizures. The narrator begins experiencing seizures at the age of eleven, significantly following Hassan's death. She believes that her disease is a 'disgraceful act', a 'secret', 'a sin without the possibility of forgiveness, a flaw it was necessary to hide, a little scandal blemishing the family that must not get out beyond the most intimate circles.'[51] The repressed memory of her brother's death is transferred to her epilepsy, which, in turn, becomes an unspeakable experience that exists outside discourse. It is a secret, a disgrace, a flaw, a little scandal that she must hide. The narrator politicises and sexualises her disease when she declares, 'the convulsions of my body strip me naked'.[52] The term she uses to describe the devastation of her disease in the original Arabic (intifāḍāt jasadī) recalls Intifadat Muharram, which equally weakened and denuded the Shiʿi community of Qatif at the hand of the Saudi Sunni state and made them more vulnerable to oppression. Describing her humiliation during one of her seizures that occurred in public, she remembers:

My entire face was like a burst of gunfire floating on a dark and empty expanse. The faces of those women were like reverberations from a game of roulette that began as a joke and ended in a wall of blood. I saw many faces lowering their gazes toward me, most frightened, others haunted by worry. Even when it is not contagious, illness strikes fear in people's hearts, for it offers observers a live show of what could easily happen to them under similar circumstances. Illness exhibits to all watchers just how fragile our humanity is. Even so, I do not doubt even one part in one hundred that the effect of illness to witnesses to it is nothing compared to the reality of how illness disfigures a human body, gashing open the soul and mind of the invalid.[53]

The narrator's sudden seizure transforms her into a creature that causes terror, pity and disgust. Her humiliation is accentuated by the gaze of her friends who rush to help her. In their eyes, she reads the horror and the anxiety that her collapse has induced, for she is a testament to the possibility of their own demise. The violence of the narrator's epileptic seizures evokes the poetics of the abject. Kristeva observes that the abject is the human reaction of fear and disgust caused by the sight, touch, taste or smell of previously living organisms such as a corpse or even organic discharges such as blood, urine or excrement. The abject, for Kristeva, is when the system of meaning or the codified signification of the world surrounding us collapses and blurs the distinction between the subject and the object or between the self and the other. The abject in that sense is 'what disturbs identity, system, order. What does not respect borders, positions, rules.'[54] Furthermore, abjection for Kristeva is not caused by the subject's exploration of the meaning of death, but instead by the subject's transformation into a witness of his/her own death or decay. The subject is thus 'at the border of [her] condition as a living being'.[55] Thus, the corpse and bodily discharges exemplify the experience of the abject, because they force the subject to confront her own demise. Following each of her epileptic seizures, the narrator faces the abjection of her body as it begins discharging dreadful liquids such as saliva and tears.[56] As she sees, touches, tastes and smells her body's abject discharges, the narrator is reminded of her own mortality and becomes an inhabitant of a liminal space between the world of the living and that of the dead.

Kristeva's abject is not only manifest in material nature; it can also reveal itself in the texture of human memory. The abject in this sense is also the unspeakable and the traumatic, the untenable collapse of the moral and symbolic orders, the fragility of laws that allow us to fathom our world. The abject, in this context, may be read as Intifadat 1400. The link between the abjection of the narrator's body and that of the history of Qatif is clear in her portrayal of her illness. The narrator intensifies the affective description of her seizures when she observes how her 'mouth smelled disgusting, an odour something like a chemical of unknown composition or a medicine bottle filled with rotting capsules too unbearably noxious to swallow.'[57] The violence of the seizure and the repulsive chemicals she is compelled to swallow operate as a grim reminder of the suppressed memory of chemicals that the Saudi army used to repress the Qatif uprising in 1979. Here, once again, we witness the destructive and somatic powers of the many spectres that return to haunt the frail narrator and remind her of her heritage.

Words

Seba al-Herz's *The Others* reveals how the unspeakable acts of violence that each generation bequeaths to the next transform both the body and memory of oblivious descendants. Spectral haunting occurs with the suspension of physical violence and the systematic erasure of its memory. The narrator's overarching identification structure goes back to the original moment of martyrdom and unspeakable oppression of the first Shi‘i martyrs, Hassan and Hussein. Identifying with the grieving sisters Zainab and Amina, the narrator is burdened by the heritage (*irth*) of oppression but also by a sense of mourning that she cannot shake off. The Battle of Karbala, Intifadat Muharram of 1979, and the execution of Baqir and Amina al-Sadr are all unspeakable acts of violence that resurface as spectres struggling to possess her frail body. Memories of thirteen centuries of violence and pain are the abject that materialises on the level of affect, specifically through the epileptic narrator's chronic physical and mental breakdowns.

The memories of centuries of communal violence occupy the body of the narrator and by doing so they induce a generational and epistemological rupture that further alienates her from her surroundings. The narrator eschews her parents' sense of political and cultural identification, pan-Arab secular sensibility that resonates neither with her reality nor with the memory of her brother, schooled in sectarian ideology. Her self-conscious misrecognition of the icons that rooted her parents in the wider Arab world sets her free to create new identity structures. Those are remarkably not Arab but probing a global consumerist Westernised culture on the one hand and a regional Shi‘i sectarian identity on the other. If the previous generations' outlook on the world has become irrelevant, so has their epistemological order. The means by which previous generations once searched for truth have, in turn, become irrelevant to the narrator's generation. Disavowing preset writing genres, mainstream Arabic literature and writers, the narrator has become distrustful of what she brands 'ideological' writings that revolve around a fixed precept about the centrality of word. Instead of modern and, one may add, secular writing genres, the narrator turns to philosophical and political texts, at the intersection of Sartre's existentialism and Baqir al-Sadr's political treatises. Instead of state-controlled traditional media, the narrator makes use of the Internet, searching on the web for audiovisual material about the events of the Qatif uprising of 1979 that points to the fault lines of secular nationalism and to the word that evokes it.

The narrator's dissatisfaction with the available epistemological model has implications on how she imagines the new intellectual. The archetype of the prophetic, exilic and secular intellectual, one who speaks truth to power, has no room in her narrative. The intellectual that Seba al-Herz puts forward, instead, has a different take on notions of power and prophecy. Barely marginal, exilic, versed in European humanism, the emerging intellectual is an image of Baqir al-Sadr and Amina al-Sadr who, because of their primordial prophetic lineage and cultural capital, do not make recourse to secular nationalism to accrue symbolic power. Although repressed, incarcerated and later executed, the new intellectuals are not alienated subjects. They are rather deeply rooted in a local sectarian communal struggle. Writers of numerous volumes on the emancipation of the Shiʿa, they did nevertheless not rely on the word alone in their struggle for collective emancipation. They led street protests, returning to praxis as a means to lead their people out of subjugation. Not another Said, Jabra or Darwish, these old/new intellectuals have resurfaced as individuals who can bridge what are now two irreconcilable worlds, that of the word and that of the street. For them, the word reflects the power of the imagined sectarian community.

The question that I raised in the beginning of the chapter becomes more pressing: does *The Others*, in effect, speak to the available critical corpus that perceives this genre merely as a literary articulation of 'feminine chatter' with 'trivial perspectives' (*qirāʾāt ṣaghīra*)? How, then, can we read the multilayered political critique inherent in al-Herz's portrayal of loss and collective memory in Saudi Arabia? It is important here to return to Madawi al-Rasheed's analytical distinction between different modes of literary resistance. Al-Rasheed reminds us that, if resistance comprises a set 'of subtle utterances, practices, silences, gestures, and rituals, then the new Saudi novel is without a doubt a textual critique of society and religion, with the state remaining beyond criticism.'[58] By examining the novel's set of multifaceted utterances, haunting silences, bodily gestures and mourning rituals, I have shown the wide, multilayered scope of its literary articulation of resistance. But to what extent can we still claim that the Saudi state ideology is beyond criticism?

The violence inherent in the narrator's epileptic seizures appears as a reproduction of the violence of losses that she has endured both as an individual and as a member of multiple religious, gendered and historical communities. The abjection of the narrator's disease alienates her not only from her body but also, as al-Rasheed observes, from the national body. The narrator's chronic bodily dysfunction is symptomatic of her inability to accept and condone the Saudi state exercise of power and its politics of erasure. As such, the narrator inadvertently exposes the very ideological fabric of her national community: the fragile nature of Saudi religious nationalism and the normalisation of grief in a contemporary Saudi Shiʿi community prevented from completing its work of mourning. But the novel's critical scope is even wider. It extends to secular Arab nationalism as an ideology that does not allow a sectarian narrative, one that gives voice to the narrator's heritage of communal violence.

The narrator de-territorialises major tenets of pan-Arab nationalist sentiments. First, the narrator's structure of identification transcends Arab nationalist borders and iconography. It is Arab in its idiom yet Shiʿi in its essence, probing thereby the secular liberal understanding of what constitutes the Arab subject in the twentieth century. Neither secular nor nationalist, the subject that emerges from al-Herz's narrative is at the margin of liberal, secular and pan-Arab ideologies. The narrator's iconoclasm dislocates consecrated and celebrated historical events from their political and national contexts. For instance, the reader witnesses the detachment of the term *intifada* from its Palestinian semantic field and its subsequent recodification within a Saudi Shiʿi historical specificity. One reads in this process of appropriation a staging of the narrator's own uprising against the centrality of the Palestinian question that inadvertently sidelined other transnational grievances that are at odds with secular anticolonial nationalism.

Beyond the critique of ideology, Seba al-Herz probes the very structure of the political novel. The subtle layering of the past and present, the political and historical, the individual and collective, and the global and the local complicates the rapport between the political and the aesthetic. Al-Herz conducts a discursive rupture with the representation of political violence and collective mourning, not by examining the workings of the dominant ideology and ideological subjects but by probing their fault lines and their incapacities. She is interested in the unspoken, the silenced and the repressed, searching for meaning in that which is denied representation. As such, the political emerges in *The Others* at the instance of the breakdown of ideologies.

The Others is equally significant because it challenges pre-existing critical paradigms. As it deconstructs, displaces and demystifies secular-nationalist prophetic models, *The Others* simultaneously revives Shiʿi iconography and eschatology. The reiteration of religious motifs in literary texts probes the viability of critical categories that classify literary texts under regional, nationalist and gendered categories. As such, through its emphasis on sectarian transnational ideological structures, *The Others* profoundly challenges the centrality of the secular Arabic literary tradition and invites critics to look beyond the available analytical tools that read literature within the scope of nationalism. The narrative that emerges from *The Others* is as Saudi as it is Iraqi or Lebanese and, at the same time, is neither.

The author's own subject position can be read as a rebellion not only against pre-existing ideological and critical models but also against the very representation of the contemporary prophetic Arab intellectual. Al-Herz's anonymity is at odds with the omnipresent and omniscient writer, with whose voice al-Herz repeatedly wrestles. As she identifies herself simply as a 'twenty-six-year-old woman from Qatif', al-Herz eschews the intellectual genealogy (*irth*) that her predecessors have bequeathed to her. Al-Herz's anonymity transforms her, in turn, into a spectral figure that haunts the Arabic literary canon and challenges its tenets.

Notes

1. Madawi al-Rasheed notes that by 2008 Saudi women novelists had published 143 novels, 97 of which had appeared since 2000: Al-Rasheed, *A Most Masculine State*, p. 178. Al-Rasheed ties this literary proliferation to the absence of restrictive laws on fiction, whereas civil society organisation and assembly are strictly controlled and criminalised. Ibid. p. 202.
2. Al-Rasheed, *A Most Masculine State*, p. 214.
3. Ibid. p. 240.
4. Anonymous, 'Tafrat al-Riwaya al-Nisaʾiyya fi-l-Saʿudiyya'.
5. Oueiss, 'Al-Katiba al-Saʿudiyya Zaynab al-Hifni', p. 18.

6. Douaihy, 'Zahirat al-Riwaʾiyyat al-Saʿudiyyat', p. 9.
7. The term *infilāt* is commonly used in police regimes to describe deterioration in security (*infilāt amnī*). The expression is commonly used by official state media across the Arab world to warn against unlawful political protests or congregations.
8. Sharafeddine, 'Al-Waqiʿ bi-Asmaʾ Mustaʿara!'.
9. Douaihy, 'Zahirat al-Riwaʾiyyat al-Saʿudiyyat', p. 9.
10. Ibid. p. 9.
11. Booth looks in particular at the ways in which her English translation of *Girls of Riyadh* was eventually watered down in order to present Western readers with a domesticated representation of the narrative. Booth also shows how publishers pay attention to details such as cover art in order to market this literary genre to a Western audience. See Booth, '"The Muslim Woman" as Celebrity Author'.
12. Al-Ghadeer, 'Reviews', p. 299.
13. Al-Rasheed argues that the self-image of these Saudi women authors is in juxtaposition to the global image of the Saudi Muslim terrorist. She writes: 'Like the successful Saudi businesswoman, entrepreneur, and scientist, these novelists "normalize" and "humanize" Saudi society – and in particular its women – by confirming their membership in the neoliberal globalized commercial and business world elite. The country can then be known not only for its violent men but for its young, educated female authors who write texts such as *The Girls of Riyadh*, *Women of Vice*, *The Return*, and *The Others*, all of which delve into prohibited territories kept away from the public gaze.' See Al-Rasheed, *A Most Masculine State*, p. 218.
14. Al-Rasheed, *A Most Masculine State*, p. 241.
15. Wazen, 'Tahaddiyat al-Riwaya al-Nisaʾiyya al-Saʿudiyya'.
16. Ibid.
17. Anonymous, 'Al-Muqrin: Fi Riwayati al-Qadima'.
18. Anonymous, 'What to Read on Vacation: *The Others*'.
19. Seggel, 'The Veiled and the Shadowed'.
20. Al-Rasheed, *A Most Masculine State*, p. 241.
21. See the back cover of the English translation of the novel.
22. Al-Herz is not alone in publishing anonymously. Warda Abdel Malak and Faiza Said are just a few of many Saudi writers who publish under pen names.
23. An interesting exception is a BBC documentary featuring footage by local activists who clearly demonstrate the evolution of the conflict from peaceful protests to an armed conflict. See Anonymous, 'Saudi Arabia's Hidden Uprising'.

24. See Louër, *Transnational Shiite Politics*, p. 161.

25. Trofimov, *The Siege of Mecca*, p. 186.

26. The original Arabic reads:

«الآخرون» سردٌ لعلاقاتٍ مبتورة وناقصة ومختلّة ومأزومة.

Al-Abdelli, 'Seba al-Herz'.

27. Hirsch, *Family Frames*, pp. 22–4.

28. Al-Herz, *The Others*, p. 85.

29. Al-Musawi, *Islam on the Street*, p. 14.

30. Ibid. p. 14.

31. Al-Herz, *The Others*, p. 86.

32. Ibid. p. 38.

33. In the original Arabic text, 'ideology' is transliterated in Arabic letters.

34. Al-Herz, *The Others*, p. 118.

35. Ibid. p. 124.

36. Scott, *Omens of Adversity*, p. 103.

37. Ibid. p. 103.

38. Ibid. p. 103.

39. Abraham and Rand, 'Notes on the Phantom', p. 290.

40. Ibid. p. 290.

41. Ibid. p. 176.

42. Derrida, *Specters of Marx*, p. 9.

43. Ibid. p. 7.

44. Al-Herz, *The Others*, p. 65.

45. Ibid. p. 65.

46. Ibid. p. 84.

47. Walbridge, 'Muhammad Baqir Al-Sadr'.

48. Al-Herz, *The Others*, p. 207.

49. Abraham, 'Notes on the Phantom', p. 175.

50. Al-Herz, *The Others*, p. 7.

51. Ibid. p. 110.

52. Ibid. p. 261.

53. Ibid. p. 105.

54. Kristeva, *Powers of Horror*, p. 4.

55. Ibid. p. 3.

56. Al-Herz, *The Others*, pp. 105–6.

57. Ibid. p. 106.

58. Al-Rasheed, *A Most Masculine State*, p. 241.

5

The Political Remains

Grasp your own reality and grasp your name and learn how to write your own proof. You, you and not your ghost, were the one driven out into this night.

Mahmoud Darwish, *In the Presence of Absence*

Mahmoud Darwish speaks of his transcendence as a subject of history in a present that shall usher in a future of certainty: 'I have found a *terra firma* saturated with history. I draw my strength from it because I look through the prisms of past and future. Thus, the present appears less fragile, more like a passage toward a more certain history.'[1] He reveals himself as a historical subject and a subject of history interpolated by a teleology that draws on the materiality of dispossession and exile, the transience of the present, and the impending future. Endowed with the prophetic word, the intellectual speaks in the name of the disenfranchised truth and emancipation to power, refiguring thereby the tragedy of displacement from an individual affliction to a catalyst for collective salvation. In this sense, the temporal stability in the triangulation of the past/present/future is intrinsic to the ways in which the intellectual-prophet conceives of himself and his peers.

Examining the yield of that prophetic legacy in literature, *The Unmaking of the Arab Intellectual* has shown how the predicament of the prophecy has been profoundly disturbed in a contemporary era emerging from the vestiges of modern ideologies of emancipation. In the context of consecutive aftermaths, if the present has lost its prospects, so has the intellectual who inhabits it. Since the 1990s, contemporary novelists and filmmakers who identify with different historical and literary generations have depicted their engulfing anxiety about the demise of ideological paradigms, that *terra firma* or Mount Nebo on which the intellectual once stood overlooking the impending future. In their individual ways, Rashid al-Daif, Rawi Hage, Elia Suleiman, Seba al-Herz and Rabee Jaber have reckoned with the intellectual's arduous journey from prophecy to disenchantment. Their refiguring of the prophecy transforms the ways in which we read the prophetic intellectual as a modern and modernising subject, political commitment as a literary ethos, exile as a catalyst for change, and nationalism as an ideology of emancipation.

Contemporary writers have thus experienced, internalised and subsequently exorcised the spectre of the intellectual-prophet that had hitherto personified the stable triangulation of past/present/future and the inevitable transition to a future of certainty and liberation. Theirs is a cynical, ambivalent, mournful and irreverent revisiting of the portrait of the Arab intellectual. Facing the scepticism of modernist epistemologies and aesthetics, they have to defend their apparent cynicism. As they watch the collapse of ideological paradigms and their icons, they have to demonstrate all the ways in which they are still committed to notions of atonement and salvation. They have to reiterate their attachment to language as a vessel for truth and eschew the celebration of meaningless and apolitical individualism.[2] But to what extent can we read their disenchantment with the prophetic legacy as a post-political gesture?

The contemporary texts that I probe in *The Unmaking of the Arab Intellectual* have deconstructed *iltizām* as a literary ethos along with the intellectuals who have channelled it in their writing but kept a tight grip on the political thread. Contemporary writers have not simply forgone the prophecy but have pointed to the fault lines apparent in its formal, linguistic and conceptual dissonance. The intellectual figures that these narratives probe are not the object of gratuitous critique but, as Hanan Toukan observes in her research on contemporary artists, 'are although admired, often also bemoaned and interrogated through different art forms for embodying a failed aesthetics of resistance.'[3] I concur with her observation about how contemporary artists, and in our case writers, return to their predecessors 'to understand their critical role in the life, death and afterlife of a botched modernist project of liberation where the centrality of writing was an unquestionable tool in the collective experience of subjugation and hence resistance and commitment to change.'[4] Contemporary writers do not surrender the political. Rather, they reconfigure it by displacing its tenets. Close readings have shown how the political unravels: first, it professes a contemporary subjectivity that is reflexive and retrospective; second, it ultimately transcends canonical literary tropes and genres, and in so doing reimagines modern literary parameters.

The Political Remained/Renamed

The texts that I have examined probe teleologies predicated on the stable triangulation of past/present/future temporalities without, however, discarding the past as a unit of analysis. The subject of return and reckoning with the past has become what Scott calls 'a pervasively recurrent question'.[5] As such, the past in these texts continues to be a site for confronting contested memories and the articulation of contemporary anxieties. Each in turn, the different novelists and cineastes, revisit the past as a means of making sense of the troubled contemporary moment. There appears an overarching sentiment that the past, no matter how one wishes to delineate and historicise it, cannot be accepted as a given in the temporal prism of past/present/future. It must be archived, debunked, unearthed, demystified and confronted.

For al-Daif, the romantic (self-) Orientalising undertones of the Syrians' early encounter with the West and the historiographies, iconologies and narratives that emerge from it are at the core of his contemporary critique. The teleological and concordant vision of time that Jurji Zaidan predicted informs al-Daif's contemporary disenchantment. At fault is the false start of the *naḥḍa* intellectual, fostering what will later become a paradoxical, ambivalent and already defeated Levantine experience of modernity. At the intersection of nostalgia, irony and the absurd, al-Daif portrays Jurji Zaidan and his friend as modern subjects consumed by the questions that animate their generation of Ottoman-Syrian scholars. Looking westward for modern epistemologies, al-Daif's protagonists delineate the contours of a nascent pan-Arab identity and envision a future abounding with progress, one that would ultimately liberate premodern Syrians from what they think are the shackles of traditions. Al-Daif represents the two friends in a discursive paradox: they are the historical subjects capable of initiating that change on the one hand and, from a contemporary standpoint, the historical subjects responsible for its demise. As he provincialises the West by exposing the fault lines of its own troubled modernity encumbered by race, class and warfare, al-Daif renders futile the teleological modernist discourse of *nahḍa* intellectuals who have found in the West a model for liberation. The past for al-Herz is the unspoken that falls outside state discourse and that is experienced somatically. It is the occult, constituted of suppressed memories of ungrievable losses that return to haunt individuals oblivious to transgenerational violence and a legacy of martyrdom and oppression that cuts across consecutive Shiʿi generations.

If al-Daif debunks the past and al-Herz unearths it, Jaber demystifies and deromanticises it. The past, in Jaber's narrative, is a temporality of loss – of the intellectual and his city – that is just like any other: deeply ordinary, personal, solitary and impervious to ideology and its attempts to permeate it. As he challenges the eminence of the collective memory discourse prevalent in post-war Lebanon, Jaber particularises past losses, previously collectivised and nationalised by Elias Khoury's rendering of the post-war intellectual and the generation with which he identifies. Depoliticised and dehistoricised, the historical and ideological construct of a 'generation of ruins' (*jīl al-kharāb*) no longer entails a community of intellectuals reckoning with the legacy of the civil war but, rather, a community of individuals simply united by an age threshold and a collective fixation on illness and ageing. Designified, the past for Jaber makes no ideological injunctions on the contemporary. As he resituates the intellectual in the language of the ordinary and the banal, Jaber suggests an alternative interpretation of the post-war intellectual, by redefining the trope of political commitment that had mobilised previous generations of intellectuals. Hage portrays the past as a temporality overburdened with the violence of wars and displacement, one that remains uncertain to the end, as it is intertwined with the hallucinations and lies of those who carry its legacy. For Suleiman, the past of dispossession and trauma is conflated with the present – one of repetition, ennui and a sense of detachment that operates as a means to resist Israeli cultural hegemony. Either way, the legacy of the past, its urgency and tragedy, is disconnected and isolated from the oblivious inhabitants of the present yet continues to hover over them.

The displacement of the prophetic legacy was facilitated not only by the contemporary reclaiming the past and its ensuing fissuring of triangulated temporalities, but also by articulating narratives that decentre nationalism as an overarching paradigm. In Seba al-Herz's *The Others*, the narrator's sensibilities are at once engrained in local identities (i.e. Qatif) and virtually connected to transnational networks that nurture and inform her sectarian identity (i.e. Iraq, Iran, Lebanon). As she rejects Saudi religious nationalism, the narrator draws on filial, transnational and religious structures of identity that organise her experience of loss. The narrative ushers in the trope of the militant Shiʿi intellectual by pointing to the interstices of local, transnational, traditional and nonsecular modes of representation and liberation, which ultimately disturb the nationalist sensibilities of the prophetic intellectual. The protagonist of *Chronicle of a Disappearance* exhibits a similar discomfort with nationalism as a paradigm for liberation. Suleiman's protagonist is uncomfortable around the fossilisation of Palestinian nationalist motifs and proceeds to question them by reimagining a Palestinian experience of the ordinary, one that embraces and complicates counter-narratives of fissured and ambivalent national identities. For Rawi Hage, the experience of displacement relates little to Lebanese or Algerian exceptional narratives of trauma and war but more to a condition of displacement that interpolates all survivors of the new world order, whether from Afghanistan or Congo, as equal victims of capitalism and a postcolonial experience of displacement.

Decentring nationalism as ideology of emancipation has implications for how different protagonists represent the stateless intellectual in exile. Hage and Suleiman probe the intellectual's mystification of exile and the discursive idealisation of the prophetic word. In their portrayal of the exilic intellectual, they revisit the legacy of their predecessors, Edward Said and Jabra Ibrahim Jabra, and displace the discursive binaries in which the two intellectuals define exilic subjectivities on ethical and aesthetic grounds. Hage and Suleiman deromanticise exile by reinscribing it within wider political and collective narratives of displacement experienced not only by displaced intellectuals but also by refugees and immigrants. Their critical undertaking ultimately balances between refugees and exiles, the two categories to which Said and Jabra had assigned different signifiers. In so doing, Hage and Suleiman question the centrality of the intellectual's exilic word, the *sine qua non* of his prophecy.

The previous chapters have revealed how loss, whether caused by dispossession, displacement or war, is the catalyst for the prophecy. The prophet in this sense codes the tragedy of displacement as a collective condition and mourns it accordingly. The dead intellectual signifies the demise of his community; his suicide comments on its oblivion. Although mourning remains an overarching motif, the contemporary texts examined here show us how loss is experienced intimately, in terms that are embedded in each writer's experience of the present. Not extrapolating collective meaning from personal loss, mourning is an intimate and somatic condition. In this context, loss emerges specifically from the collapse of the representational 'we' and the rise of the affective 'I', rendering Saadallah Wannous's lament 'We are both the mourned and the mourners' all the more incongruous in a contemporary era in which the very sense of a unified and unifying community, based on language, nation and displacement, has been reconfigured.[6] Al-Daif's narrator mourns the sudden tragic death of the *nahḍa* intellectual by pondering the predicament of his ungrieved death, his dissected body and unrealised prophecy. He mourns by pointing to the absence of his legacy, but more strikingly by reminding us that this intellectual left no mourners behind, no community of believers.

A reconfiguration of the politics of mourning is particularly pronounced in Jaber's portrayal of the suicidal intellectual. Rabee Jaber probes the idealisation of the intellectual from the vantage point of a self-effacing and self-defeating interlocutor. He writes a counter-narrative of the trials of the intellectual and situates it, not in a messianic discourse – the perennial narrative of suicide as a selfless act of political protest – but, rather, in the intellectual's personal and intimate melancholic afflictions aggravated by existential angst. The melancholic suicidal intellectual in Jaber's novel is not a prophet but merely an individual, alienated by the world and disenchanted with the word. As the intellectual's suicide cannot be a site of ideological projection, mourning, for Jaber, operates as an injunction to return, not to an ideologically codified word, but rather to text. The return to the text reiterates Jaber's image, to borrow Abbas Baydoun's words, as a pastiche artist, a composer of/in paper (*muʾallif waraqī*), who elides the singularity of authorship that has framed the intellectual's prophecy. For al-Herz, mourning is not a communal affair either. Although the wrongful deaths of Shiʿi political figures – such as the martyred brothers Hassan, Hussein and Baqir al-Sadr – have scarred the community's collective memory, they are experienced somatically, prediscursively, through the collapse of the body of the narrator as the sisters of several Shiʿi martyrs.

The displacement of the prophecy is articulated in parallel to a critique of the public sphere that fashioned the intellectual and was fashioned in return. The public sphere of the intellectual-prophet was constituted by cultural institutions such as cafés, literary journals, op-eds and literary circles. The cafés that invited Jabra and his protagonist Walid Masoud to reflect on modernism in poetry and the arts operated as platforms for the Iraqi literary and artistic vanguard. The literary venues of Baghdad, as well as those of Paris, are all too present in these contemporary novels, but they are voided of their status and political signifiers. The café in *Chronicle of a Disappearance* is a derelict space stuck in the past. It is where friends discuss the banality of the ordinary in conversations that amount to nothing. The Artista Café of *Cockroach* is not the Parisian Deux Magots, where Sartre and de Beauvoir conversed with French intellectual icons about Freedom and Being. It is a rundown hangout of the Canadian underworld where welfare recipients, whether exiles or refugees, go to resuscitate cigarette butts and borrow money. Intellectual spaces such as lecture halls and cultural institutions are equally the object of criticism. Even when invited to speak about his project, the intellectual in *Chronicle of a Disappearance* is misrepresented and continuously interrupted, and his word is never heard. The public sphere is central to Jaber's critique. The narrator bypasses *al-Mulhaq*, the most distinguished and subversive literary journal of the post-war era. The motives of Rizqallah's suicide, the narrator observes, cannot be found in *al-Mulhaq* and the words of its writers, but elsewhere, in the depth of the dead intellectual's correspondence, diary and personal photographs, among other intimate writings. The narrator in *The Others* has also lost faith in the magazine of her local *ḥusayniyya*, as it is too didactic. Instead, she participates in the virtual public sphere, one that is pluralistic, more accepting of ambivalent subjectivities, and less invested in silencing processes. As such, the intellectual-prophet's public sphere emerging from the symbolic power of conference rooms, cafés, literary journals and magazines has become, in these contemporary texts, a space where prophecies are stripped of their platforms and voided of their signifiers.

The discursive deconstruction of the intellectuals' prophecy entails a parallel dismantlement of the cultural field in which they operate. Although the protagonists of the different texts examined in *The Unmaking of the Arab Intellectual* respond to a distinctive cultural capital, their self-fashioning is based on a simultaneous recognition of their predecessors' cultural icons and their disavowal of them. They know exactly what constitutes the Arab literary canon but explicitly shun it by means of parodying it, neutralising it and most importantly, rejecting its structured and structuring hierarchical power. Walid Masoud's cultural capital, meticulously evoked by his infatuation with Henri Purcell, translations of Shakespeare and discussions about sculpture, is revisited in these contemporary writings. When the Israeli police raid E. S.'s home, they find on the shelf a Japanese language textbook, a novel by Sonallah Ibrahim, short stories by Karl Kraus and albums of Arab pop music icons. The incompatible elements of this selection confuse both the viewer and the invading officers because of how little they reveal. If they reveal anything, it is that E. S. knows what constitutes 'high' culture, what drives the accumulation of a higher cultural capital, but does not care to parade it or organise it. He has a taste for literature but does not shun the sarcastic, popular, cursory content of other writings. He attempts to learn not the idiom of Arab exiles such as French or English but Japanese, a linguistic and cultural field that falls outside the economy of Arab cultural distinction. Hage's protagonist is a cockroach, indeed, but one who knows his classics. He knows Foucault and Sartre and recognises Trotsky when he hears the Professor quoting him. But he refuses to inherit the complex structure of stratification and classification that endows its intellectual exilic carrier with distinction. The fatigue from the cultural capital associated with the intellectual materialises in the protagonist of Jaber's novel. The disinterested narrator is a learned subject, a highly literate individual, whose interests encompass Abu Tammam, Lewis Carroll, Fernando Pessoa and children's literature. He is drawn to reading not as a way to engage public debates but in order to learn more about the object of his search. Similarly, although Seba al-Herz's protagonist recognises the canon – she knows Naguib Mahfouz and has read Yusuf al-Sibai – she fashions an alternative political and literary sensibility. Her position toward the Arabic canon is not necessarily binary or relational – carrying the canonical legacy or rebelling against it – but is rather framed by an overarching sense of ennui that drives her elsewhere, where Shiʿi philosophy, Jean-Paul Sartre and Hollywood converge and deviate.

The 'conscience, consciousness, and eloquence', of the intellectual, from Jurji Zaidan to Mahmoud Darwish, is predicated on a vision of the Arabic language as a vessel of emancipation. If language has been at the core of the prophecy, its reconfirmation becomes necessary for the articulation of emerging contemporary poetics. The narrative language of the different texts examined could not be more distinct, more idiosyncratic. Seba al-Herz's narrative register does not conceal her infatuation with classical Arabic, technological jargon and global Anglophone culture equally. Her reliance on seemingly conflicting registers and jargons is strikingly different from Rashid al-Daif's neoclassical register that conjures innocence by flaunting a romantic nationalist lexicon. Al-Daif's narrative language seethes with irony, one that sarcastically appropriates and critically rethinks the project of linguistic reform stipulated by none other than Jurji Zaidan. Jaber's laconic and repetitive description of the circumstances surrounding the suicide of Ralph Rizqallah is characteristic of his writing, indeed, but it also parodies the narrative language of his precursors, particularly of Khoury's war and post-war novels. It channels such language, almost mimics it. It uses Khoury's syntax to decentre Khoury's field of meaning.

The portrait of the intellectual-prophet who stands on Mount Nebo, endowed with the divine word, speaking truth to power in the name of the disenfranchised, has been fundamentally altered. His new portrait reeks with death, disintegration and absence. The *nahda* intellectual of al-Daif's historical metafiction is a dedicated young scholar who defeats the high tides of Western modernity but ends up dying twice: death strikes when he returns to Syria as a corpse that is ultimately stolen, dissected and discarded by the same modern subjects whose consciousness he had helped to stir. Death strikes later, when his secular, nationalist and modernist legacy fails to overcome the thrust of the sectarianism and violence of the Arab Levant. Suleiman tackles the omnipotence associated with Arab intellectual-prophets by pointing to their silence. The exilic intellectual Suleiman imagines is not only invisible but also redundant to the plot: the present-absentee that is unseen and unheard, merely observing the slow collapse of intellectual authority. The loss of E. S.'s word and interlocutors is predicated on a more alarming loss triggered by his invisibility to occupation. As they raid his apartment, the Israeli police find a dreamy, unassuming intellectual posing no danger to the state, precisely because he has lost his monopoly on the word, if not the word altogether, and has become invisible, absent. In his characteristic humour and irreverence, Rawi Hage portrays the Professor as a carcass of the politically committed intellectual. A sickly, preposterous and utterly void simulacrum of a Sartrian and Saidian intellectual, Hage's intellectual inhabits the cafés of the Canadian underworld alongside the ragged and the wretched, neutralising thereby the presumed symbolic power of his prophecy. Equally debunking the prophecy of the intellectual, Jaber portrays the post-war intellectual not as a messianic figure dying for the sake of his national community nor one that is endowed with the mystique of Jabra's Walid Masoud. Rather, he is a lone melancholic individual, battling existential angst triggered by the first symptoms of ageing. He is a disaffected ordinary man uninterested in speaking truth to power, ultimately ending his life because he has lost his word.

The different authors whose works I address here have articulated their dissent from the archetype of the intellectual-prophet not only discursively but also performatively. They have pointed to the limits of the intellectual's prophecy and simultaneously suggested an alternative mode of enacting the contemporary intellectual. The omniscient, omnipotent and omnipresent writer so closely linked to the construction of the Arabic literary canon, one that evokes, 'conscience, consciousness, and eloquence' is unrecognisable in their contemporary writings.[7] As she conceals her identity behind a pen name, al-Herz puts forward a vision of the intellectual as a phantomlike entity whose presence is revealed only through the political havoc it wreaks, eschewing thereby the omnipresence of Arab intellectuals who tower over their own text. Al-Daif's anachronistic narration that disturbs temporal teleology suggests that Arab intellectuals are both historical subjects and objects of their writings. He historicises the troubled journey of Jurji Zaidan from the future, a contemporary temporality that abounds with disenchantment, specifically in the aftermath of war, which renders his positioning and his reading of Zaidan all the more tragic. Rabee Jaber narrates the tragedy of the intellectual's suicide from a comparatively self-reflexive and self-effacing positionality. Unlike Elias Khoury's lofty presence as a novelist, editor and catalyst of post-war Lebanese culture, Jaber lives outside the Lebanese cultural field and does not aspire to lead it or transform it, although he unavoidably does. Instead, he is another fleeting writer who exists as a *muʾallif waraqī*, a writer of/in paper and text.

Perhaps the most significant challenge in *The Unmaking of the Arab*

Intellectual is its transgeneric approach, which facilitated the placing of Suleiman's feature film in conversation with Said's essays and Jabra's novel on exile. This approach ultimately proposes a methodology that captures the magnitude of the question of intellectual displacement, one that invites us to widen the scope of research and conduct cross-generic readings that nevertheless acknowledge and attend to the aesthetic specificities of genres and media. As it is intimately tied to the ways in which the intellectual's reality is rendered and reproduced, genre has been central to the self-fashioning of the intellectual. The decentring of the archetype would not have been possible without revisiting in parallel the genre construction and canonisation processes. The texts and films that I address in this book could not be more distinctive, yet they all return specifically to the question of genre to formulate their political critique. Al-Daif revisits the historical novel, which matured during the *nahḍa* and was critical to Jurji Zaidan's historiographical and literary political project. As he parodies the historical novel, al-Daif challenges its three constructs – literature, history and historical subjectivity – in a move that ultimately displaces Zaidan's *nahḍa* project. The historical metafiction of al-Daif sheds doubt on what exactly constitutes the literary, what constitutes historical truth and what drives historical subjects. Genre is also the crux of Jaber's subversion of the war novel of his predecessors. Jaber borrows the theme and structure of Khoury's novels, particularly the motif of the search driven by an original moment of loss and search for truth. Jaber parodies the motifs, narrative and even language of his predecessor, only to tell a counter-narrative about the uneventful suicide of a non-messianic intellectual. Hage pushes the critique of the war novel further. His protagonist does not inhabit the fractured urban landscape of Beirut, which has hitherto operated as the vector of the memory discourse. Rather, he carries the scars of the civil war within him and narrates trauma against the backdrop of a new trauma in the making, that of his uneasy navigation of a self-congratulating welfare system. The critique of genre in Seba al-Herz's *The Others* touches on the chick-lit genre, a presumably feminised, cursory and apolitical mode of writing that she uses to narrate a deeply political and a necessarily historical novel. The subversion of the chick-lit genre in this context constitutes the first emancipatory moment that will set the historical narrative of oppression free.

As it reveals the hitherto discounted political critique inherent in the contemporary Arabic literary moment, *The Unmaking of the Arab Intellectual* seeks to open an entire literary and intellectual corpus up for reconsideration, thereby charting an additional layer to what constitutes the political. My analysis of Seba al-Herz's depiction of the intellectual draws on critical studies examining sidelined literary genres that evoke nonsecular feminine poetics. Putting *The Others*, the first and last novel by an obscure Saudi woman writing under a pseudonym, in dialogue with influential and critically acclaimed works decentres notions of canonicity and representation. Such an approach is important precisely because it demonstrates the ways in which some literary genres, national literatures and authors invite critical attention and are more prone to canonisation than others, thereby sentencing other writers to silence. The importance of *The Others* is that it is indeed contemporary insofar as it burns the effigy of the secular, nationalist, omnipresent, omniscient and omnipotent intellectual in a register that defies logocentrism and challenges the masculinist ethos that is prevalent in the literary tradition and its criticism. Placing *The Others* in this collection brings to the fore a new mode of depicting the contemporary intellectual in a poetics of loss that is autochthonous and divorced from previous modes of mourning.

The preceding chapters have shown how the political manifests in the ways in which structures of power – of intellectuals and their words – are displaced and repoliticised. Specifically, the political crystallises in the interstices of al-Daif's modernist prescriptive ethos and his nostalgic rapture with the premodern, an approach that sets his historiographic irony in opposition to Jabra's unapologetic modernism. The political is articulated in Suleiman's silence, self-effacement and cynicism, which caution us against the perils of fetishising and commodifying Palestinian nationalism and the intellectual that embodies it. Jaber's conception of the political lies in his rejection of the intellectual's messianicity resulting from his objectification and ideological codification. By unearthing repressed narratives of transgenerational violence and reinscribing them on the narrator's aching body, al-Herz understands the political at the intersection of the ideological and the corporeal; where spectral hauntings are more truthful and real than the secular-nationalist intellectual tradition from which she hails.

A Post-contemporary Poetics?

Mahmoud Darwish left behind an *oeuvre* that is complete; complete because it sets the parameters of its own canonisation and simultaneously transcends it and points to its finitude. Addressed to power, his poetics of loss and exile returns to consecrate him as the prophetic figure divided between his individual trials and nationalist project. Although consumed with the present traces of past tragedies, Darwish's poetry looks beyond itself, projecting itself onto a future free of its own edicts. In his penultimate book *In the Presence of Absence* (2006; English trans. 2011), Darwish writes a 'text' of both poetry and prose. His text stretches the doubleness of the prose and poetry further and reaches out to a genre that is both an elegy and a biography of the self, looking simultaneously at the past and attempting to rethink the unchartered future. The text reckons with the multiple losses that the poet has endured yet looks beyond the present in a poetic discourse that operates like a testament, foreseeing the future in its own end, or foreseeing its end in the future. One could read in Darwish's testament a premonition about the end of his own prophecy and the predicament of the prophetic word. Darwish's last testament leaves us at a loss: when the prophet himself looks beyond his prophecy, when he recognises his power yet anticipates its end – its mutation, in both discourse and form – how are we, readers and critics, to experience the remains of the prophecy? What becomes of the intellectual in the future of the contemporary world that we inhabit? Stripped of his prophecy, monopoly of the written word and his ability to speak truth to power, what authority and influence will remain for the intellectual?

The upheavals that the Arab world has witnessed since 2011 have made these questions all the more timely and have brought them back to where the prophecy started: to the intellectual's mastery of the word and his ability to speak truth to power in order to pave the way for a future of emancipation. The intellectual's role, as Foucault writes, is

> no longer to place himself 'somewhat ahead and to the side' in order to express the stifled truth of the collectivity; rather, it is to struggle against the forms of power that transform him into its object and instrument in the sphere of 'knowledge', 'truth', 'consciousness', and 'discourse'.[8]

Despite the contemporary displacement of prophecy, intellectuals may still be critical of the very constructs that have canonised and elevated them.

Elias Khoury conveys the predicament of the post-2011 intellectual, particularly his loss of the word. Although he has written hundreds of eulogies of friends he had lost to assassination, suicide or illness, Khoury stands speechless before the death of a Palestinian toddler burned alive by Israeli settlers in 2015. In 'Speech is Dead, So Are Elegies', Khoury searches for words to no avail and thus reflects on the link between mourning and inheritance:

> Speech is dead and no one is entitled to elegize the victim. The taste of ash in our mouths has turned speech into ash, without a spark of life. Speech is dead, because all that is said today has been said a thousand times before in the eloquence of the Arabic language. Reiteration is pointless. Enough. Let us shut up, for language no longer diffuses our anger. It has become ash diluted in the blood of children. No one is entitled to elegize anymore, for he who elegizes [yarthī] inherits [yarith]. This is the parallel that the language of our ancestors created when it entwined the letters of these two words – 'elegy' [rithāʾ] and 'inheritance' [irth] – where neither one materializes without the other.[9]

Khoury, here, embraces the paradox of using the word as a means to lament its demise. Khoury points to the end of the intellectual's prophecy and the intellectual's inalienable right to speak in the name of his community. He who has seen violence, survived it and lamented its scars countless times in novels, eulogies and editorials, has now declared the word dead. The senselessness of the child's death has set the word ablaze and reduced it to a lifeless abject matter. The assonance, or linguistic entanglement, between elegising (yarthī) and inheriting (yarith) engenders an additional dictum: he who has lost the ability to mourn is not entitled to carry the legacy. Speechless and disarmed of the word that is at the core of his mission, the intellectual is now stripped of his prophecy.

Intellectuals have lost their platform, their Mount Nebo, or at least their monopoly over it. The cultural institutions and publications that mediate intellectual communication and which have been responsible for the emergence of the public sphere, from *al-Hilal* and *al-Muqtataf* to *Hiwar* and

Shiᶜr, either ceased to exist or became unrecognisable. Op-eds and cultural supplements that provided platforms for Lebanese, Syrian and Palestinian intellectuals have had to terminate or circumscribe their literary and cultural supplements. In the last few years, political and financial crises in Arab media have led to the closure of influential media platforms. In Lebanon alone, renowned literary journals – including the established journal *al-Adab*, the short-lived journal *Kalamun*, the cultural supplement of *al-Mustaqbal*, *al-Mulhaq* and the daily *al-Safir*, – have been shut down.[10] Turning to electronic media and art conferences, intellectuals are reinventing themselves as interlocutors of artists and activists.

Due to the receding influence of print media, Arab intellectuals have had to adapt to the new lines of communication and possibilities that the web offers and evade the financial burden and political censorship of traditional media. The recent proliferation of electronic journals and magazines has, indeed, provided new platforms for intellectuals, but has also created a new set of challenges. The democratisation of speech has constituted a potential threat to intellectuals, whose claim to the word is curtailed, scrutinised and potentially undermined by a series of public modes of engagement that questions their centrality. The democratisation of media and platforms has empowered cultural actors who are now increasingly articulate and more attentive to the intricacies of the contemporary Arab world currently undergoing upheaval. The intellectual-prophets, the Jabras and Walid Masouds of our era, who once had power over the word and were, in turn, empowered by it, have been excluded from traditional cultural institutions. They now compete with a new sense of authority, the authority of the outraged social media subject, the likes of al-Herz's narrator, who lurks online awaiting the first mistake to dispel and displace the intellectual in hashtags and mentions that encircle the intellectual and declare the prophecy dead.[11]

Underlying the convergent critiques that emerge from contemporary literature is a collective interest in re-examining the power of the word – narrative, poetic or philosophical – thought to achieve collective salvation. Although hailing from different literary fields and generic traditions, Rashid al-Daif, Rabee Jaber, Seba al-Herz, Rawi Hage and Elia Suleiman articulate a critique of the intellectual-prophet from a shared contemporary sensibility that traverses their works. They have all returned to the intellectual in a discourse that is simultaneously retrospective and self-reflexive; retrospective because they critically portray the intellectual as a construct of an incongruous past, and self-reflexive because they search for the remainder of the intellectual's prophecy in their own unsettling experience of the contemporary. As such, burning the effigy of the prophet-intellectual is as personal, as political and as public as the act of writing is; it is a public exorcism of an intimate state of possession, one that undoubtedly triggers an affective reaction to that which is being ejected from the contemporary literary body. The intellectual-prophet standing on Mount Nebo, overlooking the Promised Land, is now displaced by the disarmed and disillusioned intellectual, akin to Jaber's Rizkqallah, standing before a cliff – back turned to the city, arms open in the shape of a cross – jumping into the clear sea. In the contemporary era of consecutive aftermaths, intellectuals may still stand on Mount Nebo, but their prophecy has fallen.

Notes

1. Darwish, 'Mahmoud Darwish', p. 83.
2. See, for instance, Sabry Hafez who made similar claims in examining 1990s Egyptian literature. Hafez, 'The Transformation of Reality'.
3. Toukan, 'Whatever Happened to *Iltizām*?', p. 339.
4. Ibid. p. 339.
5. Original emphasis. Scott, *Omens of Adversity*, p. 75.
6. Wannous, *Al-Aᶜmal al-Kamila*, p. 493.
7. Foucault and Deleuze, 'Intellectuals and Power', p. 207.
8. Ibid. pp. 207–8.
9. The original Arabic reads:

   من يرثي هو الذي يرث، هذه هي المعادلة التي اجترحتها لغة العرب عندما جعلت من كلمتي الرثاء والإرث متداخلتي الحروف بحيث لا تنهض كلمة منهما من دون الأخرى.

   Khoury, 'Khilis al-Haki wa Intaha al-Rithaᶜ'.
10. The last paper issue of *al-Adab* appeared in 2012. After a hiatus of three years, it reappeared in an electronic format. See http://www.al-adab.com/index (last accessed 23 May 2016).
11. On the hashtag-as-raid phenomenon and the traces of online activism on the literary fields, see El-Ariss, 'Fiction of Scandal'.

Bibliography

al-Abdelli, Mishaal, 'Seba al-Herz: Al-Akharun Sard li-ᶜAlaqat Mabtura wa Naqisa wa Mukhtalla wa Maʾzuma', *Al-Hayat*, 21 March 2007, http://goo.gl/SE9M5O (last accessed 21 May 2016).

Abdel-Malek, Anouar, *Contemporary Arab Political Thought* (London: Palgrave Macmillan, 1983).

Abraham, Nicolas, 'Notes on the Phantom: A Complement to Freud's Metapsychology', in Nicholas Thomas Rand (ed. and trans.), *The Shell and the Kernel: Renewals of Psychoanalysis*, vol. 1 (Chicago: University of Chicago Press, 1994).

Abraham, Nicolas, and Nicholas Rand, 'Notes on the Phantom: A Complement to Freud's Metapsychology', *Critical Inquiry* 13, no. 2 (Winter 1987), pp. 287–92.

Abu-Rabiᶜ, Ibrahim M., *Contemporary Arab Thought: Studies in Post-1967 Arab Intellectual History* (London: Pluto Press, 2004.)

Abu-Remaileh, Refqa, 'Palestinian Anti-Narratives in the Films of Elia Suleiman', *Arab Media & Society*, no. 5 (Spring 2008), http://www.arabmediasociety.com/?article=670 (last accessed 19 May 2016).

Aghacy, Samira, 'Contemporary Lebanese Fiction: Modernization without Modernity', *International Journal of Middle East Studies* 38, no. 4 (2006), pp. 561–80.

———, 'Elias Khoury's *The Journey of Little Gandhi*: Fiction and Ideology', *International Journal of Middle East Studies* 28, no. 2 (1996), pp. 163–76.

———, *Masculine Identity in the Fiction of the Arab East Since 1967* (Syracuse: Syracuse University Press, 2009).

Allen, Roger, 'Rewriting Literary History: The Case of the Arabic Novel', *Journal of Arabic Literature* 38, no. 3 (1 January 2007), pp. 247–60.

al-Amir, Yusri, and Rashid Al-Daif, 'Hiwar maᶜ Rashid al-Daif: ᶜAn al-Khawf wa-l-Bawh wa Inhiyar al-Siyasa', *al-Adab*, 1999.

Anderson, Betty, *The American University of Beirut: Arab Nationalism and Liberal Education* (Austin: University of Texas Press, 2011).

Anonymous, 'Al-Muqrin: Fi Riwayati al-Qadima', *Aafaq*, 11 December 2008, http://goo.gl/fx4kHQ (last accessed 20 May 2016).

———, 'Al-Riwaʾi Rashid al-Daif, Dayf Shabab al-Safir', *al-Safir*, 31 October 2012.

———, 'Saudi Arabia's Hidden Uprising', BBC News, http://www.bbc.com/news/world-middle-east-27619309 (last accessed 21 May 2016).

———, 'Tafrat al-Riwaya al-Nisaʾiyya fi-l-Saʿudiyya' *Al-Hayat*, 1 November 2011.

———, 'What to Read on Vacation: *The Others*', *NYMag.com*, http://nymag.com/arts/books/features/57867/index3.html (last accessed 5 October 2015).

Antoon, Sinan 'Mahmud Darwish's Allegorical Critique of Oslo', *Journal of Palestine Studies* 31, no. 2 (1 January 2002), pp. 66–77.

Arendt, Hannah, 'We the Refugees', in Marc Robinson (ed.), *Altogether Elsewhere: Writers on Exile* (Winchester, MA: Faber and Faber, 1994).

El-Ariss, Tarek, 'Fiction of Scandal', *Journal of Arabic Literature* 43, no. 2–3 (2012), pp. 510–31.

———, *Trials of Arab Modernity: Literary Affects and the New Political* (New York: Fordham University Press, 2013).

al-Ashqar, Youssef Habshi, *Al-Zill wa-l-Sada* (Beirut: Dar al-Nahar li-l-Nashr, 1989).

———, *La Tanbut Judhur fi al-Samaʾ* (Beirut: Dar al-Nahar lil-Nashr, 1971).

Aufderheide, Patricia, 'An Interview with Elia Suleiman', *Visual Anthropology Review* 13, no. 2 (1 September 1997), pp. 74–8.

Bardawil, Fadi A., 'The Inward Turn and its Vicissitudes: Culture, Society, and Politics in Post-1967 Arab Leftist Critiques', in Malika Bouziane, Cilja Harders and Anja Hoffmann (eds), *Local Politics and Contemporary Transformations in the Arab World*, Governance and Limited Statehood Series (London: Palgrave Macmillan, 2013).

———, 'When all this Revolution Melts into Air: The Disenchantment of Levantine Marxist Intellectuals', PhD dissertation (Columbia University, 2010).

Barthes, Roland, *S/Z: An Essay*, trans. Richard Miller (New York: Hill and Wang, 1975).

Baydoun, Abbas, 'Bukir Rabee Jaber: Min al-Tajrib al-Thaqafi ila al-Buʿd al-Shaʿbi', *al-Safir*, 4 February 2012.

———, 'Man Yaqraʾ Rabee Jabir?', *al-Safir*, 18 May 1999.

Benjamin, Walter, *Illuminations: Essays and Reflections*, ed. Hannah Arendt, trans. Harry Zohn (New York: Schocken Books, 1969).

Bin Hamza, Hussein, 'Rashid al-Daif: Al-Adab Laysa Mihnati', http://www.al-akhbar.com/node/156971 (last accessed 20 May 2014).

Bitton, Simone, *Mahmoud Darwich: As the Land is the Language* (Seattle: Arab Film Distribution, 1997). [documentary]

Booth, Marilyn, ' "The Muslim Woman" as Celebrity Author and the Politics of Translating Arabic: Girls of Riyadh Go on the Road', *Journal of Middle East Women's Studies* 6, no. 3 (1 October 2010), pp. 149–82.

Boullata, Issa J., 'Living with the Tigress and the Muses: An Essay on Jabra Ibrahim Jabra', *World Literature Today* 75, no. 2 (1 April 2001), pp. 214–23.

Boullata, Kamal, and Mirène Ghossein (eds), *The World of Rashid Hussein, a Palestinian Poet in Exile* (Detroit: Association of Arab-American University Graduates, 1979).

Boustani, Sobhi, 'Intertexte et mémoire dans l'écriture romanesque de Rabi Jabir: Essai sur le roman Ralph Rizqallah Fi Al-Mir°at', in Luc Deheuvels, Barbara Michalak-Pikulska and Paul Starkey (eds), *Intertexuality in Modern Arabic Literature since 1967* (Manchester: Manchester University Press, 2009), pp. 83–102.

———, 'Le héros chez Rashid Ad-da‘if: La quête d'une identité', *Middle Eastern Literatures* 12, no. 1 (April 2009), pp. 43–57.

Bzih, Shawqi, 'Beirut Madinat al-‘Alam li-Rabee Jaber', *al-Safir*, 16 January 2004.

Caiani, Fabio, *Contemporary Arabic Fiction: Innovation from Rama to Yalu* (New York: Routledge, 2007), http://www.myilibrary.com?id=95518 (last accessed 26 May 2016).

cooke, miriam, 'Beirut Reborn: The Political Aesthetics of Auto-Destruction', *Yale Journal of Criticism* 15, no. 2 (2002), p. 409.

———, *Nazira Zeineddine: A Pioneer of Islamic Feminism* (New York: Oneworld, 2010).

———, *War's Other Voices: Women Writers on the Lebanese Civil War* (Syracuse: Syracuse University Press, 1996).

al-Daif, Rachid, *Learning English*, trans. Adnan Haydar and Paula Haydar (Northampton, MA: Interlink Books, 2007).

al-Daif, Rashid, *Dear Mr. Kawabata*, trans. Paul Starkey (London: Quartet Books, 1999).

———, *Tablit al-Bahr* (Beirut: Riyad al-Rayyis, 2011).

———, *Who's Afraid of Meryl Streep*, trans. Paula Haydar and Nadine Sinno (Austin: University of Texas Press, 2014).

Dakhli, Leyla, *Une Génération d'intellectuels Arabes: Syrie et Liban, 1908–1940* (Paris: Karthala Editions, 2009).

Darraj, Faysal, *Al-Dhakira al-Qawmiya fi-l-Riwaya al-ᶜArabiyya min Zaman al-Nahda ila Zaman al-Suqut* (Beirut: Markaz Dirasat al-Wahda al-ᶜArabiyya, 2008).

———, 'Transfigurations in the Image of Palestine in the Poetry of Mahmoud Darwish', in Hala Khamis Nassar and Najat Rahman (eds), *Mahmoud Darwish, Exile's Poet: Critical Essays* (Northampton, MA: Interlink Books, 2008).

Darwish, Mahmoud, *Aᶜras* (Beirut: Dar al-ᶜAwda, 1977).

———, *Al-Diwan, al-Aᶜmal al-Ula*, vol. 1 (Beirut: Dar al-ᶜAwda, 2005).

———, 'Edward Said: A Contrapuntal Reading', trans. Mona Anis, *Cultural Critique* 67, no. 1 (2007), pp. 175–82.

———, 'Fi Bayt Ristus', https://www.youtube.com/watch?v=QLVKmFnlJRs (last accessed 25 April 2016).

———, 'In Pablo Neruda's Home, on the Pacific', trans. Fady Joudah (Port Townsend: Copper Canyon Press, 2007).

———, *In the Presence of Absence*, trans. Sinan Antoon (New York: Archipelago, 2011).

———, *La Taᶜtadhir ᶜAmma Faᶜalt* (Beirut: Riyad al-Rayyis, 2004).

———, *Madih al-Zill al-ᶜAli* (Beirut: Dar al-ᶜAwda, 1983).

———, 'Mahmoud Darwish', trans. Pierre Joris, *Boundary* 2 26, no. 1 (Spring 1999), pp. 81–3.

Deheuvels, Luc-Willy, Barbara Michalak-Pikulska and Paul Starkey, *Intertextuality in Modern Arabic Literature since 1967* (Manchester: Manchester University Press, 2006).

Derrida, Jacques, *Specters of Marx: The State of the Debt, the Work of Mourning, and the New International*, trans. Peggy Kamuf (New York: Routledge, 2006).

———, *The Work of Mourning* (Chicago: University of Chicago Press, 2003).

Di-Capua, Yoav, 'Arab Existentialism: An Invisible Chapter in the Intellectual History of Decolonization', *The American Historical Review* 117, no. 4 (1 October 2012), pp. 1061–91.

———, 'The Intellectual Revolt of the 1950s and the "Fall of the Udabaʾ"', in Georges Khalil and Friederike Pannewick (eds), *Commitment and Beyond: Reflections on/of the Political in Arabic Literature since the 1940s* (Wiesbaden: Reichert, 2015), pp. 89–104.

Douaihy, Jabbour, 'Zahirat al-Riwaʾiyyat al-Saᶜudiyyat', *Annahar*, 6 January 2007.

Dupont, Anne-Laure, *Gurgi Zaydan, 1861–1914: Écrivain réformiste et témoin de la renaissance arabe* (Damascus: Institut Français du Proche Orient, 2006).

————, 'How Should History Be Written? The Impact of European Orientalism on Jurji Zaidan's Work', in Thomas Philipp and Georges C. Zaidan (eds), *Jurji Zaidan's Contributions to Modern Arab Thought and Literature* (Bethesda: The Zaidan Foundation, 2013), pp. 85–122.

————, 'What is a *kātib ᶜāmm*? The Status of Men of Letters and the Conception of Language According to Jurji Zaydan', *Middle Eastern Literatures* 13, no. 2 (August 2010), pp. 171–81.

al-Eid, Yumna, 'Rabee Jaber la Yudawwin al-Tarikh Bal Wujud al-Insan', http://goo.gl/aoAtVJ (last accessed 17 May 2016).

Elshakry, Marwa, 'Between Enlightenment and Evolution: Arabic and the Arab Golden Ages of Jurji Zaidan', in Thomas Philipp and Georges C. Zaidan (eds), *Jurji Zaidan's Contributions to Modern Arab Thought and Literature* (Bethesda: The Zaidan Foundation, 2013), pp. 123–44.

————, 'Muslim Hermeneutics and Arabic Views of Evolution', *Zygon: Journal of Religion & Science* 46, no. 2 (June 2011), pp. 330–44.

————, *Reading Darwin in Arabic, 1860–1950* (Chicago: University of Chicago Press, 2014).

el-Enany, Rasheed, *Arab Representations of the Occident: East-West Encounters in Arabic Fiction* (New York: Routledge, 2006).

————, 'The Quest for Justice in the Theatre of Alfred Farag: Different Moulds, One Theme', *Journal of Arabic Literature* 31, no. 2 (1 January 2000), pp. 171–202.

————, 'Tawfiq al-Hakim and the West: A New Assessment of the Relationship', *British Journal of Middle Eastern Studies* 27, no. 2 (2000), pp. 165–75.

————, 'Theme and Identity in Postcolonial Arabic Writing', *Cross/Cultures*, no. 119 (2009), pp. 1–36.

Fayyad, Mona, 'Lam Naᶜud bi-Manᵓa', *Mulhaq al-Nahar*, 11 April 1995.

Foucault, Michel, 'The Political Function of the Intellectual', *Radical Philosophy* 17, no. 13 (1977), pp. 126–33.

————, 'Power, Moral Values, and the Intellectual: An Interview with Michel Foucault', *History of the Present*, no. 4 (Spring 1988).

————, 'Truth and Power', in *Power/Knowledge: Selected Interviews and Other Writings, 1972–1977*, ed. Colin Gordon (New York: Vintage, 1980).

Foucault, Michel, and Gilles Deleuze, 'Intellectuals and Power', in *Language, Counter-Memory, Practice: Selected Essays and Interviews by Michel Foucault*, ed. Donald F. Bouchard (Ithaca: Cornell University Press, 1980).

Frangie, Samer, 'Historicism, Socialism and Liberalism after the Defeat: On the

Political Thought of Yasin Al-Hafiz', *Modern Intellectual History* 12, no. 2 (August 2015), pp. 325–52.

al-Ghadeer, Moneera, 'Reviews', *Journal of Arabic Literature* 37, no. 2 (2006), pp. 293–302.

Ghosn, Katia (ed.), *Rachid el-Daïf: Le Roman Arabe dans la tourmente de la modernisation* (Paris: Demopolis, 2016).

Hafez, Sabry, 'The Transformation of Reality and the Arabic Novel's Aesthetic Response', *Bulletin of the School of Oriental and African Studies* 57, no. 1 (1994), pp. 93–112.

Hage, Rawi, *Cockroach* (New York: W. W. Norton & Co., 2010).

———, 'Portrait of Edward Said', *West Coast Line*, Spring 2010, p. 143.

———, 'To Roam a Borderless World', *Globe and Mail*, 13 June 2008, sec. Comment.

Hajjar, Bassam, 'Al-Taᶜasa Huna, Bala Aᶜrif', *Mulhaq al-Nahar*, 4 November 1995.

Halabi, Zeina G., 'The Bereaved and the Disappeared – and Beirut Makes Three', *The Legal Agenda*, 7 October 2015, http://english.legal-agenda.com/article.php?id=726&folder=articles&lang=en (last accessed 15 May 2016).

———, 'The Day the Wandering Dreamer Became a Fida'i: Jabra Ibrahim Jabra and the Fashioning of Political Commitment', in Georges Khalil and Friederike Pannewick (eds), *Commitment and Beyond: Reflections on/of the Political in Arabic Literature since the 1940s* (Wiesbaden: Reichert, 2015), pp. 156–70.

Hamzah, Dyala, 'Introduction', in Dyala Hamzah (ed.), *The Making of the Arab Intellectual: Empire, Public Sphere and the Colonial Coordinates of Selfhood* (New York: Routledge, 2012).

Harlow, Barbara, *Resistance Literature* (New York: Routledge, 1987).

Hartman, Michelle, *Native Tongue, Stranger Talk: The Arabic and French Literary Landscapes of Lebanon*, Middle East Studies Beyond Dominant Paradigms (Syracuse: Syracuse University Press, 2014).

Haugbolle, Sune, *War and Memory in Lebanon* (Cambridge: Cambridge University Press, 2010).

Hayek, Ghenwa, 'Rabi Jaber's Bayrut Trilogy: Recovering an Obscured Urban History', *Journal of Arabic Literature* 42, no. 2/3 (April 2011), pp. 183–204.

al-Herz, Seba, *The Others* (New York: Seven Stories Press, 2009).

Hill, Tom, 'Staging the Sublimation of Cliché: Elia Suleiman's Silences in The Time That Remains (2009)', *Jerusalem Quarterly*, no. 48 (Winter 2011), pp. 78–90.

Hirsch, Marianne, *Family Frames: Photography, Narrative, and Postmemory* (Cambridge, MA: Harvard University Press, 1997).

Hlehel, Alaa, 'Al-Riwaʾi al-Filastini Alaa Hlehel: Jili Istabdal Surat al-Batal bi-l-la-Batal', *Al-Qabas*, http://alqabas.com/42603/ (last accessed 23 May 2016).

Hout, Syrine, *Post-War Anglophone Lebanese Fiction: Home Matters in the Diaspora* (Edinburgh: Edinburgh University Press, 2012).

Hutcheon, Linda, *Narcissistic Narrative: The Metafictional Paradox* (Waterloo, ON: Wilfrid Laurier University Press, 1980).

———, *A Poetics of Postmodernism: History, Theory, Fiction* (New York: Routledge, 1988).

Jaber, Rabee, 'Al-Katib wa-Aslafuh', *al-Hayat*, 31 May 2005.

———, *Ralph Rizqallah Fi Al-Mirʾat* (Beirut: Dar al-Adab, 1997).

Jabra, Jabra Ibrahim, *In Search of Walid Masoud*, trans. Roger M. A. Allen and Adnan Haydar, First English Edition (Syracuse: Syracuse University Press, 2000).

———, *The First Well: A Bethlehem Boyhood*, trans. Issa Boullata (Fayetteville: University of Arkansas Press, 1995).

———, 'The Palestinian Exile as Writer', *Journal of Palestine Studies* 8, no. 2 (1 January 1979), pp. 77–87.

Jeha, Shafik, *Darwin and the Crisis of 1882 in the Medical Department* (Beirut: American University of Beirut Press, 2004).

Johnson, Rebecca Carol, 'The Politics of Reading: Recognition and Revolution in Jabra Ibrahim Jabra's In Search of Walid Masoud', in Philip F. Kennedy and Marilyn Lawrence (eds), *Recognition: The Poetics of Narrative: Interdisciplinary Studies on Anagnorisis* (New York: Peter Lang, 2009).

Kaplan, Caren, *Questions of Travel: Postmodern Discourses of Displacement* (Durham, NC: Duke University Press, 1998).

Kassab, Elizabeth Suzanne, *Contemporary Arab Thought: Cultural Critique in Comparative Perspective* (New York: Columbia University Press, 2010).

Kassir, Samir, *Beirut*, trans. Malcolm DeBevoise (Berkley: University of California Press, 2011).

———, *La guerre du Liban: de la dissension nationale au conflit régional, 1975–1982* (Paris: Karthala-CERMOC, 1994).

Kendall, Elisabeth, *Literature, Journalism and the Avant-Garde: Intersection in Egypt* (New York: Routledge, 2006).

Khalidi, Rashid, 'Remembering Mahmud Darwish (1941–2008)', *Journal of Palestine Studies* 38, no. 1 (2008), pp. 74–7.

Khalil, Georges, Friederike Pannewick and Yvonne Albers, 'Introduction: Tracks and Traces of Literary Commitment – On Iltizām as an Ongoing Intellectual Project', in Georges Khalil and Friederike Pannewick (eds), *Commitment and Beyond: Reflections on/of the Political in Arabic Literature since the 1940s* (Wiesbaden: Reichert, 2015).

Kharrat, Edwar, *Al-Hasasiyya Al-Jadida: Maqalat fi al-Zahira al-Qasasiyya* (Beirut: Dar al-Adab, 1993).

Khoury, Elias, *Bab al-Shams* (Beirut: Dar al-Adab, 1998).

———, 'Beyond Commitment', in Georges Khalil and Friederike Pannewick (eds), *Commitment and Beyond: Reflections on/of the Political in Arabic Literature since the 1940s* (Wiesbaden: Reichert, 2015).

———, *The Journey of Little Gandhi*, trans. Paula Haydar (Minneapolis: University of Minnesota Press, 1994).

———, 'Khilis al-Haki wa Intaha al-Ritha^c', *Al-Quds al-^cArabi*, 3 August 2015, http://www.alquds.co.uk/?p=382081 (last accessed 23 May 2016).

———, 'The Memory of the City', *Grand Street*, no. 54 (1 October 1995), pp. 137–42.

———, 'The Poet is Dead: Elias Khoury Remembers his Friend Mahmoud Darwish', *Arab Studies Journal* 17, no. 1 (Spring 2009), pp. 100–9.

———, 'Ralph Rizqallah: Al-Khayar al-Akhir', *Mulhaq al-Nahar*, 4 November 1995.

———, 'Rashid Hussein: Al-Ghai'b al-Hadir', *Majallat al-Dirasat al-Filastiniyya*, no. 96 (Fall 2013), pp. 54–62.

———, 'Risala ila Ralph Rizqallah: Al-Ihtijaj Intiharan', *Mulhaq al-Nahar*, 4 November 1995.

———, 'Thaqafat Ma Ba^cd al-Iltizam', *Bidayat*, no. 7 (Winter 2014), http://www.bidayatmag.com/node/159 (last accessed 26 May 2016).

———, *Zaman al-Ihtilal* (Beirut: Mu'assasat al-Abhath al-^cArabiyya, 1985).

Khoury, Elias, and Sonja Mejcher, 'Interview with Elias Khoury: The Necessity to Forget and to Remember', *Banipal*, no. 12 (2001), http://www.banipal.co.uk/selections/48/151/elias-khoury/ (last accessed 15 May 2016).

Khuri-Makdisi, Ilham, *The Eastern Mediterranean and the Making of Global Radicalism, 1860–1914* (Berkley: University of California Press, 2010).

———, 'Inscribing Socialism into the Nahda: Al-Muqtataf, Al-Hilal, and the Construction of a Leftist Reformist Worldview, 1880–1914', in Dyala Hamzah (ed.), *The Making of the Arab Intellectual: Empire, Public Sphere and the Colonial Coordinates of Selfhood* (New York: Routledge, 2012).

Klemm, Verena, 'Different Notions of Commitment (*Iltizam*) and Committed Literature (*Al-Adab al-Multazim*) in the Literary Circles of the Mashriq', *Arabic & Middle Eastern Literature* 3, no. 1 (2000), pp. 51–62.

Kristeva, Julia, *Desire in Language: A Semiotic Approach to Literature and Art* (New York: Columbia University Press, 1980).

———, *Powers of Horror: An Essay on Abjection*, trans. Leon S. Roudiez, Reprint edition (New York: Columbia University Press, 1982).

Kundera, Milan, *The Unbearable Lightness of Being* (New York: Harper & Row, 1984).

Kurzman, Charles, and Lynn Owens, 'The Sociology of Intellectuals', *Annual Review of Sociology*, no. 28 (2002), pp. 63–90.

Lapierre, Maude, 'Refugees and Global Violence: Complicity in Rawi Hage's Cockroach', *Journal of Postcolonial Writing* 50, no. 5 (3 September 2014), pp. 559–70.

Levy, Lital, 'Partitioned Pasts: Arab Jewish Intellectuals and the Case of Esther Azhari Moyal (1873–1948)', in Dyala Hamzah (ed.), *The Making of the Arab Intellectual: Empire, Public Sphere and the Colonial Coordinates of Selfhood* (New York: Routledge, 2012).

Limbrick, Peter, 'Contested Spaces: Kamal Aljafari's Transnational Palestinian Films', in Terri Ginsberg and Andrea Mensch (eds), *A Companion to German Cinema* (Oxford: Wiley-Blackwell, 2012).

Litvin, Margaret, *Hamlet's Arab Journey, Shakespeare's Prince, and Nasser's Ghost* (Princeton, NJ: Princeton University Press, 2011).

Louër, Laurence, *Transnational Shiite Politics: Religious and Political Networks in the Gulf* (New York: Hurst/Columbia University Press, 2008).

Lyotard, Jean-François, 'The Wall, the Gulf, and the Sun: A Fable', in Bill Readings and Kevin Paul Geiman (trans.), *Political Writings* (Minneapolis: University of Minnesota Press, 1993).

Makdisi, Saree, 'Laying Claim to Beirut: Urban Narrative and Spatial Identity in the Age of Solidere', *Critical Inquiry* 23, no. 3 (1 April 1997), pp. 661–705.

Massad, Joseph A., *Desiring Arabs* (Chicago: University of Chicago Press, 2008).

Meier, Daniel, 'The Palestinian Fidâ'i as an Icon of Transnational Struggle: The South Lebanese Experience', *British Journal of Middle Eastern Studies* 41, no. 3 (15 May 2014), pp. 322–34.

Mejcher-Atassi, Sonja, 'The Arabic Novel between Aesthetic Concerns and the Causes of Man: Commitment in Jabra Ibrahim Jabra and ʿAbd Al-Rahman Munif', in Georges Khalil and Friederike Pannewick (eds), *Commitment and Beyond: Reflections on/of the Political in Arabic Literature since the 1940s* (Wiesbaden: Reichert, 2015).

Mostafa, Dalia Said, 'Literary Representations of Trauma, Memory, and Identity in the Novels of Elias Khoury and Rabi' Jābir', *Journal of Arabic Literature* 40, no. 2 (July 2009), pp. 208–36.

———, 'Re-Cycling the Flâneur in Elias Khoury's The Journey of Little Gandhi', *Middle East Critique* 18, no. 2 (2009), pp. 95–115.

Munif, Abd al-Rahman, *Al-Qalaq wa-Tamjid al-Hayah: Kitab Takrim Jabra Ibrahim Jabra* (Beirut: Al-Muʾassasa al-ʿArabiyya li-l-Dirasat wa-l-Nashr, 1995).

al-Musawi, Muhsin J., *Islam on the Street: Religion in Modern Arabic Literature* (Lanham: Rowman & Littlefield Publishers, 2009).

———, *Trajectories of Modernity Arabic Poetry and Tradition* (London: Routledge, 2006).

Najjar, Iskandar, 'ʿAn Shay Aswad, Riwayat Rabee Jaber: tadaʿiyat al-Thakira, wa-l-Mawt wa-l-Hijra wa-l-Amakin', *al-Safir*, 22 February 1995.

Nikro, Norman Saadi, *The Fragmenting Force of Memory: Self, Literary Style, and Civil War in Lebanon* (Newcastle: Cambridge Scholars, 2012).

Nora, Pierre, 'Between Memory and History: Les Lieux de Mémoire', *Representations*, no. 26 (1989), pp. 7–24.

———, *Realms of Memory: Rethinking the French Past*, vol. 1, Conflicts and Divisions (New York: Columbia University Press, 1996).

Oueiss, Mohammad, 'Al-Katiba al-Saʿudiyya Zaynab al-Hifni fi Liqaʾ Qahiri', *Al-Hayat*, 6 April 2011, p. 18.

Pannewick, Friederike, 'From the Politicization of Theater to Individual Humanism: Towards a New Concept of Engagement in the Theater of Saadallah Wannous', in Georges Khalil and Friederike Pannewick (eds), *Commitment and Beyond: Reflections on/of the Political in Arabic Literature since the 1940s* (Wiesbaden: Reichert, 2015).

Philipp, Thomas, 'Language, History, and Arab National Consciousness in the Thought of Jurjî Zaidân (1861–1914)', *International Journal of Middle East Studies* 4, no. 1 (1973), pp. 3–22.

Philipp, Thomas, and Georges C. Zaidan (eds), *Jurji Zaidan's Contributions to Modern Arab Thought and Literature* (Bethesda: The Zaidan Foundation, 2013).

Philipp, Thomas, and Jirjī Zaydān, *Gurgi Zaidan: His Life and Thought* (Wiesbaden: Orient-Institute, 1979).

Prokhoris, Sabine, and Christophe Wavelet, 'Entretien avec Elia Suleiman', *Vacarme* 8, no. 2 (1999), pp. 67–72.

al-Rasheed, Madawi, *A Most Masculine State: Gender, Politics and Religion in Saudi Arabia* (Cambridge: Cambridge University Press, 2013).

Rastegar, Kamran, 'Introduction', *Middle Eastern Literatures* 16, no. 3 (1 December 2013), pp. 227–31.

———, 'Literary Modernity between Arabic and Persian Prose: Jurji Zaydan's Riwayat in Persian Translation', *Comparative Critical Studies* 4, no. 3 (1 October 2007), pp. 359–78.

———, *Surviving Images: Cinema, War, and Cultural Memory in the Middle East* (Oxford: Oxford University Press, 2015).

Readings, Bill, 'Foreword', in Bill Readings and Kevin Paul Geiman (trans.), *Jean-François Lyotard: Political Writings* (Minneapolis: University of Minnesota Press, 1993).

Rizqallah, Ralph, 'Madkhal ila al-Taʿasa', *Mulhaq al-Nahar*, 4 November 1995.

Said, Edward W., 'Arabic Prose and Prose Fiction after 1948', in E. W. Said, *Reflections on Exile and Other Essays* (Cambridge, MA: Harvard University Press, 2000), pp. 41–60.

———, 'The Mind of Winter', *Harper's*, 1 September 1984.

———, 'Reflections on Exile', in E. W. Said, *Reflections on Exile and Other Essays* (Cambridge, MA: Harvard University Press, 2000), pp. 173–86.

———, *Representations of the Intellectual: The 1993 Reith Lectures* (New York: Vintage, 1996).

———, *The World, the Text, and the Critic* (Cambridge, MA: Harvard University Press, 1983).

Sakr, Rita, 'Imaginative Migrations: An Interview with the Lebanese-Canadian Writer Rawi Hage', *Journal of Postcolonial Writing* 47, no. 3 (1 July 2011), p. 346.

Salibi, Kamal S., *Beirut wa-l-Zaman: Qiraʾa fi Riwayat Rabee Jaber al-Thulathiyya* (Beirut: Dar Nilsun, 1999).

Sayigh, Yezid, *Armed Struggle and the Search for State: The Palestinian National Movement, 1949–1993* (Oxford: Oxford University Press, 1999).

Scott, David, *Omens of Adversity: Tragedy, Time, Memory, Justice* (Durham, NC: Duke University Press, 2014).

Seggel, Heather, 'The Veiled and the Shadowed', *The Gay & Lesbian Review*, 1 January 2010, http://www.glreview.org/article/article-453/ (last accessed 20 May 2016).

Seigneurie, Ken, 'Anointing with Rubble: Ruins in the Lebanese War Novel', *Comparative Studies of South Asia, Africa and the Middle East* 28, no. 1 (2008), pp. 50–60.

———, 'Introduction: A Survival Aesthetic for Ongoing War', in Ken Seigneurie (ed.), *Crisis and Memory: The Representation of Space in Modern Levantine Narrative* (Wiesbaden: Reichert, 2004).

——, *Standing by the Ruins: Elegiac Humanism in Wartime and Postwar Lebanon* (New York: Fordham University Press, 2011).

Sharafeddine, Maher, 'Al-Waqi᷂ bi-Asma° Musta᷂ara!', Qantara.de, http://goo.gl/3VuKW9 (last accessed 23 January 2010).

al-Shaykh, Khalil Muhammad, 'Sirat Jabra Ibrahim Jabra wa Tajalliyatuha fi A᷂malihi al-Riwa°iyya wa-l-Qasasiyya', in ᷂Abd al-Rahman Munif (ed.), *Al-Qalaq wa-Tamjid al-Hayah: Kitab Takrim Jabra Ibrahim Jabra* (Beirut: Al-Mu°assasa al-᷂Arabiyya li-l-Dirasat wa-l-Nashr, 1995).

Sheehi, Stephen, 'Towards a Critical Theory of Al-Nahdah: Epistemology, Ideology and Capital', *Journal of Arabic Literature* 43, no. 2–3 (1 January 2012), pp. 269–98.

Suleiman, Elia, 'The Hidden Conscience of Estimated Palestine', *UTS Review: Cultural Studies and New Writing* 2, no. 2 (November 1996).

——, 'The Occupation (and Life) Through an Absurdist Lens', *Journal of Palestine Studies* 32, no. 2 (1 January 2003), pp. 63–73.

Suleiman, Elia, and Richard Porton, 'Notes from the Palestinian Diaspora: An Interview with Elia Suleiman' *Cineaste* 28, no. 3 (Summer 2003).

Suleiman, Susan Rubin, *Authoritarian Fictions: The Ideological Novel as a Literary Genre* (New York: Columbia University Press, 1983).

Taras, Ray, 'Manichean Taxis and Murderous Readers', *World Literature Today* 87, no. 4 (August 2013).

Toukan, Hanan, 'On Delusion, Art, and Urban Desires in Palestine Today: An Interview with Yazid Anani', *Arab Studies Journal* 22, no. 1 (Spring 2014), pp. 208–29.

——, 'Whatever Happened to *Iltizām*? Words in Arab Art after the Cold War', in Georges Khalil and Friederike Pannewick (eds), *Commitment and Beyond: Reflections on/of the Political in Arabic Literature since the 1940s* (Wiesbaden: Reichert, 2015).

Toukan, Oraib, ' "We, the Intellectuals": Re-Routing Institutional Critique', *Ibraaz: Contemporary Visual Culture in North Africa and the Middle East*, http://www.ibraaz.org/essays/98#_ftnref24 (last accessed 20 June 2015).

Trofimov, Yaroslav, *The Siege of Mecca: The Forgotten Uprising in Islam's Holiest Shrine and the Birth of Al Qaeda* (New York: Random House, 2007).

Trotsky, Leon, *Literature and Revolution*, ed. William Keach (Chicago: Haymarket Books, 2005).

Walbridge, John, 'Muhammad Baqir Al-Sadr: The Search for New Foundations', in Linda S. Walbridge (ed.), *The Most Learned of the Shi*ᶜ*a: The Institution of the Marja*ᶜ *Taqlid* (New York: Oxford University Press, 2001).

Wannous, Saadallah, *Al-A*ᶜ*mal al-Kamila* (Damascus: Al-Ahali, 1996).

Wazen, Abdo, 'Tahaddiyat al-Riwaya al-Nisaʾiyya al-Saᶜudiyya [Challenges of the Saudi women novelists]', *Al-Arabiya*, 5 June 2006, http://goo.gl/6IHoUl (last accessed 20 May 2016).

Yaqub, Nadia, 'Refracted Filmmaking in Muhammad Malas's The Dream and Kamal Aljafari's The Roof', *Middle East Journal of Culture and Communication* 7, no. 2 (1 January 2014), pp. 152–68.

Yeshurun, Helit, '"Exile Is So Strong Within Me, I May Bring It to the Land" A Landmark 1996 Interview with Mahmoud Darwish', *Journal of Palestine Studies* 42, no. 1 (September 2012), pp. 46–70.

Zaidan, Jurji, *The Autobiography of Jurji Zaidan: Including Four Letters to His Son*, trans. Thomas Philipp (Washington: Three Continents Press, 1990).

———, 'Honesty in Speech as a Form of Superior Conduct', in Thomas Philipp and Georges C. Zaidan (eds), Kamran Rastegar (trans.), *Jurji Zaidan's Contributions to Modern Arab Thought and Literature* (Bethesda: Zaidan Foundation, 2013).

Zaidan Foundation, 'First Fifty Years of al-Hilal', http://zaidanfoundation.org/ZF_Website_AlHilal.html (last accessed 20 April 2015).

Index

Note: f signifies film still; n signifies note

EU representative:
Easy Access System Europe
Mustamäe tee 50, 10621 Tallinn, Estonia
Gpsr.requests@easproject.com

www.ingramcontent.com/pod-product-compliance
Lightning Source LLC
Chambersburg PA
CBHW070839030726
47504CB00005B/1154